Authority

Authority

Essays

Andrea Long Chu

FARRAR, STRAUS AND GIROUX

NEW YORK

Farrar, Straus and Giroux
120 Broadway, New York 10271

Printed in the United States of America
First edition, 2025

The essays collected here first appeared in the following publications: "Hanya's Boys,"
"Holier Than Thou," "Big Cry Country," "Cunt!," "The Opera Ghost," "Finish Him,"
"The Mixed Metaphor," "Likely People," and "You Must Decide" in *New York*; "On
Liking Women," "Bad TV," "Pink," and "China Brain" in *n+1*; "Psycho Analysis,"
"Metro-Goldwyn-Myra," and "Join the Club" in *Bookforum*; "Angel in the Wings"
and "Oh No" in *Artforum*; "Girl Eat Girl" and "Sick Leave" on the *New Yorker*
website; "Votes for Woman" on the *Jewish Currents* website; and "No One
Wants It" on the website *Affidavit*.

Library of Congress Cataloging-in-Publication Data
Names: Chu, Andrea Long, 1992– author.
Title: Authority : essays / Andrea Long Chu.
Description: First edition. | New York : Farrar, Straus and Giroux, 2025. |
    Includes index.
Identifiers: LCCN 2024038314 | ISBN 9780374600334 (hardcover)
Subjects: LCSH: Authority. | LCGFT: Essays.
Classification: LCC BF637.A87 C48 2025 | DDC 155.9/2—dc23/eng/20241011
LC record available at https://lccn.loc.gov/2024038314

Our books may be purchased in bulk for promotional, educational, or business
use. Please contact your local bookseller or the Macmillan Corporate and
Premium Sales Department at 1-800-221-7945, extension 5442, or by email at
MacmillanSpecialMarkets@macmillan.com.

www.fsgbooks.com
Follow us on social media at @fsgbooks

1   3   5   7   9   10   8   6   4   2

To J,
who will always be the boss of me

Contents

Preface

I got the title for this book from Frank Rich, the recovering theater critic, who wrote to me last year to say that, while he had personally wished never to think of *The Phantom of the Opera* again, he admired the authority I had brought to a genre as arcane as musical theater. A few weeks later, my editor at *New York* magazine called to let me know I had won the Pulitzer Prize—news so shocking that I immediately doubted it when we hung up. It turned out she was telling the truth.

This book collects work published between 2018 and 2023. Roughly half of it comprises my freelance book reviews, as well as a series of literary essays I wrote for *n+1*, a little magazine forever dear to my heart. Much of this work centers on themes of desire and disappointment that obsessed me greatly in those days. The other half consists of essays written for *New York* magazine, where I have worked as a critic since 2021. There I have had the enormous privilege of writing five or six longform pieces a year with the time and budget to comprehensively research the topic at hand while benefiting from an ever-deepening relationship with a terrific editor. This, for the reader eager to skip to the end, is the secret of all real authority: money.

I also include here two new essays: "Criticism in a Crisis" and "Authority." The first is a polemic and a statement of purpose; the second is an intellectual history and, I think, a work of political philosophy. Each in its way represents an attempt to *historicize* the peculiar tendency among critics to gnash their teeth over the state of criticism during any given period, including our own. I am hardly the first to point this tendency out, but I have never encountered a serious analysis of it.

With the exception of grammatical errors and a few infelicities of language—I seem to have used the phrase *Icarian optimism* twice in the span of a year—the old essays appear here as originally published. Here and there, I have restored a sentence that was cut for space. Where irresistible, I have added postscripts. The impulse to tidy up is, as you might expect, hardest to suppress when it comes to work that may now strike the author as juvenilia. "I would not deny being one of those critics who educate themselves in public, but I see no reason why all the haste and waste involved in my self-education should be preserved in a book," wrote the art critic Clement Greenberg. Alas, haste and waste is all there is. If there is any profit in looking back at these essays now, I hope it is because the crooked path I was blazing in those days may now, in the gentler light of dusk, assume the character of a perfect line. Perhaps I was up to something after all.

Brooklyn, New York
April 2024

Authority

Criticism in a Crisis

In the summer of 2023, I was commissioned by the 92nd Street Y, the storied arts center on the Upper East Side, to give a lecture on the state of criticism today. This sounded to me like something Susan Sontag would have done, a thought with which I flattered myself immensely, and as the date approached I began to entertain the notion that I really did have something big and serious to say about how the critic might go about resolving the crisis in criticism that we have heard so much about lately. By *the critic*, I meant myself.

Then a bulldozer tore through a fence across the sea, and within hours Hamas fighters had massacred more than a thousand people in southern Israel. In retaliation for the events of October 7, Israel's far-right government launched a brutal siege of Gaza that, as of this writing, has killed thirty-three thousand people. (The count is almost certainly an underestimate.) It was clear that this was the next bloody phase in Israel's long campaign of occupation and genocide in Palestine—what Rashid Khalidi has called the hundred years' war on the Palestinian people. In the weeks that followed, many writers and artists in the United States who dissented from the overwhelmingly pro-Israel consensus were subject to a swift wave of suppression. The editor of *Artforum*, for whom I wrote two of the pieces in this collection, was fired for publishing a letter of solidarity with the Palestinian people; an award-winning writer exited *The New York Times* after signing a different open letter calling for an end to the occupation; and brave student protesters across the country were doxed, physically threatened, and disparaged by the media, which for weeks seemed to devote itself to regurgitating Israeli propaganda and casting doubt over the "true" death toll in Gaza.

Among the institutions taking a hard pro-war stance was the 92nd Street Y itself, which began life in 1874 as the Young Men's Hebrew Association. On October 8—one day after the Hamas attack—the Y had issued a statement of unconditional support for Israel that spoke ominously of "a time for war and a time for peace." Two weeks later, the Y's leadership abruptly pulled the plug on a book talk with the novelist Viet Thanh Nguyen, whom I happened to have met just the night before, on account of his having signed yet another open letter calling for a ceasefire, this one published in the *London Review of Books* and bearing the names of hundreds of writers, including myself. The decision to disinvite Nguyen made national news and drew swift rebukes from longtime friends of the Y, with several announcing their intention to withdraw from their upcoming events. The entire staff of the Y's Unterberg Poetry Center, including its beloved director of eighteen years, bravely resigned in protest—leaving leadership with little choice but to cancel the center's entire fall slate.

So there I was, trying to think about this fabled crisis in criticism, when a set of real-world crises—concerning the rights of nations and the claims of the soul—became impossible to ignore. I hope the war on Gaza will have done for my generation of writers what the Vietnam War did for earlier generations: that is, it will have shot a beam of moral clarity through a complacent intelligentsia. For what a war like this one asks the left-wing critic to do is to distinguish between a political crisis with clear actors and material stakes, on the one hand, and the self-aggrandizing existential crisis that criticism is always going through, on the other.

We plainly do not lack for the former. The past decade alone has seen the continued militarization of the police, family separations at the border, the criminalization of abortion and gender-affirming health care, a harrowing pandemic, and the literal blotting out of the sun here in New York by wildfires burning hundreds of miles away. And yet what have we been yodeling about here in the Alps of *Kultur*? The idea that young people, besotted with their own identity categories and invented grievances, have gotten a vise grip on the culture industry, which they are blackmailing into making bad movies. The fact that the left itself often cannot resist complaining about "wokeness"—I implicate here some of the essays in this very book—has increasingly struck me as a serious intellectual failure. It is undoubtedly true that political consciousness is easily commodified in the age of social media; this, we may observe without great controversy or, indeed, effort. But to sound the alarm about a public that is too busy virtue signaling or playing the victim to get around to the serious business of *reading* is to take one's place in the grand parade of idiocies that marches in circles around the sacred cathedral of art. Thus one finds the anti-woke leftist darkly reminding his comrades that it is fascism which aims to aestheticize politics. One dearly wishes he remembered the second half of the Walter Benjamin quote: "Communism replies by politicizing art."

Let us do just that. We may begin by asking whether this supposed crisis in criticism is a historical one. We are certainly *told* that it is. I might have opened my talk at the 92nd Street Y by observing that today's critics are succumbing to the "perdition of egotism"; that they are reducing art to a "statement being made in the form of a work of art"; that they are viewing everything through a "religio-political color-filter"; that they are building their reputations on the "violence and extremity of [their] opposition to other critics"; that they are ossifying "the living tissues of literature"; that they are practicing "little more than a branch of homiletics"; that they are trying to "limit the subject-matter at the disposal of the artist"; that they are demonstrating a "resolute avoidance of shades and distinctions"; that they are getting by on a "sententious, cavalier, dogmatical tone"; and that almost all of them are "amateurs of literature" who are frankly angling to "grow important and formidable at very small expense."

None of these observations, I think, would have been terribly controversial today. Nor would they have been mine: they are taken, in fact, from Cynthia Ozick, Susan Sontag, Northrop Frye, T. S. Eliot, Virginia Woolf, H. L. Mencken, Oscar Wilde, Matthew Arnold, William Hazlitt, Samuel Taylor Coleridge, and Samuel Johnson, writing in 2007, 1966, 1957, 1932, 1923, 1919, 1891, 1864, 1822, 1817, and 1759, respectively. This illustrious cohort cannot be said to have agreed on much. Yet when they sat down to write about the state of their art, each of them concluded that criticism was in the midst of a terrible crisis that bore the unmistakable signature of their exact historical moment. The same crisis in criticism has been, it seems, a unique product of the rise of the British newspaper *and* a singular effect of the social alienation that followed the First World War *and* an inescapable feature of the decadence of postwar American capitalism. You will see the problem here: any one of these arguments is fatal to all the others.

This is not to say that each successive critic, in presenting a contemporary diagnosis, has been unaware of the chronic character of the disease. "I was complaining not long ago of this prostitution of literary criticism as peculiar to our own times," wrote Hazlitt in 1822, "when I was told that it was just as bad in the time of Pope and Dryden, and indeed worse." But most critics, or at least the ones we still read today, have contented themselves with the simple *noticing* of this pattern, which they either write off as a droll irony of the job or take as validation of their own urge to cry wolf. Consider A. O. Scott in 2016, acknowledging that "in every generation, the majority of critics can be counted on to do it wrong" while also decrying, as if inventing this idea, the "polarized climate of ideological belligerence in which bluster too often substitutes for argument." It is certainly easy to note that criticism has always been in crisis. Yet almost never has this perpetual cycle of amnesia and epiphany led critics to ask whether the purported crisis is *real*, and not just a façade that hides something else. One marvels at this failure of curiosity, especially in a population so preoccupied with itself; one begins to wonder if it really is a failure at all.

It will be necessary to resist the vanity of presentism. When it is claimed today, for instance, that the internet has democratized criticism to a historically unprecedented degree—a worrisome development, given what most critics think of democracy—this certainly *feels* true: one is tempted to say that if Gutenberg made everyone a reader, then Zuckerberg made everyone a writer. But the umbrage taken by the scribbling classes at the putative explosion of opinions online reflects a much older grudge against literacy itself. "All men being supposed able to read, and all readers able to judge, the multitudinous Public, shaped into personal unity by the magic of abstraction, sits nominal despot on the throne of criticism," Coleridge wrote in 1817, but he might as well have been writing for *The Atlantic* last week. The more relevant changes to the profession are the material ones—the decline of print, the merging of the publishing houses, the evaporation of staff writing positions, the pressure to churn out ad-supported content. And even these are less novel than supposed: Henry James once described the periodicals of his day as a "huge, open mouth which has to be fed."

So we must disaggregate our legitimate fears over the degeneration of legacy media in the digital age from what may be the oldest idea in the history of criticism: the idea that there are simply *too many critics*. No profession has a higher opinion of itself or a lower opinion of its practitioners. "Criticism is a goddess easy of access and forward of advance," wrote Samuel Johnson in 1759, observing that while art takes genius and science takes effort, "every man can exert such judgment as he has upon the works of others." One of the primary tasks of the responsible critic has always been to protect criticism from "the critics"—typically spoken of in the writhing plural. (Alexander Pope called them "half-form'd insects on the banks of Nile.") This typically involves an anxious distinction between criticism, which is an art, and mere "book reviewing," which is a job. Cynthia Ozick has claimed that the critic is like an architect, whereas the reviewer is like a stonemason—as if nothing could be more demeaning to criticism than an association with *labor*. But the sheer volume of abuse to which the lowly book reviewer has been subjected since the eighteenth century is proof enough that criticism has never actually succeeded at insulating itself from the unwashed masses. Its many treatises on proper conduct amount, in retrospect, to a succession of crudely painted NO TRESPASSING signs that imply, above all, the ubiquity of trespassers.

The crisis in criticism thus depends on the mythological figure of the Bad Critic, whose badness must be constantly, hysterically reaffirmed in order to make the good critic look good. To cite the crisis is to participate in a kind of ritual sacrifice, one by which a secret society of serious people may pin its sins on writers with less money or clout. For no critic escapes the pitfalls of moralizing, or restricts herself to the work of art in its purity, or resists the temptation to smuggle in all manner of intellectual contraband; no critic manages to cut out her heart and hide it under the floorboards without leaving a little trail of blood. All that separates the serious critic from the common reviewer is a good mop. In a book of Ozick's from 2000, for instance, we are warned of the "extremist" notion that Jane Austen should be made to endure postcolonial critique simply because Sir Thomas Bertram happened to own one measly sugar planta-tion in the West Indies. Yet in the same book, we may read the author's celebrated essay on a shameful stage adaptation of Anne Frank's diary that was guilty of nothing less than the "appropriation" (this very word!) of the memory of the Holocaust. Why the sudden change of tune? Be-cause the second thing comports with Ozick's own politics; the first thing does not.

So there is no keeping politics out of criticism. There is only regu-lating the flow of traffic. The idea of *art for art's sake*, which continues to enjoy great prestige among the literati today, may give the appear-ance of tranquil isolationism; in fact, it is a frantic deportation program. One finds an excellent expression of this in the introduction to a slim 1941 volume called *The Intent of the Critic*, edited by Donald Stauffer, a minor literary critic of the midcentury. "When we encounter a writer who is primarily or solely the preacher, the politician, the sociologist, the psychologist, the philosopher, the rhetorician, the salesman, the patron, the blood-relative, or the schoolmate, we must recognize him as such," wrote Stauffer. This is clearly an invitation to paranoia. If a critic says that *Hamlet* is a document of Shakespeare's filial grief, why then, he is an unconscious Freud. If another says that autofiction dramatizes late-capitalist alienation, he is nothing but Marx in Groucho glasses. Noth-ing less than constant vigilance will keep the bad critic out. If he cannot be physically prevented from writing reviews then he must at least be defined out of existence. "He fails to be a literary critic because his prime interest is not in literature as it exists," wrote Stauffer. "His heart is over-seas." That final metaphor is telling: the bad critic, like a homesick sol-dier who lets the enemy slip behind lines, has forgotten his duty not just to literature but, perhaps, to his country as well.

It would seem absurd to us to claim that the health of the republic turns on one person's review of the latest film or novel. Yet the absurdity of this thought is an ideological accomplishment, not a natural given. It would not have been so absurd in the context of medieval Christian-ity, where one's response to the beauty of a cathedral, for example, was directly linked with one's place in a spiritual hierarchy, not to mention the divinely mandated political order. Even today, the religious right reg-ularly treats Hollywood like a battleground for the soul of the nation.

This may strike us as illiberal—but that is my point. To the extent that the crisis in criticism has any historical validity at all, it should be understood as a barely sublimated crisis of confidence in liberalism, both as a concrete system of political organization and as a general civic attitude. Adam Gopnik has claimed in its defense that liberalism is a temperament before it is an ideology; a more honest claim is that liberalism is an ideology of good temper. We find it only natural today to rate a critic on the basis of her mental attitude—her poise, her catholicity, her scrupulousness—rather than the ideological content of her judgments. This is the corollary to art for art's sake: *criticism for the sake of criticism.* Hence the paradox of well-regarded critics like James Wood, Zadie Smith, or Adam Kirsch who write with great moral *intensity* but little moral *clarity*. We expect the good critic to leave his own values at the door but not his nose for valuing; we then applaud him for how many other values he can root up without eating them.

Enough of this. We must oppose the scapegoating of the bad critic at every level. I do not mean we should abandon all standards; standards are our whole line of work. It is true that of the criticism being published today, a little is excellent, a little more is adequate, and the lion's share is a dog's breakfast. But bad criticism is bad not because it has been deflowered by political ideology but for all the typical reasons that writing is bad: it is poorly paid, hastily edited, and written mostly by freelancers with so little in the way of financial security, development opportunities, or access to good health care that they may go their entire careers without finding out whether or not they are genuinely untalented. Meanwhile, the vast majority of the advice lobbed their way—that the critic should write with wit, have a sense of tradition, strive to be truthful but prepare to be wrong—is basically identical to the stock advice doled out to *all* writers. Whatever one makes of it, I see little point in rehearsing it. Here is some better advice: *Pay people.* If we really want a "critical mass of critics," as Ozick has called for, then we will have to substantially improve the economic reality of being a critic in this country. That this needs to be stated so emphatically is a sign that it will not happen any time soon. There is no higher truth of criticism than what W. H. Auden once said of his own book reviews: "I wrote them because I needed the money."

We are speaking of the material conditions of being a critic. We should speak the same way of the critic's objects. The endless debate about whether book reviewing has been too positive or too negative in any given decade is not only a tiresome waste of energy but also a calculated diversion. At heart, it is an objection to the simple fact that *all art originates in the world*. It is never possible to separate the work of art from its "umbilical cord of gold," as Clement Greenberg once put it, nor does the artist herself deserve any special immunity because some corporation decided to publish, produce, or exhibit her work. Indeed, when critics claim that art must be considered "on its own" simply because it is art, they are appealing precisely to the *social* character of art—that is, to its putative status as a protected category within society. I myself have often been characterized as writing "takedowns" of certain authors, a distinction I do not terribly resent. Why shouldn't a book review be personal? It is my understanding that persons are where books come from. My patient copy editors at *New York* have noticed that I like to speak of literature in the past tense—"Dickens wrote," instead of the more standard "Dickens writes." I suspect this is because I am more invested in the material activity of writing than the eternal present of literature. One does not step outside of history just because one is dreaming up a world; no author has ever managed to solve the irritating problem of their own concrete existence. How many reviews could we be spared if we only acknowledged that many novels are really, as Scrooge said to the ghost of Marley, "an undigested bit of beef, a blot of mustard, a crumb of cheese"?

I am talking about what Fredric Jameson in 1981 called the "scandal of the extrinsic"—the way that a material "accident" can leave a formal mark on a work of art. His example was the late nineteenth-century transition from the three-volume lending-library novel to the cheaper one-volume format, and the consequent modification of the "inner form" of the English novel as such. (We might also think of the three-act structure of the American sitcom, an artifact of an obsolete advertising model that nonetheless continues to exert significant narrative force even on streaming platforms.) Jameson's famous maxim—"Always historicize!"—remains fine advice for any critic today, albeit with an important addendum. The history of criticism itself attests to just how easy it is for the critic to lapse into *false* historicism—namely, the belief that the present age must be uniquely disastrous just because it is ours. This is really an evolved form of presentism; it has no interest in history other than as a dark backdrop for its glittering narcissism. We may amend the maxim accordingly: *Always historicize—but only if you have to!* Providence there may be in the fall of every sparrow, but history is more discriminating. It takes real historical knowledge and (can it be?) real political values to tell a genuinely new development from the cheap novelties peddled by the social catastrophists.

When I say that the critic must have values, I mean this in both senses of the phrase: the critic cannot *help* but have moral and political beliefs, and therefore he must give serious thought to what he actually believes. Anyone who claims to have no horse in the great derby of American political life is either lying or misinformed about himself; either way, the public has a right to know which horse is his. "Not only should the critic realize the necessity of coordinating his esthetic values with values in all other spheres of life, but he has a duty in a democracy to tell the public what they are," wrote Auden in 1941. "If I find, for instance, that he believes in automatic progress I shall no more trust him than I would trust a philosopher who liked Brahms." This is a small ask, though many critics have historically perceived it as a grave affront. One does not have to require that every critic annually release her moral tax returns in order to claim that, minimally, the reading public has a right to judge her by her actual, sincerely held values and not just by how politely she applies them in the company of strangers.

Now I am not saying that the critic's values must be leftist ones if she is to be recognizable as a critic. The tools of criticism are equally available to the right and the left—in fact, criticism is dominated by the center in the United States, at least in its public, journalistic form—and I see no reason to try to isolate some radical germ within criticism in order to define this fact away. I came of age in an academic literary field littered with inflated political claims; one could not swing a dead white man around campus without hitting a scholar who was purporting to extract the revolution in vitro from the work of some German filmmaker or queer performance artist. This involved, among other things, a basic ignorance of the public sphere, which even the most civic-minded academics still tend to imagine rather as European monks once imagined the elephant. In truth, there is nothing inherently emancipatory, empowering, or even particularly enlightening about criticism. By insisting on the generic radicalism of "critical thinking," the academic critic hopes to spare herself the labor of defending her actual political beliefs. If only! I myself desire a robust culture of left criticism, both inside and outside the academy, and I have tried to contribute to one over the years. But I have done this not because I believe that all critics should be leftists but because I think leftist values like prison abolition or the right to change sex are substantively superior to others, and I think everyone—critic or no—should agree with me.

Still, I have occasionally been accused, even by others who share my politics, of reducing the work of art to a ship's manifest of ideas. Why bother refuting this? It is true that I tend to treat a novel like an argument, which I am told amounts to riding roughshod over the delicate nuances of fictionality. When a character decides to bomb a hospital and when a journalist advocates for the bombing of a hospital, these are surely different things, and neither of them is a bomb. But I strenuously object to the claim that novels are somehow *more* complex than ideas, on the grounds that the latter can nominally be expressed in plain descriptive prose. It is a rather pernicious form of commodity fetishism, one that can blind even the best critic to the fact that authors very often do have easily identified and reasonably coherent ideologies. I am amazed at how often we labor to suppress the *living character of ideas*, which flow through the same obscure affective channels that fiction writers never tire of claiming for themselves. (To them, I say: Stop reducing ideas to novels!)

If that makes me an ideologue, so be it. I do not think I write in the spirit of polite debate. There is no reason to insist on a false mutuality of reader and writer: it is odd, and probably not very ethical, to insist to the passenger that she is the one flying the plane. What the critic always knows for sure about her readers is that they are not, at this very moment, reading the book under consideration; they are reading her review of it. These are the only readers worth writing for: one's own. I do not write to persuade the reader; I write to give her a chance to experience herself as the subject of thought, as if I am reading aloud what is already written on the inside of her own skull. I agree with the late Peter Schjeldahl that the everyday business of the critic lies in conveying certain "heightened states of mind." Indeed, if our digital age has shown us anything, it is not that everyone's a critic; it is that actually *being* a critic is, for most people and certainly for most critics, an experience of anxiety, resentment, distress, and failure. If I have made that experience a bit more tolerable, then I have done my job.

That said, I cannot bring myself to endorse that long tradition within criticism, going back at least to the nineteenth century, which says that the critic is an artist in her own right, and not merely a handmaiden to the arts. "Criticism is really creative in the highest sense of the word," wrote Oscar Wilde in 1891. "The critic occupies the same relation to the work of art that he criticizes as the artist does to the visible world of form and color." This idea remains popular among critics today—especially, I think, professional reviewers, who resent the perennial accusation that they are barnacles and parasites—and I do think it is notionally true, in the sense that prose cannot do without style, and style will always be available for aesthetic evaluation. But the irony of this claim, which is a transparent bid to increase the prestige of criticism with the public, is that it locates the critic's worth in the formal qualities of her prose rather than her judgments. It betrays, in other words, a basic lack of confidence in criticism as a genre of assertive prose, one whose primary aim is to actually communicate actual ideas. The young Sontag was so enamored of the flight to abstraction in modernist painting that she sometimes supposed that criticism could participate in modernism itself. But this could not be: the critic always had to assume the possibility of meaning, even as the modernist realized he *didn't*. (This is what made him a modernist!)

If criticism really is an art, then it is the lowest and most concrete of all the arts. I am personally inclined to think of it as one of the higher crafts. It is, perhaps, a nobler instance of what Matthew Arnold called the "journeyman-work of literature"—dictionaries, translations, and the like. It may be beautiful; it *must* be functional. "Criticism can talk, and all the arts are dumb," wrote Northrop Frye, who happened to be an excellent writer of similes. "The axiom of criticism must be, not that the poet does not know what he is talking about, but that he cannot talk about what he knows." This is why, if it is a choice between left-wing art and left-wing criticism, I will choose the latter every time. One recalls what Baldwin said of the protest novel: that we receive "a very definite thrill of virtue from the fact that we are reading such a book at all." The problem of much (though not all) "political" art is very often that the artist is trying too hard to be her own critic, premasticating the work so that all we have to do is swallow. Let us make this our motto instead: *Art for art's sake—and criticism for the sake of everything else.* This seems more than fair to me. I am not advocating that we push criticism to the margins in the name of respecting the artist's vast natural freedom. I am saying that art's autonomy, as a social convention, necessarily depends on the critic's responsibility to the outside world. Art need not mean anything in itself—but only because the critic works to ensure that it will mean something for *us.*

This is the supreme task of the critic: to restore the work of art to its original worldliness. The artist creates by *removing* something from the world; the critic's job is to *put it back.* I am speaking of the difference between eternity and history, leisure and work, exchange-value and use-value. The artist is free to ascend the brightest heaven of invention if he wishes—it is up to the critic to pull him down to earth again. This means that the good critics and the bad critics cannot be told apart by looking at their fingernails: they are all down in the mud, every last one of them. The genuinely good critic, I think, must know the difference between an existential crisis, whose elements may be freely swapped around without any appreciable effect on the whole, and an actual historical event, whose meaning emerges from the gritty particularity of its parts. This is only possible in practice, and never just in theory.

For who is to say if the critic is right? The rest of us, of course. The only measure of judgment is *more judgment*: that is what it means to try to live together with other human beings. It is to them—to everyone else—that the critic owes her allegiance, not to art or the state or even the abstract totality of society. And sometimes, overseas is precisely where her heart belongs.

2024

I

Hanya's Boys

By the time you finish reading *A Little Life*, you will have spent a whole book waiting for a man to kill himself. The novel, the second from the author Hanya Yanagihara, begins as a light chronicle of male friendship among four college graduates in New York City before narrowing its focus to Jude, a corporate litigator whose decades-long struggle to repress a childhood of unrelenting torments—he was raised by pedophiles in a monastery, kidnapped and prostituted in motels, molested by counselors at an orphanage, kidnapped again, tortured, raped, starved, and run over with a car—ends in his suicide.

An unlikely beach read with a gothic riptide, *A Little Life* became a massive bestseller in 2015. Critics lavished praise on the book, with one declaring it the long-awaited "great gay novel" for its unsparing approach to Jude, who falls in love with his male best friend. (An unexpected pan in *The New York Review of Books* prompted an indignant letter from Yanagihara's editor.) *A Little Life* would go on to win the Kirkus Prize and was a finalist for the National Book Award and the Man Booker Prize; it has since been adapted for the stage by the celebrated director Ivo van Hove, and last month, readers of *The New York Times* nominated it next to finalists like *Beloved* and *1984* for best book of the past 125 years.

But Yanagihara's motivations remained mysterious. The author was born in Los Angeles to a third-generation Hawaiian Japanese father and a Seoul-born Korean mother; her father, a hematologist-oncologist, moved the family around the country for work. She has lived in Manhattan since her twenties, but her heart is in Tokyo and Hawaii. (She has called the last "the closest thing that Asian Americans have to Harlem.") Her first novel, *The People in the Trees*, about a doctor who discovers immortality on an island paradise, was well but quietly received in 2013. That book featured homosexuality and pedophilia; not until *A Little Life* would these be revealed as consistent preoccupations. *The People in the Trees* took Yanagihara eighteen years to write, off and on, during which time she worked as a publicist, book editor, and magazine writer. *A Little Life*, which she wrote while an editor at large at *Condé Nast Traveler*, took only eighteen months.

How to explain this novel's success? The critic Parul Sehgal recently suggested *A Little Life* as a prominent example of the "trauma plot"— fiction that uses a traumatic backstory as a shortcut to narrative. It's easy to see Jude as a "vivified DSM entry" perfectly crafted to appeal to "a world infatuated with victimhood." But Jude hates words like *abuse* and *disabled* and refuses to see a therapist for most of the novel, while Yanagihara has skeptically compared talk therapy to "scooping out your brain and placing it into someone else's cupped palms to prod at." (Jude's sickest torturer turns out to be a psychiatrist.) More compelling about *A Little Life*—and vexing and disturbing—is the author's omnipresence in the novel, not just as the "perverse intelligence" behind Jude's trauma, in the words of another critic, but as the possessive presence keeping him, against all odds, alive. *A Little Life* was rightly called a love story; what critics missed was that its author was one of the lovers.

This is Yanagihara's guiding principle: if true misery exists, then so might true love. That simple idea, childlike in its brutality, informs all her fiction. The author appears unable, or unwilling, to conceive love outside of life support; without suffering, the inherent monstrosity of love—its greed, its destructiveness—cannot be justified. This notion is inchoate in *The People in the Trees*, which features several characters kept on the brink of death and ends with a rapist's declaration of love. In *A Little Life*, it blossoms into the anguished figure of Jude and the saintlike circle of friends who adore him. In Yanagihara's new novel, *To Paradise*, which tells three tales of people fleeing one broken utopia for another, the misery principle has become airborne, passing aerosol-like from person to person while retaining its essential purpose—to allow the author to insert herself as a sinister kind of caretaker, poisoning her characters in order to nurse them lovingly back to health.

Two years after *A Little Life* was published, Yanagihara joined *T* magazine, *The New York Times'* monthly style insert, as editor. She has called the

publication "a culture magazine masquerading as a fashion magazine"—
though you'll have to sift through many pages of luxury advertisements
to confirm that. During her time at *Condé Nast Traveler*, the publication
sent her on a staggering twelve-country, twenty-four-city, forty-five-day,
$60,000 journey from Sri Lanka to Japan for a 2013 issue called, incred-
ibly, "The Grand Tour of Asia." "A trip to India isn't complete without
a stop at the legendary Gem Palace," she wrote in a photo spread titled
"The Plunder," "and a few souvenir diamonds"—four diamond bangles,
to be exact, priced up to $900 each. "When we wear a piece of custom
jewelry," she once told readers of *T*, "we are adding ourselves to a legacy
as old as the Romans, the Greeks, the Persians—older."

This may be surprising. But it is easy to forget that *A Little Life* is an
unapologetic lifestyle novel. Jude's harrowing trials are finger-sandwiched
between Lower East Side gallery openings, summers on Cape Cod, holiday in Hanoi. Critics remarked on its mouthwatering (or eye-rolling)
spread of culinary delights, from duck à l'orange to escarole salad with
pears and jamón, followed by pine-nut tart, tarte Tatin, and a home-
made ten-nut cake Yanagihara later described as a cross between Danish
rugbrød and a Japanese milk bread she once ordered at a Tokyo bakery.
The book inspired the celebrity chef Antoni Porowski to publish a recipe called "Gougères for Jude," based on the canapés Jude makes for a
New Year's party before cutting his arms so badly he requires emergency
medical attention; it can be found on the website for Boursin, the French
herbed-cheese brand.

Yanagihara's onslaught of horrors effectively allowed readers to block
out, like a childhood trauma, the fact that they were reading luxury
copy. Her first book was quite literally a travelog narrated by a pedo-
phile; in *To Paradise*, Yanagihara has not lost the familiar voice of a
professional chronicler of wealth. Here are rose-hued Oriental carpets,
dark-green douppioni-silk drapes, wood floors polished with macadamia
oil; here are wok-fried snow peas, ginger-wine syllabub, a pine-nut tart
(another one!). As in *A Little Life*, Yanagihara cannot help giving cheer-
ful directions as she maneuvers her characters, tour guide–like, through
New York. "We'll cut across Christopher, and then go past Little Eight
and east on Ninth Street before turning south on Fifth," a minor character proposes during a crisis.

Perhaps I am being ungenerous. Surely novelists should describe things! Better, they should evoke them, like the dead, or the Orient. Yanagihara has a tourist's eye for detail; this can make her a very engaging narrator. Here's that holiday in Hanoi from *A Little Life*:

> [He] turned down an alley that was crowded with stall after stall of small, improvised restaurants, just a woman standing behind a kettle roiling with soup or oil, and four or five plastic stools. . . . [He] let a man cycle past him, the basket strapped to the back of his seat loaded with spears of baguettes . . . and then headed down another alley, this one busy with vendors crouched over more bundles of herbs, and black hills of mangosteens, and metal trays of silvery-pink fish, so fresh he could hear them gulping.

And here's days twenty-three and twenty-four of that "Grand Tour of Asia" from *Condé Nast Traveler*:

> You'll see all the little tableaux . . . that make Hanoi the place it is: dozens of *pho* stands, with their big cauldrons of simmering broth, . . . bicyclists pedaling by with basketfuls of fresh-baked bread; and, especially, those little street restaurants with their low tables and domino-shaped stools. . . . [The next day] you'll pass hundreds of stalls selling everything for the Vietnamese table, from mung bean noodles to homemade fish paste to Kaffir limes, as well as vendors crouched over hubcap-size baskets of mangoes, silkworms, and fish so fresh they're still gulping for air.

Now it is no crime to put your paid vacation into your novel. My point is that Yanagihara remains at heart a travel writer. She seems to sense that wealth can be tilted, like a stone, to reveal the wriggling muck beneath. In a few cases, she is even making a political point, as with her abiding interest in the colonization of Hawaii. But more often in these books, wealth's rotten underbelly is purely psychological: There are no wrongful beach houses in *A Little Life*, no ill-gotten hors d'oeuvres. Luxury is the backdrop for Jude's extraordinary suffering, neither cause nor effect; if

anything, the latter lends plaintiveness to the former. This was Yanagihara's first discovery, the one that cracked open the cobbled streets of
SoHo and let something terrible slither out—the idea that misery be-
stows a kind of dignity that wealth and leisure, no matter how sharply
rendered on the page, simply cannot.

The new novel, *To Paradise*, is not a novel at all. It is three books
bound into a single volume: a novella, a brace of short stories, and a full-
length novel. The conceit is that its three tales are set in 1893, 1993, and
2093 in alternate versions of a Washington Square town house. The first
is a Henry James–esque period romance: David, a wealthy scion with a
secret history of nervous breakdowns, rejects a proposal from the boring
Charles to flee west with roguish pauper Edward. The second, a weird
postcolonial fable, finds gay paralegal David hosting a dinner party with
his older HIV-positive boyfriend, Charles, in honor of a terminally ill
friend, while David's father, the rightful king of Hawaii, lies dying in a
psychiatric facility. The third book, the novel-length one, is a fitful attempt at speculative fiction complete with surveillance drones ("Flies"),
boring names ("Zone Eight"), and a biodome over Central Park. In this
New York ravaged by a century of pandemics, brain-damaged lab tech
Charlie discovers her husband Edward's infidelity, while her grandfather, a brilliant virologist, reveals his role in creating the current totalitarian government. (In a desultory bid to sew the three parts together,
Yanagihara has given multiple characters the same name, without their
being meaningfully related.)

The third part of *To Paradise* may sound topical, but Yanagihara has
a lifelong fascination with disease. She was a self-described "sickly child"
whose father used to take her to a morgue where a pathologist would
show her the cadavers, folding back the skin flaps like flower petals so
the young girl could sketch their insides. Years later, *The People in the
Trees* would center on a zoonotic disease that extends the sufferer's life
span while rapidly degrading cognitive function. In *A Little Life*, Jude's
history of abuse is equally a nutrient-rich soil for infection: his venereal
diseases, acquired from clients; his cutting, which results in septicemia;
his maimed legs, which, after decades of vascular ulcers and osteomyeli-
tis, must finally be amputated. That's to say nothing of the many minor
characters in the novel who are summarily dispatched by strokes, heart

attacks, multiple sclerosis, all kinds of cancer, and something called Nishihara syndrome, a neurodegenerative disease so rare the author had to make it up.

Like its predecessor, *To Paradise* is a book in which horrible things happen to people for no reason. The agents of misery this time have become literally inhuman: cancer, HIV, epilepsy, functional neurologic disorder, a toxic antiviral drug, the unidentified viral hemorrhagic fever that will fuel the next pandemic. A virus makes perfect sense as Yanagihara's final avatar after three novels. The anguish it visits on humanity—illness, death, social collapse—is just an indifferent side effect of its pointless reproductive cycle. Biologists do not even agree on whether viruses are living organisms. A virus wants nothing, feels nothing, knows nothing; at most, a virus is a little life.

This is ideal for Yanagihara: pure suffering, undiluted by politics or psychology, by history or language or even sex. Free of meaning, it may more perfectly serve the author's higher purpose. Reading *A Little Life*, one can get the impression that Yanagihara is somewhere high above with a magnifying glass, burning her beautiful boys like ants. In truth, Jude is a terribly unlovable character, always lying and breaking promises, with the inner monologue of an incorrigible child. The first time he cuts himself, you are horrified; the fiftieth, you wish he would aim. Yet Yanagihara loves him excessively, cloyingly. The book's omniscient narrator seems to be protecting Jude, cradling him in her cocktail-party asides and winding digressions, keeping him alive for a stunning eight hundred pages. This is not sadism; it is Munchausen by proxy.

Yanagihara herself provides a perfect image for this kind of love. Jude's lover, Willem, trying to prevent him from cutting himself, hugs Jude so tightly he can barely breathe. "Pretend we're falling and we're clinging together from fear," Willem tells him; for a brief moment, the fiction of imminent death cuts through Jude's self-loathing and allows him to crumple helplessly into his lover's suffocating embrace. As he loses consciousness, Jude imagines them falling all the way to the earth's core, where the fires melt them into a single being whom even death cannot part.

If disease is Yanagihara's angel of death, gay men are her perfect patients. The majority of her protagonists to date are gay men, or at least men-loving men, and she approaches them with a distinct preciousness. When Jude finally reveals the details of his horrific childhood to Willem, the two are lying on the floor of a literal closet. In *A Little Life*, this tendency could be fobbed off as a literary technique in line with Yanagihara's stated desire to make the novel "operatic," but in *To Paradise*, her sentimentality has begun weeping like a sore. "We could never be together in the West, Edward. Be sensible! It is *dangerous* to be like us out there," pleads one David. "If we couldn't live as who we are, then how could we be free?" The entire first book of *To Paradise* is set in an alternate version of nineteenth-century New York preposterously founded on the freedom of love; you'll forgive me for being unmoved, at this moment in history, by the poignancy of marriage equality.

And then there is the matter of AIDS. It's true that *To Paradise* is not an AIDS novel; the actual crisis, which unfolds here just as it did in reality, is little more than a faint backdrop for a hundred pages. But this is only because Yanagihara appears to see all diseases as allegories for the human immunodeficiency virus. Charles's ex-boyfriend Peter may only be dying of "boring old cancer, I'm afraid," but the virus hovers over his farewell party and lingers through the novel's succession of pandemics. The next Charles, persona non grata in a fascist state of his own design, will join other mildly oppressed gay men of New York in seeking love and support in a riverside rowhouse on Jane Street in the West Village— three blocks from the real-life AIDS memorial in Hudson River Park. This detail is mawkish in the extreme, a shameless attempt to trade on the enviable pathos of a disease transmitted through an act of love.

When *A Little Life* was first published, the novelist Garth Greenwell declared it "the most ambitious chronicle of the social and emotional lives of gay men to have emerged for many years," praising Yanagihara for writing a novel about "queer suffering" that was about AIDS only in spirit. This was a curious claim for several reasons. First, many of the novel's characters, including Willem and Jude, fail to identify as gay in the conventional sense. Second, Yanagihara herself is not gay, though she says she perfunctorily slept with women at Smith College. (If *A Little Life* was opera, it was not *La Bohème*; it was *Rent*.) Now perhaps the great gay novel should move beyond the strictures of identity politics; Yanagihara has stubbornly defended her "right to write about whatever I want." God forbid that only gay men should write gay men—let a hundred fairies bloom. But if a white author were to write a novel with Asian American protagonists who, while resistant to identifying as Asian American, nonetheless inhabited an unmistakably Asian American milieu, it might occur to us to ask why.

Why, then? "I don't know," Yanagihara told one journalist. To another, she insisted, "I don't think there's anything inherent to the gay-male identity that interests me." These are baffling, even offensive responses given that she has had almost a decade to come up with better ones. But I do not think Yanagihara, an author who believes in fiction as a conscious act of avoidance, is being dishonest. "A fiction writer can hide anything she wants in her fiction, a power that's as liberating as it is imprisoning," she has written, explaining her refusal to go to therapy despite the urging of her best friend, the man to whom *A Little Life* is dedicated and whose social circle inspired the book's friendships. "As she grows more adept at it, however," Yanagihara continues, "she may find she's losing practice in the art of telling the truth about herself."

That may well be. Regardless of Yanagihara's private life, her work betrays a voyeuristic kind of love for gay men. By exaggerating their vulnerability to humiliation and physical attack, she justifies a maternal posture of excessive protectiveness. This is not an act of dehumanization but the opposite. There is a horrible piety to Jude, named for the patron saint of lost causes; he has been force-fed sentimentality like a foie-gras goose. When the author is not doling out this smothering sort of love through her male characters (Willem, for instance), she is enacting it at the level of her own narration. The conspicuous absence of women in her fiction may even express Yanagihara's tendency, as a writer, to hoard female subjectivity for herself.

This brings us to Charlie, a narrator in *To Paradise* and Yanagihara's only female protagonist to date. Charlie is a technician who takes care of mouse embryos at an influenza lab in Zone Fifteen. The antiviral drug that saved her life as a child has left her affectless and naïve, pitifully incapable of comprehending the extent of her own loneliness. After Charlie is raped by two boys her age—the only rape in this whole book, if you can believe it—her grandfather Charles desperately tries to ensure her safety by marrying her off to a homosexual like himself. But it is with Charlie, who longs for her husband to touch her even as she knows he never will, that the sublimation of romantic love will finally slouch into despair. When Charlie follows him to a gay haven in the West Village, having discovered notes from his lover, she is heartbroken. "I knew I would never be loved," Charlie thinks. "I knew I would never love, either." But this isn't entirely true. After Charlie's husband dies of an unknown illness, the only woman Yanagihara has ever asked readers to care about will lie next to his corpse and kiss him for the first time—the space between them closed, at last, by death.

There is no paradise for Charlie. The odd and tuneless phrase *to paradise* provides a destination but withholds any promise of arrival. Perhaps this is why Yanagihara has tacked it half-heartedly onto the last sentence of each of the novel's three books. Doom shadows every character who decides to abandon one apocryphal heaven on earth for another: the plutocratic northeast for the homophobic west, the colonized state of Hawaii for a delusional kingdom on the beach, totalitarian America for the unknown New Britain. Every paradise is a gossamer curtain; behind it lies a pit of squalor, disease, torture, madness, and tyranny. Freedom is a lie, safety is a lie, struggle is a lie; even the luxuries Yanagihara has spent her career recording are lies in the end. For paradise, insofar as it means heaven, also means death.

Not even love will save Yanagihara's characters. Her fantasies of suffering and illness are designed only to produce a very specific kind of love, and this love is not curative but palliative—it results, sooner or later, in the death of the thing. If this is fatalism, it is not the sanguine fatalism of Prospero, another rightful king on another island paradise, reminding his audience that "we are such stuff / As dreams are made on, and our little life / Is rounded with a sleep." No, it is the exsanguinating fatalism of Jude, who, out of love for his boyfriend, will try to show "a little life"—a phrase he learned from his pimp—while Willem makes love to his reluctant body. The same phrase appears in *The People in the Trees*, where it describes the bleak vegetative state that befalls the islanders whose disease has stretched out their life spans. In *To Paradise*, Charles reflects on a set of immune-compromised twins, explaining that he never became a clinician because he "was never convinced that life— its saving, its extension, its return—was definitively the best outcome."

The twins die, possibly by suicide, and Charles goes on to design death camps. "There's a point," Yanagihara once said of Jude, at which "it becomes too late to help some people."

These are difficult words to read for those of us who have passed through suicidal ideation and emerged, if not happy to be alive, then relieved not to be dead. It is indeed a tourist's imagination that would glance out from its hotel window onto the squalor below and conclude that death is the opposite of paradise, as if the locals did not live their little lives on the expansive middle ground between the two. But even Yanagihara's novels are not death camps; they are hospice centers. *A Little Life*, like life itself, goes on and on. Hundreds of pages into the novel, Jude openly wonders why he is still alive, the beloved of a lonely god. For that is the meaning of suffering: to make love possible. Charles loves David; David loves Edward; David loves Charles; Charlie loves Edward; Jude loves Willem; Hanya loves Jude. Misery loves company.

2022

Girl Eat Girl

In 1996, after a private plane crashes in the Canadian wilderness, its passengers, the members of a varsity girls' soccer team, must go to extreme lengths to stay alive. Meanwhile, in the present day, a group of haunted survivors, now tabloid-famous, struggle to live normal, suburban lives while guarding the truth of what happened in the woods. The short answer? They ate one another.

This is *Yellowjackets*, Showtime's gripping new drama, which concludes its first season on Sunday. Beyond making inescapable comparisons to ABC's *Lost*, critics have praised the show for its unsparing look at the trauma of female adolescence and its long-toothed effects. Appropriately, three of the present-day survivors are played by Melanie Lynskey, Juliette Lewis, and Christina Ricci, all former teen actresses from the nineties. "You could say that we are all bonded by the trauma of having been very young and very famous," Ricci has said. The creators of *Yellowjackets* have called trauma "a big theme" of the show, expressing their interest in exploring it from a "personal" angle rather than a clinical one. Several critics have followed suit, with one reviewer insisting that, even in a crowded field of shows claiming to be about trauma, *Yellowjackets* was the real deal.

The series appears to neatly bolster Parul Sehgal's recent claim that the trauma plot has cannibalized all others. "With the trauma plot, the logic goes: Evoke the wound and we will believe that a body, a person, has borne it," she writes. For Sehgal, the trauma plot transcends genre. It bites into the diasporic epic, the novel of manners, the uplifting sports comedy. It gnaws character down to the bone of backstory. Its game is wide-ranging: television shows like *Ted Lasso*, *WandaVision*, *Fleabag*;

fiction by Hanya Yanagihara, Jason Mott, Karl Ove Knausgaard; even superhero movies. Should *Yellowjackets* be added to this vast ward, or does it have something new to tell us about the form?

I'll let that question hang there, like the strung-up carcass of a delicious midfielder, while I tell you more about the show. The two timelines of *Yellowjackets* are separated by twenty-five years. The first follows the stranded girls as they bury the dead, hunt game, and fend off wolves and madness while still finding time to make out in the lake. It's a terrifically acted ensemble, which includes Jackie, a shoo-in for homecoming queen; the wallflower Shauna, pregnant by Jackie's boyfriend, Jeff; and the high-achieving Taissa. There's also the burnout Natalie, the born-again Laura Lee, the loony Lottie, and the sociopathic Misty, who secretly destroys the plane's black box to preserve her newfound importance as the group's medic.

The second timeline picks up in 2021 and focuses on just four survivors. Shauna is now a housewife married to Jeff, whom she suspects of infidelity; Natalie is a drug addict living out of a motel; Taissa is an affluent candidate for the state senate. ("You're the queer Kamala!" a photographer gushes.) Meanwhile, Misty, now realized by a terrifying Christina Ricci, is a hospice nurse by day and a "citizen detective" by night. All of them are trying to forget what happened; when they start receiving threats of blackmail, and letters marked with an ominous symbol from the woods, they scramble to protect themselves.

This is the genius of *Yellowjackets*: it is not one show but two. One is a survival drama, with elements of horror and coming of age; the other is a suburban thriller, a few highway stops short of a soap. The survival drama, as a form, tends to explore how long characters who are cut off from civilization can retain their humanity before descending into madness or instinct. It is no accident that it includes, almost invariably, a plane crash—a monument of mankind's hubris, struck down to the animal earth. The classic of the genre is *Alive*, the 1993 film about the real-life Uruguayan rugby team, portrayed by Ethan Hawke and others, who were forced to eat their loved ones after a plane crash in the Andes.

By comparison, the premise of the suburban thriller, neither revolutionary in its observation nor untrue, is that something dark and desperate lies beneath the surface of the American middle class, especially as represented by the family sitcom. (The exemplar is *Breaking Bad*, AMC's landmark drama about a terminally ill chemistry teacher turned crystal-meth kingpin.) Driven from their enormous kitchens or wood-paneled bungalows by sexual frustration, financial anxiety, or medical crises, characters turn to infidelity, blackmail, drug trafficking, and murder, even as they drive minivans and make pot roasts. They launder money; they fold laundry. A good litmus test for this genre is whether a character who has just committed a crime might reasonably be expected to attend a parent-teacher conference the next day.

I labor these distinctions to show you that *Yellowjackets* inhabits two genuinely distinct forms, each with its own proper set of interests and goals. I am not referring to genre hybridity, a more or less omnipresent phenomenon, in which multiple genres are crossbred into something new. What I'm talking about, to borrow a chemistry metaphor, is *genre chirality*—two genres like two hands, mirroring each other but not superimposable, capable of doing the television equivalent of patting one's head and rubbing one's belly at the same time.

This structure allows *Yellowjackets* to take the same seed crystals of character and grow them in pleasingly different ways. Consider the matter of affect. The survival drama is built, counterintuitively, around hope: the teenage Shauna should be dead (hunger, wolves, plane crash), but, by some miracle, she isn't. As often as the girls may be thwarted by Mother Nature or good old adolescent rancor, there is always a chance that they'll make it back to civilization. This is true even for those characters absent from the 2021 storyline; indeed, it is strongly implied by the resurfacing of the symbol from the woods. By contrast, the suburban thriller's reigning affect is unhappiness: the middle-aged Shauna should be happy (house, family, kitchen island), and yet she couldn't be more miserable. When she kills, skins, and stews a rabbit from her garden, we cannot help thinking that the rabbit is her husband.

Here we find another distinction, at the level of drama, between the fatal error and the bad decision. In the past, the girls at first fail to ration their food supplies, believing that they will be rescued. Laura Lee is killed trying to fly an abandoned plane; psilocybin mushrooms, accidentally added to a stew, drive the girls to a bloodthirsty orgy. These are understandable but critical missteps made by desperate people trying to do the right thing. But, in the present, the very same characters, languishing in suburbia, go looking for trouble: Shauna has an affair; Natalie blackmails her sponsor; Misty kidnaps and blackmails a campaign fixer posing as a journalist. This is why the adults of *Yellowjackets*, despite having access to money and modern amenities, can feel more stuck than their literally stranded teenage counterparts. In the past, our heroines are trapped in the wilderness; in the present, they're trapped in themselves.

Perhaps the most interesting thing about the two timelines of *Yellowjackets* is their relationship to time itself. Strangely, it is not quite right to say that the teen narrative comes "before" the adult one. Rather, they both take place in the perpetual present of their own diegeses, the past no more a direct cause than the future its inevitable outcome. Sometimes, the gap between a character and her other self is so vast that it can be disorienting: Juliette Lewis's Natalie is sour, restless, almost elastic in her physicality, while her younger self, played by Sophie Thatcher, is sharply observant, a coiled spring. In other cases, the woods seem to have left no imprint at all. "When did we become these people who lie and cheat and do awful things?" Shauna asks her husband after she murders her lover with a kitchen knife. "We've always been these people," he replies quietly.

Each timeline is capable of provoking, by some hidden mechanism, a narrative shudder in the other. It is not until the adult Taissa awakens in a tree outside her house, gnawing on her own hand, that we realize that the menacing tree woman seen by her troubled son is not a shadow from his mother's past but his actual mother. Here the future explains the past: We realize with horror that, in 1996, Lottie has not hallucinated a teenage Taissa blankly shoveling dirt into her mouth, and we fear the worst. Sure enough, teen Taissa will sleepwalk into another tree, leaving her girlfriend to be mauled by a wolf.

Another way to put this is that *Yellowjackets*—unlike *Lost*, say—does not rely on backstory for character development. We do get a few flashbacks, always internal to the survival drama: Lottie's hallucinations as a little girl, Laura Lee's near-death experience at Bible camp. But the teenage arc, taken as a whole, is not merely a series of flashbacks, nor is the adult arc an extended flash-forward; these are two stories taking place at different times, simultaneously. The one exception is a horrific sequence, in the pilot, in which an unidentified girl is hunted, bled, cooked, and eaten by, presumably, what's left of the 1996 state champions. Clearly, the hunt takes place well into the girls' time in the woods, but it is not part of the teen timeline—at least not yet. The sequence is at once a terrifying vision and a harrowing memory; never revisited (thus far), it forms an invisible spine that connects the series' two arcs like ribs, curving out and around without touching.

This is the show's darkest mystery: How will the girls come to eat one another? Will cannibalism be an unthinkable act of survival, or something worse—the ultimate bad decision, an act of hatred, or even an act of bright and hideous joy? The survival drama would see the girls do it because they *had* to; in a suburban thriller, they would do it only because they *wanted* to. This has put the show's two genres on a collision course; its greatest pleasure lies in anticipating, from a safe distance, the destruction of one by the other.

Speaking of which, I think the blood has finally drained from my question: Is *Yellowjackets* about trauma or not? You could say that the chirality I've been describing is intrinsic to trauma—that to be traumatized is precisely to be thrown from one genre into another, without knowing how or why. Or you could say that this structure is what elevates the show above the trauma discourse, by scrambling cause and effect, damage and desire. My point is that a show can be overdetermined in its meaning at the level of cultural context—critical response, fan reactions, the stated desires of its creators—and still be wonderfully underdetermined at the level of the text itself. These two levels require distinct genres of criticism; where they touch lies the greatest mystery, and the reddest meat. The trick is figuring out how to keep them both alive at once. Genres, like girls, have a way of eating each other up.

2022

The Opera Ghost

In 1988, *New York* magazine ran a cover story about the arrival of a new Broadway show. Described as an "old-fashioned, romantic musical that assaults the senses," *The Phantom of the Opera* told the tale of a deformed composer—the masked Phantom—who falls tragically in love with a beautiful soprano. The actual composer, Andrew Lloyd Webber, had written it for his mistress-turned-wife, Sarah Brightman; their affair had been all over the tabloids back in London. Interviewed at the couple's $5.5 million duplex in Trump Tower, Lloyd Webber called the show his "favorite" to date, all due respect to his previous hit *Evita*. In any case, it was hard to argue with a record-breaking $18 million in advance tickets. *Phantom* might have been a British musical based on a French novel, but the show's fin-de-siècle grandeur fit perfectly with the decadence of the Reagan years: opulent architecture, sexual nostalgia, rock-and-roll pyrotechnics. (Plans to release a flock of live pigeons had been scrapped before the London premiere.) Even the unforgiving Frank Rich, in an otherwise blistering review for *The New York Times*, admitted, "It may be possible to have a terrible time at *The Phantom of the Opera*, but you'll have to work at it."

Now *Phantom* is finally closing. In its thirty-five-year run, the longest in Broadway history, *Phantom* has grossed over $1.3 billion and exceeded twenty million viewers; two weeks ago, it brought in a record-setting $3 million from ticket holders eager to pay their respects. The official cause is the pandemic, but the fact is that having a terrible time at *Phantom* today takes no effort at all. The production is simply miserable, succumbing in its old age to anemic tempos and wretched acting; there is a shocking amount of dead air for a show in which the performers never stop singing. Emilie Kouatchou, marketed a little too proudly as the first Black actress to play Christine on Broadway, is a capable soprano doomed to a thankless role that often involves begging men to "guide" her. It is hard to ignore that *Phantom* has always been a classic rape fantasy; its appeal hinges entirely on the charisma of its titular bodice ripper, a self-described ugly virgin who plots violent attacks on the public from his basement. Fans have long speculated that the extravagant title song, in which the Phantom ferries Christine across a fog-covered subterranean lake, relies on body doubles and prerecorded vocals. Only the famous chandelier still thrills: its ominous ascent during the organ overture (also likely pretaped) remains a true coup de théâtre. It hangs menacingly over the orchestra section, a Chekhov's light fixture; but at the act break, it will "fall" lightly back onto the stage like Peter visiting the Darlings. (To ensure brand continuity, Lloyd Webber's first new Broadway show in almost a decade, *Bad Cinderella*, has opened around the block to poor reviews.)

Why did anyone ever like this? To dismiss *Phantom* as just another spectacle for a spectacular age (one could just as easily praise it for this, and many did) would be to contradict the Phantom himself. Lloyd Webber's previous work, such as the gaudy colossus *Cats*, had earned him the reputation of an opportunist with few principles beyond the British pound. By comparison, *Phantom* was an almost intellectual work, an artist's statement from a man whom few had ever accused of artistry. The Phantom was no entertainer, preferring to compose in literal obscurity beneath the opera house rather than betray his belief in music as the highest expression of the human spirit; he stood for devotion, not diversion.

Through *Phantom*, Lloyd Webber presented an argument for the destiny of musical theater itself. The operatic tradition had always been divided over the relationship between music and drama, and this debate had reemerged in Lloyd Webber's day. His contemporary Stephen Sondheim was a studied modernist who brought dramatic heft to musical theater in the 1970s. But Lloyd Webber had no ear for drama; his characters declaimed their emotions directly into the audience, as if by T-shirt cannon. What he offered was something different: an experience of sheer musical transcendence. This emphasis on the *musical* part of musical theater served as both a defense of his earlier endeavors, which by this reasoning could be considered serious works of art, and a vision for the future of Broadway. Night after night, the Phantom promised the audience that, for two and a half hours, *nothing*—neither plot nor character, not social issues, not even good taste—would be more important than what happened when that invisible beam of music shot across the darkened theater into their souls.

Lloyd Webber was born in postwar London to a family of music lovers. His father, an accomplished organist and little-known composer, taught composition at the Royal College of Music in London, while his mother was a successful piano teacher frustrated with her husband's professional complacency. As a teenager, Lloyd Webber wept with emotion upon hearing a radio broadcast of *Tosca*, the 1900 opera by Puccini. "This was truly theatre music that I never dreamed possible," he writes in his 2018 memoir, *Unmasked*. The young man was under considerable pressure to distinguish himself musically. His mother became so morbidly obsessed with a piano prodigy that she effectively adopted the boy into the family; meanwhile, her actual son planned a half-hearted suicide attempt. Lloyd Webber still vividly remembers the time his father played him a recording of "Some Enchanted Evening," a love song from Rodgers and Hammerstein's *South Pacific*. "Andrew," his father told him, "if you ever write a tune half as good as this, I shall be very, very proud of you."

Let no one say he didn't try. Lloyd Webber's first produced musical, *Joseph and the Amazing Technicolor Dreamcoat*, sounded like a Sunday-school pantomime written by a teenager, because it was. But by his father's death in 1982, Lloyd Webber had several smash hits under his belt: *Jesus Christ Superstar*, a rock opera; *Evita*, a sympathetic look at fascism in Argentina; and *Cats*, a show about cats. He had practically defined the British megamusical of the 1980s: breathtaking visuals, timeless themes, and above all a fully sung-through structure, usually with a strong pop influence.

The composer's work divided critics, but Lloyd Webber himself, a merry populist with a growing Pre-Raphaelite art collection, saw no contradiction between artistic integrity and commercial appeal. Early on, he had learned to promote his music by releasing concept albums and lead singles—"Don't Cry for Me Argentina" from *Evita* reached number one on the U.K. singles charts in 1977—and his shows were so profitable that Margaret Thatcher, when challenged on her government's cuts to public funding for the theater, replied, "Look at Andrew Lloyd Webber!" Indeed, given the huge moving sets and live sound mixing—a practice Lloyd Webber pioneered for the theater—it was hard to look away. His next hit, *Starlight Express*, was a synth-pop nightmare about racing trains that featured android-like actors who zoomed around the audience on roller skates. That production's director, Trevor Nunn, who had also worked on *Cats*, told the press it was like going to Disneyland: "Here is my money. Hit me with the experience."

Still, Lloyd Webber longed to be thought of as a serious composer. He was proud that *Cats* was built around a fugue, and, like Rachmaninoff before him, he wrote variations on Paganini's Caprice no. 24. He had become obsessed with the "mesmeric possibilities" of the unusual 7/8 time signature after hearing it in one of Prokofiev's piano sonatas as a youth, and he would make a self-impressed point of putting a juddering 7/8 section into every score. Yet there was something labored and prosaic about Lloyd Webber's music. His father is said to have asked his composition pupils, "Why write six pages when six bars will do?" But the younger Lloyd Webber, a self-described "maximalist," preferred to elongate his melodic lines far beyond their natural conclusions, and he was slavishly devoted to the downbeat.

This schoolboy approach did make Lloyd Webber a passable writer of pastiche: rock and pop mostly, without a hint of jazz, as well as the classical music his father had schooled him in. The tune for "Memory" from *Cats* was ersatz Puccini, originally intended for a show about a cut song from the opera *La Bohème*. The elder Lloyd Webber, an "acknowledged expert on Puccini," loved it—though the song also recalled Ravel's *Boléro*, slowed down and played in a maudlin 12/8 time. Critics noticed this sort of thing a lot. The favorite ballad from *Superstar*, "I Don't Know How to Love Him," appeared to take its plaintive melody from the second movement of Mendelssohn's Violin Concerto, and underneath "Don't Cry for Me Argentina," one could hear the Paraguayan harp plucking something like Bach's Prelude in C Major. The most puzzling thing about these borrowings was their apparent insouciance: the composer did not care. Lloyd Webber's longtime orchestrator would defend him on the grounds that there "aren't that many notes." But as the drama critic John Simon put it for *New York*, "It's not so much that Lloyd Webber lacks an ear for melody as that he has too much of one for other people's melodies."

In truth, Lloyd Webber was borrowing more than music. At twenty-one, he had fallen in love with a "deliciously open-faced" sixteen-year-old girl named Sarah Hugill, marrying her just weeks after her eighteenth birthday; now he was leaving her for Brightman, a former *Cats* actress twelve years his junior whom the tabloids dubbed "Sarah II." Guilty over the divorce and eager to challenge himself artistically, Lloyd Webber landed on the idea of *Requiem*, a Requiem Mass dedicated to his late father—with a soloist part that would show off Brightman's three-octave lyric soprano, which was clearly in demand. On a hot summer's night in 1984, Lloyd Webber went with his new wife to see a fledgling musical by the director Ken Hill, who wanted Brightman for his female lead. The production, which concerned a pretty soprano and the tortured composer who is in love with her, featured classic opera arias with new lyrics by Hill. Brightman, then eyeing actual opera, was unconvinced, but Lloyd Webber thought the show had potential as a *"Rocky Horror Picture*–type musical" and agreed to produce it and compose an original title song. It was called *The Phantom of the Opera*.

In his memoir, Lloyd Webber is at pains to minimize the role played by Hill's *Phantom* in the genesis of his own, though he briskly acknowledges that the demo he recorded for Hill was an early version of the song "The Phantom of the Opera," down to the iconic organ chords. His preferred origin story is that, during rehearsals for *Requiem*, he happened to pick up a fifty-cent copy of Gaston Leroux's original 1910 novel *Le Fantôme de l'Opéra* on Fifth Avenue, suddenly realizing that it could furnish the "high romance" he wanted to write for Brightman. The novel, set at the Opéra Garnier in 1880s Paris, is about an ingénue named Christine Daaé who believes she is being tutored by an unseen angel sent by her dead father; in fact, her teacher is the rumored Opera Ghost, a disfigured but very human composer named Erik who has fallen dangerously in love with her. The story had already been adapted many times, including as a classic 1925 silent film starring Lon Chaney; later films depicted the Phantom as, ironically, an enraged victim of musical plagiarism. But Lloyd Webber saw something else: a man in love with a voice. His Phantom would be an inverted Orpheus, beckoning his beloved to the underworld with music; here was an opportunity for passion, for real gravity. For the first time in his career, it seemed to Lloyd Webber that he might have something to say.

The Phantom of the Opera opened on the West End in 1986. To an extent, it did for the operatic arts what Cole Porter's *Kiss Me, Kate* had done for Shakespeare: it provided a night at the opera for people who, as a rule, did not go to the opera. In the English-speaking world, then as now, opera was being kept alive by an elite donor class whose tastes rarely ventured beyond the nineteenth century. (The composer Pierre Boulez remarked in 1967 that the best way to modernize opera would be to "blow the opera houses up.") What Lloyd Webber offered, alternatively, was a pleasing impression of opera—continuous singing, throbbing vibrato, very high notes—without the infamous longueurs or unintelligible vowels. Critics agreed that the score was his most mature, incorporating modest experiments alongside the opera pastiche; here and there, one caught a glimpse of genuine musical intelligence. But the true star of *Phantom* was music itself; there was simply so much of it. By the third hour, one felt like the weary opera managers, after receiving yet another letter from the Phantom: "Far too many notes for *my* taste / And most of them about Christine!" It was the first show for which Lloyd Webber shared a book credit, and his characters discussed music incessantly: who should sing it, how to market it, what gave it value. In essence, Lloyd Webber had written a reply to critics who saw him (positively or not) as a purveyor of theatrical delights, countering that the experience of listening to music was a matter of grave artistic importance.

Opera had a significant conceptual role to play in *Phantom*. Act one began with a lumbering rehearsal for the fictional *Hannibal*, a caricature of nineteenth-century *grand opéra* complete with dancing slave girls and a large fake elephant. Lloyd Webber's stated target of parody was the hugely successful Giacomo Meyerbeer, remembered today for his elaborate stage effects. The direct parallels between the two men—Meyerbeer's *Le Prophète* had even featured roller skates back in 1849—might not have escaped Lloyd Webber himself. This, *Phantom* assured its audience, was opera at its most tedious, and it was perfectly natural to dislike it. A great deal of the plot was devoted to the Phantom's attempts to replace Carlotta, a fussy coloratura soprano with a thick Italian accent, with his beloved Christine. "We smile because she represents the old way with opera, but she is not a figure of fun," Lloyd Webber writes of Carlotta, whose interpretation of a *Hannibal* aria is turgid and self-indulgent. By contrast, Christine's rendition has a clearer, poppier quality, helped along by the fact that the melody bears more resemblance to a Linda Ronstadt ballad than a Meyerbeer aria. For the Phantom, only Christine's voice offers a way out of opera and into "a new sound"—even if that sound happens to be 1980s pop.

There was a touch of history in this. In late nineteenth-century Paris, the true phantom was *grand opéra* itself, treading the boards even as successors emerged both at home and across the Atlantic. French and English operettas were becoming wildly popular in America—a parody of opera for a nation with little native operatic tradition—and by the early twentieth century, comic opera had come together with minstrelsy and vaudeville to form the basis of what today we call musical theater. At first, the musical comedy resembled a plotless revue—until the arrival of *Show Boat* in 1927, a melodrama about miscegenation with lofty aspirations. "Is there a form of musical play tucked away somewhere in the realm of possibilities which could attain the heights of grand opera and still keep sufficiently human to be entertaining?" wondered its playwright and lyricist, Oscar Hammerstein II. In his later "book musicals" with the composer Richard Rodgers, resurrecting opera came to mean something very specific: smoothly integrating the music into the play to produce a single dramatic whole. "Some Enchanted Evening" might have sounded like a sweeping love song when played in one's sitting room, but in the context of *South Pacific*, it was a widower's tongue-tied expression of affection for a woman he barely knew.

For Lloyd Webber, the benefit of drama was to give definite shape to the abstract emotionality of music: a melody might sound sad, but only a lament could be tragic. But for this very reason, the music in *Phantom* rarely served a dramatic *end*—rather, it strutted around the stage like it owned the place. As the lyricist Charles Hart reported, the director Hal Prince was so focused on making *Phantom* into a crowd-pleaser that "any actor looking for motivation had to go and look elsewhere as far as Prince was concerned." Lloyd Webber evidently felt the same about Hart's lyrics, recalling with amusement how the beleaguered lyricist ended up tossing the word *somehow* into "Wishing You Were Somehow Here Again" to sop up the extra notes. But Lloyd Webber preferred for the music to talk over the words, as when the Phantom showed up at the masquerade ball: the revelers, having just got done singing about how good masks are for hiding one's identity, nevertheless recognize him instantly thanks to the massive organ chords that introduce him—and which, diegetically speaking, they *cannot hear*.

The debate over these competing priorities—music and drama—was as old as opera itself. "In an opera, the poetry simply has to be the obedient daughter of the music," Mozart wrote in 1781, arguing that Italian opera had overcome its "miserable librettos" by ensuring that "music reigns supreme and everything else is forgotten." Other composers, like the imperious Richard Wagner, saw music as a powerful organ of expression with no inherent content—that is, music was very good at saying things but had nothing of its own to say. In his 1851 polemic *Opera and Drama*, Wagner contended that the worst opera composers used music to produce "effects without causes," forgoing dramatic action to send impressions of feeling straight into the listener's ears. In the American musical-theater tradition, this tension would be borne out by Rodgers's own career as a composer. In his earlier partnership with the lyricist Lorenz Hart, Rodgers had written the melodies first, crafting sparkling tunes for forgettable plays, whereas with Hammerstein, the words had come first, requiring a more mature Rodgers to compose music with a clear dramatic purpose in mind. The former duo produced classic songs; only the latter produced classic *musicals*.

In one telling, Hammerstein's vision won out. For the 1957 musical *West Side Story*, the classically trained Leonard Bernstein wrote a complex, often operatic score around a recurring musical interval—the tritone, as immortalized in the melody for "Maria." But when it came time to write a "mad aria" for Maria to sing over her lover's dead body, Bernstein recalled, he "never got past six bars," realizing that the tragic climax called for precisely no music at all. To be clear, drama didn't have to be Shakespearean in order to have structural priority: Meredith Willson's

The Music Man, also from 1957, was a fully integrated musical with a corn-fed plot. Nor did a show have to be full of action in order to be dramatic, as with the thematically linked vignettes of Sondheim's *Company*. The point is that, in all these cases, music served at drama's pleasure. Sondheim, himself a protégé of Hammerstein's, took this to extremes in the seventies, veering away from the traditional song form in favor of accretive harmonic shapes that provided rich subtext for his lyrics—so much so that critics began complaining of having nothing to hum. The prickly composer seemed to mock this criticism in his 1979 masterpiece, *Sweeney Todd: The Demon Barber of Fleet Street*, in which a flamboyant Italian barber is so distracted by his own melodiousness that he loses a shaving contest to Sweeney, who remains perfectly silent throughout.

At the same time, musical theater was always grappling with a kind of royalist impulse, one that aspired to set music atop its rightful throne. By the eighties, it was as if Lloyd Webber, ever the Tory, had sent the megamusical to America to reclaim the colonies for the crown, armed with terroristically hummable tunes. Wagner had long ago despaired of the effects of the "naked, ear-delighting, absolute-melodic melody" on the opera-going public—what we would call an earworm. (Sure enough, as soon as *South Pacific* opened in 1949, Frank Sinatra and Perry Como had both released covers of "Some Enchanted Evening.") Bernstein agreed: "An F-sharp doesn't have to be considered in the mind; it is a direct hit." Even Sondheim, who admitted to being "not a huge fan of the human voice," ended up writing a pretty aria for his silly *barbiere*. Later in the original *Sweeney Todd* score, the triumphant orchestral blast that ended Sweeney's murderous "Epiphany" was abruptly undercut by a soft, sickly chord, thus tingeing his elation with moral uncertainty. But for the national tour, the sickly chord would be omitted—not for dramatic reasons but presumably because this allowed the singer, who had just pulled off a musical tour de force, to be rewarded with applause.

This is what *The Phantom of the Opera* stood for: not opera itself, for which it frankly had limited patience, but rather what it imagined to be operatic *values*, in particular the elevation of melody over everything else. If Hammerstein had wanted to dig up opera's bones, Lloyd Webber wanted to raise its spirit. (His hero had always been Rodgers anyway.) But he was so focused on musical effects that he seemed to cut corners when it came to the actual music. For all the banging on about it, the Phantom never even bothered to clarify what his "music of the night" actually was. He cannot have meant his pallid avant-garde opera, which better resembled a children's piano exercise than a work of French modernism. "If the Phantom is supposed to be such a brilliant musician," a woman once asked Lloyd Webber, "why does he write such horrible music?" As for "The Music of the Night" itself, no single Lloyd Webber melody has been more accused of plagiarism: its opening notes recall both *Tosca* and Lerner and Loewe's *Brigadoon*, followed by a long, indisputable borrowing from Puccini's *La Fanciulla del West*. It would seem that, even as he demanded that Christine submit to his music, the Phantom was singing someone else's.

But if the Puccini operas he admired had placed music over drama, it was Lloyd Webber's innovation to install *music-loving* over music it-self. The Phantom was not a musical genius but an aficionado. "Close your eyes and surrender to your darkest dreams!" he urged the audience, pontificating on the virtues of music appreciation. That's what the music of the night really meant: music as heard in the dark, such that its sole quality became its effect on the listener. This conveniently obviated the need for music that was actually *good*, as far as the critics were concerned. After all, the Phantom himself was hideous; what mattered was that his music had irresistible emotional power over a practically orgasmic Christine. "You cannot win her love by making her your prisoner!" Christine's aristocratic lover cried out to the Phantom. Yet this had always been Lloyd Webber's strategy as a composer: not to persuade but to overwhelm. In this way, Lloyd Webber was musical theater's irrepressible id, emerging from the orchestra pit to insist that at the form's core lay pure musical enthusiasm.

He wasn't entirely wrong. For centuries, people had come to the theater out of a desire to be overpowered by music; the various American plots to dethrone the megamusical could not change this. The grungy social realism of Jonathan Larson's 1996 rock opera, *Rent*, was largely a feint; if anything, *Rent* was good evidence that theater music may be even less suited to political statements than to drama. The show wore its own Puccini influences on its tattoo sleeve, and its AIDS-era anti-establishment message sounded as generic as that of the alt-rock genre from which it borrowed. At a certain point, one wished the crazy kids would stop trying to say something and just *sing*. A slightly more artful approach to political messaging would arrive in Jason Robert Brown's 1998 score for *Parade*, in which an unjust guilty verdict is read over a jaunty cakewalk and a Confederate march, played simultaneously and at different tempos. Even then, as the critic Jackson McHenry noted of the recent revival, one left the theater humming the "wrong" tune: a pretty hymn to the antebellum South. A few years later, ABBA's *Mamma Mia!* arrived on Broadway, unleashing the ongoing torrent of jukebox musicals that have forgone the hard labor of plagiarism in favor of stringing together the exact songs into which people actually do break out in real life.

The past decade has seen an even stranger heir to *Phantom*: the message musical. Atop the form, like a mad king, sits Lin-Manuel Miranda's 2015 hip-hop opera, *Hamilton*; the much-discussed decision to cast actors of color as the founding fathers concealed the fact that its cantata-like format and R&B pastiche brought it closer to *Cats* than to *Company*. (Lloyd Webber, horribly, credits the first rap in musical theater to *Starlight Express*, which is practically a work of minstrelsy.) But at least *Cats* was about cats; the message musical has taken Lloyd Webber's philosophy and affixed it, with the dramatic equivalent of spirit gum, to its earnest social causes. The British musical *Six*, a girl-power pop concert presented by the wives of Henry VIII, should be a simple excuse to hear decent impressions of Beyoncé and Adele; its needless gesture at feminist historiography is so limp that the characters openly admit it. At the logical end of this trend lies the jukebox musical *& Juliet*, now playing at the Stephen Sondheim Theater on Forty-Third Street, an excruciating retelling of *Romeo and Juliet* in which a transfeminine character is made to tearfully croak Britney Spears's "I'm Not a Girl, Not Yet a Woman." It is enough to make one long for the music of the night; at least the Phantom's message was that music shouldn't have one.

Today, it is clear that *Phantom* succeeded in remaking the musical in its own image. Not only did Lloyd Webber set Broadway on its current path of chintzy commercial nihilism, but he also reminded us, through his peculiar naïveté, that the greatest obstacle to musical theater is music itself. Perhaps this is why we love it so much. Ironic, then, that Lloyd Webber himself has rarely brought a hit to Broadway since. (His five-hundred-page memoir peters out in 1986, sparing him the embarrassment of flops like the execrable *Love Never Dies*, a sequel to *Phantom* in which Christine has given birth to the Phantom's love child.) Curiously, Lloyd Webber's new Broadway show, *Bad Cinderella*, is a pedestrian message musical; the classic story has been carved, like a stepsister's heel, into a deeply misogynistic satire of beauty standards. The title song contains an almost note-for-note quotation from Rodgers and Hammerstein's "In My Own Little Corner" from their own *Cinderella* show. It is as if, having finally accepted that he will never write a tune half as good as Rodgers, Lloyd Webber has settled for writing a tune half-composed by him.

But what's really notable about *Bad Cinderella* is its lack of ambition: it is an old-fashioned book musical with plenty of dialogue and a forgettable score. It is not a train wreck, just a train. There is something pitiful about this. It is odd to be lectured on beauty by a man who has spent his entire career blindly devoted to it. The Phantom, at least, had the courage of his convictions; he was an enlightened philistine, willing to murder in the name of beautiful music while lacking a single opinion about what made a piece of music beautiful. In the twilight of his career, Lloyd Webber has sent the ghost back to his underground lagoon, and the theater feels small and empty now. It could use a little opera.

2023

One rarely has the opportunity to write about an artist as blithely generous with his own misdeeds as Sir Andrew Lloyd Webber. So many things were left on the cutting-room floor. I will tell you one: During the original recording session for "Don't Cry for Me Argentina," the composer was notified by telephone that the forest he had purchased in Wales as part of a harebrained tax scheme had burned to the ground. "No matter your tax problem," he writes in his memoir, "don't get into forestry."

Finish Him

In the third episode of HBO's *The Last of Us*, a pair of postapocalyptic travelers search through an abandoned gas station ten miles outside Boston. "No way!" exclaims Ellie (Bella Ramsey), the savvy teenage girl whom the gruff smuggler Joel (Pedro Pascal) is tasked with transporting across the country. Most of the population has been infected by a parasitic fungus that transforms its victims into killing machines. But in this brief moment of repose, Ellie spots a relic of a more civilized era. "I had a friend who knew everything about this game," she tells Joel breathlessly, mashing the buttons of a busted arcade unit for Midway Games' classic fighting game *Mortal Kombat II*. "There's this one character named Mileena who takes off her mask and she has monster teeth and then she swallows you whole and barfs out your bones!"

It's a slyly self-referential moment for *The Last of Us*, which co-creators Neil Druckmann and Craig Mazin have lovingly adapted from developer Naughty Dog's critically acclaimed 2013 video game. In the game, Joel is a hard-bitten survivor whose daughter was shot on Outbreak Day; Ellie's mysterious immunity to the fungus may hold the key to a vaccine. As they make their way west, through bombed-out city blocks and overgrown interstates, past echolocating zombies and desperate human beings like themselves, they begin to regard each other as father and daughter. Widely considered a masterpiece of the video-game form, *The Last of Us* boasted a story whose strong characters and disturbing moral conflicts had all the makings of a buzzy television drama—so much so that *The New Yorker* asked in its preview of the series, "Can a Video Game Be Prestige TV?"

The answer is obviously yes. Before it premiered in January, critics had already crowned *The Last of Us* the best video-game adaptation ever made. In itself, this was no great honor: Outside a few passable kids' movies, competition for the title has been limited to dreck like *Resident Evil, Tomb Raider*, or the limp *Halo* series on Paramount+. Attempts to imitate gameplay directly have yielded almost universally ridiculous results. (The nauseating first-person-shooter sequence from *Doom* lurches to mind.) But, really, video-game adaptations have sucked for the same reason many movies suck: low budgets, terrible scripts, and an often comical misunderstanding of their own material. The solitary exception to this rule, until now, was 2021's *Werewolves Within*, an amiable horror comedy that, tellingly, bears even less resemblance to the virtual party game on which it is based than *Clue* bore to *Clue*.

The showrunners of *The Last of Us* have wisely exchanged action sequences for extended character beats, and thanks to the chemistry between Pascal and Ramsey, the series remains grounded in the deepening relationship between Joel and Ellie. Asked ad nauseam about the curse of the video-game adaptation, Mazin took to replying he had "cheated" by picking the best story the medium had to offer. What he probably meant was he had chosen a title whose actual gameplay, a fine but standard mix of third-person stealth and combat, mostly acted as a system of gates between one narrative sequence and the next. In this sense, HBO's *The Last of Us* represents a superb realization of a modest goal: to adapt the *narrative* of a video game without attempting to adapt the game itself.

It's worth remembering that this is standard operating procedure for prestige television, which regularly makes a point to bestow literary qualities—realism, lyricism, characterization—onto middling works of genre fiction. (An obvious example is *Big Little Lies*, elevated from beach read to serious drama by its naturalist approach and moody shots of the ocean.) That this formula should have finally been applied to a video game, and a good one, is a matter less of artistic innovation than of budget. "One of the highest compliments I can pay the show is that I wouldn't have guessed that Joel and Ellie's mordant, spiritedly macabre adventures first began in pixelated form," negged Inkoo Kang in *The New Yorker*. But the question was never whether *The Last of Us* would make for compelling television, since anyone who had played it could tell you it basically already was that. The real question, buried in the praise, was why a story with such cinematic ambitions had bothered being a video game to begin with.

To answer it, one would first need to know what a video game is. Despite enjoying a higher level of prestige than ever in their relatively brief history, video games are still reviewed largely for their recreational value—that is to say, as toys. But the chief obstacle to serious criticism is not that we fail to recognize video games can be art, which is usually just a desperate shorthand for "capable of evoking a strong response." It's that we presume to know what kind of art they would be. The first is merely a lack of attention; the second is a genuine error of judgment.

Look no further than the broad caricature of video games as "interactive," a quality that supposedly distinguishes them from more "passive" media like television or the novel. Regarding a long, claustrophobic shot from inside a moving car as Joel flees the zombie outbreak with his daughter, Sarah (Nico Parker), one otherwise admiring critic reproached *The Last of Us* for aping the interactive format of a game, noting it was "hard to resist the feeling that you should have a controller in your hand to choose which way they should turn next." Yet in the nearly identical sequence from the game's prologue, the player is responsible not for the car but just for the in-world virtual camera, which they may swivel uselessly from Sarah's terrified face to the dark road ahead to a neighbor's house burning in the distance. Indeed, the feeling of helplessness is the whole point.

The mistake here, common enough even among those literate in video games, is the breezy conflation of interactivity with control, as if the simple fact of player choice were any surer guarantee of efficacy than the existence of choice in real life. It's true you can't alter the content of a television show just by watching it, but too great an emphasis on this will obscure the fact that something similar is true of many video games. *The Last of Us* has sometimes been called an "interactive movie" by fans and detractors alike—a faintly damning term that implies, ironically, a *dearth* of consequential interaction between players and the game. And it's true: As a game about difficult moral choices, it gives the player none. There are no plot decisions, no dialogue options; there is no open world. The weight of choice is felt instead during the mundane task of inventory management, where every bullet and clean rag is precious. Meanwhile, Joel is Joel, violent and gentle, and players cannot overrule his decisions short of turning off the game and going outside to play.

To an extent, *The Last of Us* was an outlier by design, one that left a choice-shaped hole in player experience that reflected Joel's uncompromising commitment to protecting Ellie. Yet even in the most liberal of narrative video games, the majority of choices available to players are either cosmetic or mechanical. The classic example is a suit of armor that increases the computing number associated with one's defense while also lending a desirable visual panache. These things matter deeply to how a game plays: gamers were so appalled by the clothing system of *Cyberpunk 2077*, in which combat bonuses could be reaped only by rocking truly hideous pieces of streetwear, that its developer, CD Projekt Red, later added an option for players to stick with one acceptable outfit without falling behind in their armor class. But none of this had any effect on the game's narrative, which despite its many branching plotlines, romance options, and endings was still just one story that could be told only a finite number of ways. There is a big difference, in other words, between mere *customization* and true narrative control—if such a thing even exists.

A video game, then, is emphatically *not* a story you get to change; in its most elemental form, it is not a story at all. The highly visual aspect of video games can mask the fact that, as computer programs, they are naturally far more abstract than film or television. In *Left Behind*, a short companion to *The Last of Us* released in 2014, Ellie's best friend Riley takes her to a deserted mall in Boston where she shows Ellie an arcade cabinet for a *Mortal Kombat*–style fighting game. The unit is long dead, but at her friend's insistence, Ellie closes her eyes and slams the buttons while Riley describes a round of gleefully gory combat. It's an ingenious comment on the nature of video games: The narration is all but divorced from the gameplay, a mini-game in which the player may press their own buttons in order to help Ellie's imaginary avatar "defeat" her equally imaginary opponent. But the actual *game* takes place only inside Ellie's mind, her delighted face illuminated by the static glow of the defunct machine.

The lesson here is that, even in longform-narrative video games like

The Last of Us, no predetermined relation exists between gameplay, as a real-time system of potential inputs and outputs, and traditional film elements like character, narration, or image. In theory, if one happened to strike the right buttons at the right time, one could play through a video game in its entirety without a single thought to what was transpiring on-screen, like a monkey typing out Shakespeare. The long-standing appeal of *Mortal Kombat II*, for instance, was that it really *could* be played by blindly mashing the buttons, with the game smoothly converting even the most anarchic style of play into a potentially deadly flurry of punches and kicks.

This doesn't mean video games shouldn't tell stories, a pseudo-formalist position occasionally staked out by sour game-studies types, any more than cinema should limit its focus to the passage of light through a lens. The resistance of gameplay to being narrativized, and of stories to being gamified—what game bloggers sometimes call "ludonarrative dissonance"—can never be eliminated, only managed; the first question for any narrative video game is therefore how it plans to forge this foregone conclusion into a compelling aesthetic experience. In fact, many of the most interesting video games tend to amplify ludonarrative dissonance, allowing form to poke stylishly through the envelope of narrative content. Valve's puzzle-platformer *Portal* famously ends by revealing the protagonist is trapped in a gamelike research facility run by a homicidal computer whose sardonic directions the player must disobey to escape. Here was a darkly comic acknowledgment that a life wholly composed of jumping, shooting, and pushing boxes around—the life of many video-game characters—would in the real world be nothing short of torture.

To return to our initial question, then: It's true that *The Last of Us* often resembles a game that doesn't want to be one. But this tension, which the television adaptation is at pains to relieve, is precisely what made the original game such a compelling study in powerlessness. Its protagonist, after all, *also* doesn't want to be one. In early cutscenes, Joel is vehemently opposed to becoming Ellie's keeper, his fatherly grief masked as stony pragmatism; when gameplay resumes, players may feel they are pushing Joel forward against his will, overriding his reluctance with their own desire to progress in the game. Even as Joel softens to his precocious young charge, *The Last of Us* gives players few opportunities to make their Joel stronger or faster: a slight increase in his health bar, perhaps, or a new gun whose bullets are rarer than usual. Instead, the same ludic architecture that at first makes players do things Joel doesn't want to do—linear level design, few upgrades, scarce resources—slowly comes to reflect Joel's terrifyingly limited ability to protect Ellie.

What *The Last of Us* does let you do, as often as you would like, is die. In itself, this is unremarkable. The need for a death mechanic is almost as old as video games themselves. "*Finish him*," a voice booms in the HBO series as Riley (Storm Reid), playing as the bone-barfing Mileena, bests Ellie in a fully functional game of *Mortal Kombat II*. "Do *not* finish me!" Ellie yells, but soon the girls are slotting in more quarters, bribing death with pocket change. The arcade industry's pay-to-stay-alive system, which in its golden age brought in as much as $8 billion a year in quarters alone, faded with the rise of home consoles, where player death usually just meant respawning at the last checkpoint. Today, many video-game protagonists are zombies after a fashion, their bodies hijacked by an alien intelligence with crude control over their motor systems and an unlimited ability to resurrect. The studio behind last year's role-playing game *Elden Ring* has built its entire punishing aesthetic around death, giving players a single nerve-racking chance to return to the site of their demise to collect lost experience points. Recent games like *Hades* or *Deathloop* have integrated this concept on a narrative level, not only providing canonical explanations for why exactly the player keeps coming back to life but also using this de facto immortality as an opportunity for character development. ("I guess you want to die again?" purrs your ex-girlfriend in *Hades* after murdering you for the eighth or ninth time.)

What distinguishes *The Last of Us* is the *way* the player character dies. In the series, Pascal's soulful Joel is keenly aware of his own mortality—his bad knees, his hearing loss. But in the video game, Joel actually *does* die over and over. Each time, the game snatches back control of the camera, forcing players to watch as he is shot, stabbed, burned alive, beaten with a lead pipe; as shrieking zombies gouge out his eyes, snap his jaw apart, rip glistening red sinew from his neck. These cutscenes, animated with a gruesome realism far more disturbing than the blood-and-guts approach typical to the genre, often have the quality of jump scares, pouncing just as the player thinks they're safe. As in most games, Joel's deaths are shunted off into a noncanonical universe; the player retakes control of Joel at the latest checkpoint, and he has no memory of his latest fatality. But the player does, and this visceral sense of Joel's death—something that, speaking strictly from the narrative point of view, *never happens*—comes to define their relationship to both Joel and the game as a whole.

Players thus experience *two* Joels: the Joel presented in the story, a powerful father figure propelled to heroic heights by grief and love, and the version of Joel controlled by the player, a terrified man with poor aim, little endurance, and a perilously high mortality rate. As many viewers have already joked, no amount of fidelity will allow the HBO show to capture the frustration of watching Joel be repeatedly eviscerated by the same zombie. Druckmann has said the game was designed to give players the same protective relationship to Ellie that Joel develops, and this is true, in a sense: Ellie can die in just as grisly a fashion as Joel if the player misses a window to rescue her. "That's why men like you and me are here," a fellow survivor tells Joel in the show, urging him to give his life meaning by finding someone to keep safe. For Joel, this person is Ellie; but for the player, this person is *Joel*, and when he is gravely wounded late in the game, player control startlingly passes to Ellie, who must now protect her protector in the most brutal stretch of gameplay yet.

This was the game's masterstroke. Form erupts into content, the player's ludic relationship to Joel at last given narrative flesh in the person of Ellie, whose bitter determination to keep Joel alive leads to a horrific loss of innocence from which—as players of *The Last of Us Part II* already know—she may never recover. Here, we may rightly speak of interactivity: One may care *about* a character on television, but one must care *for* a character in a video game. In fact, *The Last of Us* suggested that care, by definition, means *choosing* to have no choice, holding on to another person so tightly their survival becomes an inescapable necessity. Of course, a TV show may treat these themes too, and the adaptation acquits itself admirably; the point is not that a video game, like other art forms, can show us something about love, but that love, at its most monstrous, can have the unyielding structure of a video game. This only a video game can teach. That's not a knock on the HBO show, which has genuinely demonstrated that you may adapt a video game for television by taking its story and swallowing it whole. But you'll still have to spit out the bones.

2023

Cunt!

For most scholars—I speak from recovery—academic writing is a professional genre, not a literary one, more akin to a legal memo than a novel. The famous abstruseness of what we call "theory" is usually not an effect of intellectual sophistication; more often, it's just someone doing their job. I don't mean that cruelly. I mean it as a rightful acknowledgment that scholars are workers, and like other workers, they have an inalienable right to mediocrity.

On Freedom, the new essay collection from the poet and memoirist Maggie Nelson, sits squarely in this genre. Its lyrical subtitle—"Four Songs of Care and Constraint"—is an overpromise; the chapters are "songs" exclusively in the sense that they have musical names: "Art Song," "The Ballad of Sexual Optimism," "Drug Fugue," and "Riding the Blinds." In fact, they are bits of straightforward academic criticism. They do not sing; they talk. What they say is this: if freedom-minded people are to rid ourselves of "the habits of paranoia, despair, and policing" that Nelson believes to be menacing the left—from the #MeToo movement to climate nihilism—we must learn to sit with ambiguity, risk, and indeterminacy. In doing so, Nelson says we'll be engaging in what the French philosopher Michel Foucault called "practices of freedom"—careful, patient experiments with what freedom might look like in everyday life with often conflicting results.

This is a fine, if unremarkable, thesis. But Maggie Nelson is a Guggenheim Fellow, a MacArthur Fellow, the bestselling author of nine (now ten) books, the most recent of which earned her wide recognition outside both academia and letters. Maggie Nelson could etch sentences into a grain of rice if she wanted to. So why write an academic book? Why fill chapters with ponderous quotations from writers who are, at the end of the day, talking about something else? Why hide in the endnotes arguments that could have appeared out in the open? I am in full agreement with Nelson's observation that "people read much more challenging things than they are given credit for," as she once said regarding the success of her 2015 memoir, *The Argonauts*. But I am not talking about the specter of difficulty; I am talking about clarity, novelty, and—forgive me—beauty.

Whatever else it was, *The Argonauts* was beautiful. It told the story of Nelson's love affair with the artist Harry Dodge, with whom she had a son named Iggy. There, she threaded French philosophy and psychoanalysis through raw, sensual descriptions of being pregnant while Dodge was beginning testosterone therapy: "Each time I count the four rungs down on the blue ladder tattooed on your lower back, spread out the skin, push in the nearly-two-inch-long needle, and plunge the golden, oily T into deep muscle mass, I feel certain I am delivering a gift." Nelson called the book "autotheory," a term she attributed to Paul Preciado's unfortunate book *Testo Junkie*; a more modest term might have been "high memoir."

Either way, it's true: *The Argonauts* was full of theory, including that of Nelson's mentor, Eve Kosofsky Sedgwick, by then six years dead of cancer. The field of affect theory is haunted by untimely deaths: Sedgwick at fifty-eight; four years later, her student José Esteban Muñoz at forty-six; and earlier this year, Lauren Berlant at sixty-three. These were thinkers who taught us that thinking has feelings, and this, at its best moments, is what *The Argonauts* delivered to its surprisingly wide audience: the emotional world of theory. Admittedly, as often happens in the "auto" genres, Nelson relied on her own vulnerability to insulate herself from close scrutiny. It was easy to miss, for instance, that Nelson named her son Igasho, a supposedly Native American name, on the flimsy justification that Dodge once told her he was part Cherokee, and *The Argonauts* clearly profited immensely from being someone else's transition memoir. Still, it is one thing to dryly rehearse the psychoanalyst D. W. Winnicott's theory of the "good-enough mother," which tried to imagine the mother as an ordinary person, not an ideal; it is quite another to show readers what it feels like to read about de-idealizing motherhood while raising a two-year-old.

If it sounds like I'm saying Nelson writes best when she's writing about her personal life, instead of writing essays, I suppose I am. No, the same isn't true for many women writers, even most of them; but I do think it's true for her. Fans of *The Argonauts* will find reproduced in *On Freedom* only that book's inner graduate student, eager to show she has done the reading. Take the thesis, drawn directly from the work of Sedgwick, whose famous essay "Paranoid Reading and Reparative Reading" proposed that academic critics should soften the defensive urge to pin their objects down in favor of a slower, open-minded willingness to "confer plenitude" on them. I have read, and this is not exaggerating, some forty or fifty accounts of what Sedgwick meant by paranoid and reparative reading; it is, within queer theory, a forest fully logged.

Such is Nelson's approach in *On Freedom*: to present six or seven academics on a topic and then say of one, "I like this." She does not have ideas, only opinions. I don't mean that she is not an intelligent thinker and, sometimes, a formidable stylist; I mean that she does not advance new concepts, nor is she, by her own description, interested in doing so. "The Ballad of Sexual Optimism" reads frustratingly like a series of takes that have aged poorly in the five years since Nelson began writing *On Freedom*. "Drug Fugue," by contrast, has the character of a perfectly serviceable chapter of lit-crit that's interesting only if you're already interested in drug literature. The chapter on the climate crisis, "Riding the Blinds," brings a refreshing urgency of tone, though it may be no accident that in doing so, Nelson leaves freedom behind almost altogether.

It is the forceful first chapter of *On Freedom*, "Art Song," where Nelson makes her most concerted attempt to prove herself as an essayist rather than as a memoirist, an academic, or a poet. Nelson is a regular writer of art criticism, and she taught at an art school for more than twenty years; her investment in the topic is clear, personal, and fierce. It's here that Nelson takes up arms against the "rhetoric of harm" that *On Freedom* is most interested in criticizing, and this argument about thinking is intended to resonate through the rest of the book. In fact, I'm going to spend the rest of this piece talking about it.

The rhetoric of harm goes something like this: depicting harm through art can be harmful to marginalized people, and artists who refuse to be held accountable for that harm end up furthering it, regardless of their own views on the matter. Nelson doesn't like this line of thinking. She worries it places undue restraints on artists' freedom to "give expression to complex, sometimes disturbing dimensions of their psyches"; that its hair-trigger condemnations eclipse "the slow work of looking, making, reading, or thinking"; and that it reflects a "homogenizing logic of paranoia" that divides art into good and bad, right and wrong.

If Nelson's argument sounds like one you've heard before, or perhaps have made yourself, that's because it is. I will grant that Nelson prosecutes this argument with a level of care unbecoming of the genre, which can ironically be found all over the very internet whose deleterious effects the author likes to decry. But why should we listen to yet another emissary of Generation X complain about "a world drunk on scapegoating, virtue signaling, and public humiliation"? It doesn't matter anymore whether complaints like this are legitimate. Maybe they are. But they are also *boring*.

It doesn't help that Nelson's two main examples, to which she frequently returns in "Art Song," are both from 2017: Sam Durant's sculpture *Scaffold* at the Walker Art Center in Minneapolis, a large-scale replica of gallows used to hang thirty-eight Dakota men that was eventually removed following protests and negotiations between the museum and Dakota elders, and Dana Schutz's *Open Casket*, a sort-of-abstract oil painting of Emmett Till exhibited at the Whitney Biennial in New York that became the object of national controversy when the artist Hannah Black demanded in an open letter posted on Facebook that the painting be removed and destroyed. Scandals in the art world brown like bitten apples; to discuss them now, as relevant as they may be to the point at hand, feels like an unsolicited rehashing. If there's one thing everyone should be able to agree about that letter now, it's that people sure did talk about it then.

But fine, let's talk about it. Nelson criticizes protesters for applying "the language of physical harm"—for instance, "a slap in the face," as one person described Durant's installation. It's one thing, Nelson says, to argue that neo-Nazis chanting slogans through the streets are engaged in violence. But to say that an oil painting by Schutz, a white woman, perpetrated "violence against Black communities," as some protesters put it, or that Durant's installation reinstated "the violent power of sovereignty," as the scholar Arne De Boever wrote—Nelson sees an insidious logic at work here, as if art could have power analogous to "a militarized state."

I agree that *violence* is a difficult word these days; it means too much and rarely enough. But watch what Nelson says next. When protesters and academics equate a work of art with violence, she writes, their arguments mirror "a classic prerequisite not only for censorship but also for the persecution of artists." Nelson's example is the artist and porn star Annie Sprinkle, who was once jailed on charges of sodomy after making a zine depicting her penetration by an amputee's stump. This is a surprising comparison. When a scholar like De Boever claims, in an academic monograph with a likely print run of a few thousand, that Durant's gallows "reinstated" state violence against the Dakota nation, should readers consider this speech act on par with a sex worker's literal detention by the police, simply because it "plays into the same arguments" historically used to persecute artists? Equating art with violence is bad, but equating rhetoric with violence isn't? Who is calling who the state now?

Undeterred, Nelson argues that, unlike an act of violence, even the most offensive art has a "diffuse audience with no reducible target," carries "no expressly malign (or even discernible) intent," and poses "no imminent danger to its audience." But isn't that exactly what protesters were saying—that racism could be diffuse, benign, and slow-acting? True, Nelson's picture of art does not sound like a slap in the face; it sounds more like city officials blithely allowing the runoff from the local power plant to slowly alter the quality of a municipal water supply until low-income residents begin to develop chronic illnesses.

That's Nelson's image, not mine, taken from a passage in the book's climate essay. There, she alleges that when queer writers criticize the having of children (she cites a few, including me), we are being callous in the face of the possible extinction of humanity thanks to climate change. Blasé indifference to future generations, Nelson writes, is *"arguably no different from* dumping a bunch of toxic waste guaranteed to poison whoever comes into contact with it," then disclaiming any responsibility for your actions "because you won't know the sickened people personally or won't be alive when they get sick, or because you just aren't that into people anyway, especially small ones that cry on airplanes." The italics there are mine; the murder charges, maybe not.

You see the problem with this kind of argumentation. False equivalences abound, on both sides, and the question devolves into not just which equivalences are false but which false equivalences are, as it were, falser than others. Is racism like art? Art like climate change? An open letter like the police? Nelson writes, "Acting as if the world neatly divides . . . into problematic, ethically turbulent, essentially dangerous people who should stay 'over there,' and nonproblematic, ethically good, essentially safe people who should be allowed to stay 'over here' is not our only option. After all, what I've just described is a prison." So which is worse, you tell me—a protester calling *Scaffold* a "slap in the face" or Maggie Nelson comparing that protester's speech to incarceration?

I'm being unfair. Nelson is using a metaphor, which is when you use one thing to describe a different thing. Surely it cannot in every case belittle the horrors of mass incarceration or the cause of abolition to refer to something that isn't a prison as a prison. That would make a prison of language, which has freely tended toward abstraction since we crawled out of the caves. The first words were all false equivalences: the word *fire* is not a fire. Okay then: Nelson is not saying the rhetoric of harm is a physical prison; she is being *expressive*, like an artist. "Expression needs context," she writes. We must be able to distinguish "being called a cunt in a sex game with your lover, from being called a cunt by your boss during a meeting, from seeing the word *cunt* spray-painted on a wall as you're walking by, from calling your own cunt a cunt, from reading a paragraph like this one."

This is an excellent observation, and a perfect example. In writing it, Nelson is both illustrating and exercising the freedom of expression, by which I mean both her legal right to say what she wants the way she wants to and the freedom, inherent in the nature of language, for words *not to mean what they say*. The freedom not to mean things—this is what Nelson will freely extend to works of art while in the same breath denying it to those who would advocate that these same works of art be removed or destroyed. If the protesters had wanted to be open to interpretation, they should have tried being paintings.

But hang on. "If and when we are really calling for the destruction and/or prohibition of a piece of art," Nelson replies, "it is disingenuous to argue, as has often been argued to me, that we aren't *really* calling for any of that, based on the premise that, since we lack the power to carry out such demands, they are best understood as inert performance designed to garner attention that a critique without such demands wouldn't receive." She is saying that it is disingenuous to say protesters were being disingenuous; betting that institutions will "refuse to cave in to our demands," Nelson writes, is a poor excuse for organizing. That's a reasonable retort. Let's say the protesters really did want the art removed. Nelson calls this "censorious," noting that the ACLU considers censorship to occur "whenever some people succeed in imposing their personal political or moral values" on others. Yet surely the left *should* try to impose its political values on others; if I'm not mistaken, we call this winning. The real question is how to do it without resorting to the gulags.

But Nelson feels especially protective toward art. She recalls her twenty-odd years of teaching at the California Institute of the Arts, which boasts a very broad freedom-of-expression policy: "CalArts does not censor any work on the basis of content," period. According to Nelson, this policy largely worked: "Sometimes provocative student work glistened with punk or even revolutionary spirit; at others, its transgressions sank into the mean-spirited or clichéd. The pedagogical task at hand was not to discipline people for their failures, but to help them make more interesting art." This was not always easy, but it was worth it, for Nelson, to learn to forgo the knee-jerk reactions of "suppression, shaming, or ejection" in favor of the more patient labor of "radical compassion."

Radical compassion sounds good, and it certainly makes sense for an art school, whose mission is to safeguard not just art but also, and arguably more fundamentally, an educational environment. Professional training presumes both the existence of a profession and a difference between itself and that profession; art students are taught not to be art students but to be artists. One supposes the Whitney Biennial, which courts the attention of not just New Yorkers but the entire international art world, might be held to different, possibly higher standards than a senior showcase; one at least hopes that a chef has less freedom than a culinary student.

Let's say something obvious. People have the right to make art. People have the right to write books. They also have the right to go to school for those things. (In fact, the state should pay for it!) What people do not have a right to is having their art exhibited in museums or their books published by publishers. The latter is a privilege, by which I mean it largely reflects its bearers' material resources, connections, and luck, and only to a much lesser extent their talent. It can be argued, and has, that this privilege should be redistributed to members of historically marginalized groups; good, but this would only be back pay, not freedom. Institutions like these, the museums with arms dealers on their boards, the publishing houses owned by multinational conglomerates—freedom is not to be found within the matrices of their financial decisions.

And you know what? I agree with Nelson. I agree that art is "a place to engage in open-ended experiments with extremity, wildness, satire, defiance, taboo, beauty, and absurdity, to make space for anarchic gestures and urges that might otherwise rip apart (for better or worse) social norms or fabric." I'm just far less convinced that this only describes art. Take Nelson's comments about social media, where, she writes, one finds "a chorus of disembodied strangers standing at the ready to trash-talk not only your work but also your appearance, your attachments, your demographic markers, your family, and more." One of her examples of this disinhibition is, bizarrely, the joy many of us felt at the viral video of the white supremacist Richard Spencer getting sucker punched. But it is easy to blame "new attentional technologies" for fostering rage and paranoia without noticing that these technologies represent a historically new level of abstraction in language. Twitter, too, is full of experiments with wildness and satire; think of trolling, an absurdist practice as expressive as any oil painting. Do people mean what they post? Well, do people mean what they paint?

Or consider Hannah Black's open letter to the Whitney. I am sorry to be talking about this letter again; Hannah, I'm sorry I'm talking about this letter. But here goes. Did Hannah Black mean it when she wrote of *Open Casket*, "The painting must go"? Let's assume so. What does it mean to say she meant it? In the first place, the letter was not a real letter; it was not, as far as I know, written on a piece of paper, sealed in an envelope, and delivered to the Whitney's doorstep. In the second place, it was an open letter, meaning its putative addressees—the Whitney curators and staff—were not its true audience; it was, like all open letters, a bit of theater. The letter *presumed*, in other words, that it would be multiply interpreted; in fact, according to one possible interpretation (this one), it *planned* to be.

I am not saying the open letter was a work of art. I am only saying that it is difficult to prove it wasn't, and more importantly, that Nelson should *have* to prove it if she is going to deny it the slow interpretive attention she asks readers to give to artistic work. It should never be assumed that the thing one defends has a monopoly on the qualities that first inspired one's allegiance to it. For a critic, it is easy to attack, harder to understand, hardest to understand one's attackers. Yes, the rhetoric of harm can be paranoid, flattening, and reductive; yes, it can reify "tinny stereotypes of bully and snowflake, target and troll, defender and supporter, perpetrator and victim." But reifying something doesn't actually make it real; it only pretends to, and hopes you won't notice the difference. The rhetoric of harm is just that—a rhetoric. It does not really divide the world into victims and perpetrators of harm, either literally or metaphorically. Where is its army, its police? No, a rhetoric only tries to impose its categories on the world, and that—the failure of language to manifest what it names—is what deserves our critical attention if we are to move beyond tiresome debates over whether the internet is tearing the left apart.

It is unfortunately true that those who call for more nuance usually want less of it instead; this is what's happening when liberal pundits feel sorry for Nazis. More disappointing is when a writer of stature and skill who genuinely wants us to think more carefully, as I believe Nelson does, manages not to extend that care beyond the limits of what she finds interesting, right, or true. The higher critical act, if we want to go in for that sort of thing, is not to position the subtlety of one's own views against the crudeness of those who do not share them but to draw out like water from a rock the nuances that exist within the ideas one finds the most noxious, the most strident, the most difficult to dignify.

The critic should do this work not just because it will further her understanding of the world (good), or because it is far more interesting (better), but because it will crack open a view onto unconscious processes within *herself* that are available only through (forgive me) the infinite regard of other people. This is what I've been trying to show you, modestly, in my back-and-forth with Nelson. I can only say she is being disingenuous by risking disingenuousness myself; I place on her arguments a demand for logical consistency that I implore her, at the same time, to spare other people. A few paragraphs ago, I apologized to you for talking about the Whitney letter, and then I apologized to Hannah Black. But Hannah isn't here right now; I'm only *pretending* to address her, for dramatic effect, while in fact I'm still talking to you, and you're not here either, so I'm really just talking to myself, and if I'm being really honest, I'm not talking at all—I am only, God help me, *writing*.

The freedom not to mean it, or to mean it only sometimes—whose freedoms are these? Mine? Yours? I'll tell you a secret: I am generally in favor of the artistic freedom to provoke and offend, except when I am not. I am generally opposed to the censorship of troubling or controversial speech, except for when I am not. How do I quarter that orange? Well, I exercise judgment, or at least I try to—which is to say, I gather the indeterminacy of a thing into the inconsistency of having an opinion about it. Indeed, opinions can be formed no other way. When I make a judgment about a work of art, or a political act, or a book like this one, I change not knowing what to think about it into not knowing why I think it. Like all of us—like you, like Maggie Nelson—I do this every day. It is, if nothing else, a practice of freedom.

2021

II

On Liking Women

Once a week, for a single semester of high school, I would be dismissed early from class to board the athletics bus with fifteen teenage girls in sleek cap-sleeved volleyball jerseys and short-shorts. I was the only boy.

Occasionally a girl who still needed to change would excuse herself behind a row of seats to slip out of her school uniform into the team's dark-blue colors. For more minor wardrobe adjustments, I was simply asked to close my eyes. In theory, all sights were trained on the game ahead where I, as official scorekeeper, would push numbers around a byzantine spreadsheet while the girls leapt, dug, and dove with raw, adolescent power. But whatever discipline had instilled itself before a match would dissolve in its aftermath, often following a pit stop for greasy highway-exit food, as the girls relaxed into an innocent dishabille: untucked jerseys, tight undershirts, the strap of a sports bra. They talked, with the candor of postgame exhaustion, of boys, sex, and other vices; of good taste and bad blood and small, sharp desires. I sat, and I listened, and I waited, patiently, for that wayward electric pulse that passes unplanned from one bare upper arm to another on an otherwise unremarkable Tuesday evening, the away-game bus cruising back over the border between one red state and another.

The truth is, I have never been able to differentiate liking women from wanting to be like them. For years, the former desire held the latter in its mouth, like a capsule too dangerous to swallow. When I trawl the seafloor of my childhood for sunken tokens of things to come, these bus rides are about the gayest thing I can find. They probably weren't even all that gay. It is common, after all, for high school athletes to try to squash the inherent homoeroticism of same-sex sport under the heavy cleat of denial. But I'm too desperate to salvage a single genuine lesbian memory from the wreckage of the scared, straight boy whose life I will never not have lived to be choosy. The only other memory with a shot at that title is my pubescent infatuation with my best friend, a moody, low-voiced, Hot Topic–shopping girl who, it dawned on me only many years later, was doing her best impression of Shane from *The L Word*. One day she told me she had a secret to tell me after school; I spent the whole day queasy with hope that a declaration of her affections was forthcoming. Later, over the phone, after a pause big enough to drown in, she told me she was gay. "I thought you might say that," I replied, weeping inside. A decade later, after long having fallen out of touch, I texted her. "A week ago, I figured out that I am trans," I wrote. "You came out to me all those years ago. Just returning the favor."

This was months before I began teaching my first undergraduate recitation, where for the second time in my life—but the first time as a woman—I read Valerie Solanas's *SCUM Manifesto*. The *SCUM Manifesto* is a deliciously vicious feminist screed calling for the revolutionary overthrow of all men; Solanas self-published it in 1967, one year before she shot Andy Warhol on the sixth floor of the Decker Building in New York City. I wondered how my students would feel about it. In the bathroom before class, as I fixed my lipstick and fiddled with my hair, I was approached by a thoughtful, earnest young woman who sat directly to my right during class. "I loved the Solanas reading," she told me breathlessly. "I didn't know that was a thing you could study." I cocked my head, confused. "You didn't know what was a thing you could study?" "Feminism!" she said, beaming. In class, I would glance over at this student's notes, only to discover that she had filled the page with the word *SCUM*, written over and over with the baroque tenderness usually reserved for the name of a crush.

I, too, had become infatuated with feminism in college. I, too, had felt the thrill of its clandestine discovery. I had caught a shy glimpse of her across a dim, crowded dormitory room vibrating with electronic music and unclear intentions: a low-key, confident girl, slightly aloof, with a gravity all neighboring bodies obeyed. Feminism was too cool, too effortlessly hip, to be interested in a person like me, whom social anxiety had prevented from speaking over the telephone until well into high school. Besides, I heard she only dated women. I limited myself, therefore, to acts of distant admiration. I left critical comments on the student newspaper's latest exposé of this or that frat party. I took a women's studies course that had only one other man in it. I read desperately, from Shulamith Firestone to *Jezebel*, and I wrote: bizarre, profane plays about rape culture, one where the archangel Gabriel had a monologue so vile it would have burned David Mamet's tongue clean off; and ugly, strange poetry featuring something I was calling the Beautiful Hermaphrodite Proletariat. Feminism was all I wanted to think about, talk about. When I visited home, my mother and my sister, plainly irritated, informed me that I did not know what it was like to be a woman. But a crush was a crush, if anything buttressed by the conviction that feminism, like any of the girls I had ever liked, was too good for me.

It was in my junior year of college that I first read the *SCUM Manifesto*, crossing over the East River in a lonely subway car. It exhilarated me: the grandeur, the brutal polemics, the raw, succulent style of the whole thing. Solanas was *cool*. Rereading *SCUM*, I realized this was no accident. The manifesto begins like this:

> Life in this society being, at best, an utter bore and no aspect of society being at all relevant to women, there remains to civic-minded, responsible, thrill-seeking females only to overthrow the government, eliminate the money system, institute complete automation and destroy the male sex.

What's striking here is not Solanas's revolutionary extremism per se, but the flippancy with which she justifies it. Life under male supremacy isn't oppressive, exploitative, or unjust: it's just fucking boring. For Solanas, an aspiring playwright, politics begins with an aesthetic judgment. This is because male and female are essentially styles for her, rival aesthetic schools distinguishable by their respective adjectival palettes. Men are timid, guilty, dependent, mindless, passive, animalistic, insecure, cowardly, envious, vain, frivolous, and weak. Women are strong, dynamic, decisive, assertive, cerebral, independent, self-confident, nasty, violent, selfish, freewheeling, thrill-seeking, and arrogant. Above all, women are cool and groovy.

Yet as I read back through the manifesto in preparation for class, I was surprised to be reminded that, for all her storied manhating, Solanas is surprisingly accommodating in her pursuit of male extinction. For one thing, the groovy, freewheeling females of Solanas's revolutionary infantry SCUM (which at one point stood for "Society for Cutting Up Men," though this phrase appears nowhere within the manifesto) will spare any man who opts to join its Men's Auxiliary, where he will declare himself "a turd, a lowly abject turd." For another, what few men remain after the revolution will be generously permitted to wither away on drugs or in drag, grazing in pastures or hooked into twenty-four-hour feeds allowing them to vicariously live the high-octane lives of females in action. And then there's this:

> If men were wise, they would seek to become really female, would do intensive biological research that would lead to men, by means of operations on the brain and nervous system, being able to be transformed in psyche, as well as body, into women.

These lines took my breath away. This was a vision of transsexuality as separatism, an image of how male-to-female gender transition might express not just disidentification with maleness but disaffiliation with men. Here, transition, like revolution, was recast in aesthetic terms, as if transsexual women decided to transition, not to "confirm" some kind of innate gender identity, but because being a man is stupid and boring.

I overread, perhaps. In 2013, an event in San Francisco intended as a tribute to Solanas on the twenty-fifth anniversary of her death was canceled after bitter conflict broke out on its Facebook page over what some considered Solanas's transphobia. One trans woman described having been harassed in queer spaces by radical feminists who referenced Solanas almost as often as they did Janice Raymond, whose 1979 book *The Transsexual Empire: The Making of the She-Male* is a classic of anti-trans feminism. Others went on the offensive. Mira Bellwether, creator of *Fucking Trans Women*, the punk-rock zine that taught the world to muff, wrote a lengthy blog post explaining her misgivings about the event, characterizing the *SCUM Manifesto* as "potentially the worst and most vitriolic example of lesbian-feminist hate speech" in history. She goes on to charge Solanas with biological essentialism of the first degree, citing the latter's apparent appeal to genetic science: "The male is a biological accident: the Y (male) gene is an incomplete X (female) gene, that is, it has an incomplete set of chromosomes. In other words, the male is an incomplete female, a walking abortion, aborted at the gene stage." For Bellwether, this is unequivocal proof that everything *SCUM* says about men, it also says about trans women.

Yet these are odd accusations. To call Solanas a "lesbian feminist" is to imply, erroneously, that she was associated with lesbian groups like New York City's Lavender Menace, which briefly hijacked the Second Congress to Unite Women in 1970 to protest homophobia in the women's movement and distribute their classic pamphlet "The Woman-Identified Woman." But Solanas was neither a political lesbian nor a lesbian politico. She was by all accounts a loner and a misfit, a struggling writer and sex worker who sometimes identified as gay but always looked out for number one. The dedication to her riotous 1965 play *Up Your Ass* reads, "I dedicate this play to ME, a continuous source of strength and guidance, and without whose unflinching loyalty, devotion, and faith this play would never have been written." (It was this play, whose full title is *Up Your Ass, or, From the Cradle to the Boat, or, The Big Suck, or, Up from the Slime*, that Solanas tried first to sweet-talk, then to strong-arm, Andy Warhol into producing.)

As for the matter of genetics, I suppose I ought to be offended to have my Y chromosomes' good name raked through the mud. Frankly, though, I have a hard time getting it up for a possession I consider about as valuable as a fifteen-dollar gift card to Blockbuster. The truth is, if it's hard for contemporary readers to tell men and trans women apart in Solanas's analysis, it is not because she thinks all trans women are men; if anything, it's because she thinks all men are closeted trans women. When Solanas hisses that maleness is a "deficiency disease," I am reminded of those trans women who diagnose themselves, only half-jokingly, with testosterone poisoning. When she snarls that men are "biological accidents," all I hear is the eminently sensible claim that every man is *literally* a woman trapped in the wrong body. This is what the

SCUM Manifesto calls pussy envy, from which all men suffer, though few dare to admit it aside from "faggots" and "drag queens," whom Solanas counts among the least miserable of the lot. Hence the sentiment Solanas expresses through Miss Collins, one of two quick-witted queens who grace the filthy pages of *Up Your Ass*:

> MISS COLLINS: Shall I tell you a secret? I despise men. Oh, why do I have to be one of them? (*Brightening.*) Do you know what I'd like more than anything in the world to be? A Lesbian. Then I could be the cake and eat it too.

Bellwether might object that I am, again, being too generous. But generosity is the only spirit in which a text as hot to the touch as the *SCUM Manifesto* could have ever been received. This is after all a pamphlet advocating mass murder, and what's worse, property damage. It's not as if those who expressed their disappointment over the tribute's cancellation did so in blanket approval of Solanas's long-term plans for total human extinction (women included) or her attempted murder of a man who painted soup cans. As Breanne Fahs recounts in her recent biography of Solanas, the shooting was the straw that broke the back of the camel known as the National Organization for Women (NOW), which despite its infancy—it was founded in 1966, only two years earlier—had already suffered fractures over abortion and lesbianism. As the radical feminists Ti-Grace Atkinson and Florynce Kennedy visited Solanas in prison, the latter agreeing to represent Valerie pro bono, then-president Betty Friedan scrambled to distance NOW from what she viewed as a problem that most certainly had a name, demanding in a telegram that Kennedy "DESIST IMMEDIATELY FROM LINKING NOW IN ANY WAY WITH VALERIE SOLANAS." Within the year, both Kennedy and Atkinson had left the organization, each going on to found their own, ostensibly more radical groups: the Feminist Party and the October 17th Movement, respectively. Likewise, after the Solanas tribute was canceled in 2013, folks hoping to hash out the Facebook fracas in person held a splinter event called "We Who Have Complicated Feelings About Valerie Solanas."

This is simply to note that disagreement over Solanas's legacy is an old feminist standard, the artifact of a broader intellectual habit that critiques like Bellwether's lean on. This is the thing we call feminist historiography, with all its waves and groups and fabled conferences. Any good feminist bears stitched into the burning bra she calls her heart that tapestry of qualifiers we use to tell one another stories about ourselves and our history: radical, liberal, neoliberal, socialist, Marxist, separatist, cultural, corporate, lesbian, queer, trans, eco, intersectional, anti-porn, anti-work, pro-sex, first-, second-, third-, sometimes fourth-wave. These stories have perhaps less to do with What Really Happened than they do with what Fredric Jameson once called "the 'emotion' of great historiographic form"—the satisfaction of synthesizing the messy empirical data of the past into an elegant historical arc in which everything that happened could not have happened otherwise.

To say, then, that these stories are rarely if ever "true" is not merely to repeat the axiom that taxonomy is taxidermy, though it cannot be denied that the objects of intellectual inquiry are forever escaping, like B-movie zombies, from the vaults of their interment. It is also to say that all cultural things, *SCUM Manifesto* included, are answering machines for history's messages at best only secondarily. They are rather, first and foremost, occasions for people to feel something: to adjust the pitch of a desire or up a fantasy's thread count, to make overtures to a new way to feel or renew their vows with an old one. We read things, watch things, from political history to pop culture, as feminists and as people, because we want to belong to a community or public, or because we are stressed out at work, or because we are looking for a friend or a lover, or perhaps because we are struggling to figure out how to feel political in an age and culture defined by a general shipwrecking of the beautiful old stories of history.

So when Bellwether condemns the *SCUM Manifesto* as "the pinnacle of misguided and hateful 2nd wave feminism and lesbian-feminism," this condemnation is a vehicle for a sort of political disappointment that feminists are fond of cultivating with respect to preceding generations of feminists. In this version of the story, feminism excluded trans women in the past, is learning to include trans women now, and will center trans women in the future. This story's plausibility is no doubt due to a dicey bit of revisionism implied by the moniker *trans-exclusionary radical feminist*, often shortened to TERF. Like most kinds of feminists, TERFs are not a party or a unified front. Their beliefs, while varied, mostly boil down to a rejection of the idea that transgender women are, in fact, women. They also don't much like the name TERF, which they take to be a slur—a grievance that would be beneath contempt if it weren't also true, in the sense that all bywords for bigots are intended to be defamatory. The actual problem with an epithet like TERF is its historiographic sleight of hand: namely, the erroneous implication that all TERFs are holdouts who missed the third wave, old-school radical feminists who never learned any better. This permits their being read as a living anachronism through which the past can be discerned, much as European anthropologists imagined so-called primitive societies to be an earlier stage of civilizational development caught in amber.

In fact, we would do better to talk about TERFs in the context of the internet, where a rebel alliance of bloggers like Feminist Current's Meghan Murphy and GenderTrender's Linda Shanko spend their days shooting dinky clickbait at the transsexual empire's thermal exhaust ports. The true battles rage on Tumblr, in the form of comments, memes, and doxing; it is possible, for instance, to find Tumblrs entirely devoted to cataloging *other* Tumblr users who are known "gender-critical feminists," as they like to refer to themselves. But this conflict has as much to do with the ins and outs of social media—especially Tumblr, Twitter, and Reddit—as it does with any great ideological conflict. When a subculture espouses extremist politics, especially online, it is tempting but often incorrect to take those politics for that subculture's beating heart. It's worth considering whether TERFs, like certain strains of the alt-right, might be defined less by their political ideology (however noxious) and more by a complex, frankly fascinating relationship to trolling, on which it will be for future anthropologists, having solved the problem of digital ethnography, to elaborate.

Of course, feminist transphobia is no more an exclusively digital phenomenon than white nationalism. There were second-wave feminists who sincerely feared and hated trans women. Some of them are even famous, like the Australian feminist Germaine Greer, author of the 1970 bestseller

The Female Eunuch. Few TERFs curl their lips with Greer's panache. This is how she described an encounter with a fan, in *The Independent Magazine* in 1989:

> On the day that *The Female Eunuch* was issued in America, a person in flapping draperies rushed up to me and grabbed my hand. "Thank you," it breathed hoarsely, "Thank you so much for all you've done for us girls!" I smirked and nodded and stepped backward, trying to extricate my hand from the enormous, knuckly, hairy, be-ringed paw that clutched it. The face staring into mine was thickly coated with pancake make-up through which the stubble was already burgeoning, in futile competition with a Dynel wig of immense luxuriance and two pairs of false eyelashes. Against the bony ribs that could be counted through its flimsy scarf dress swung a polished steel women's liberation emblem. I should have said, "You're a man. *The Female Eunuch* has done less than nothing for you. Piss off."

Little analysis is needed to show that disgust like Greer's belongs to the same traffic in woman-hating she and her fellow TERFs supposedly abhor. Let us pause instead to appreciate how rarely one finds transmisogyny, whose preferred medium is the spittle of strangers, enjoying the cushy stylistic privileges of middlebrow literary form. It's like watching Julia Child cook a baby.

Then again, Greer has long imagined herself as feminism's id, periodically digging herself out of the earth to rub her wings together and molt on network television. In 2015, she made waves when she criticized as "misogynist" *Glamour* magazine's decision to give their Woman of the Year award to Caitlyn Jenner, then fresh off her *Vanity Fair* photo shoot. In response to the backlash, Greer released this gem of a statement: "Just because you lop off your dick and then wear a dress doesn't make you a fucking woman. I've asked my doctor to give me long ears and liver spots and I'm going to wear a brown coat but that won't turn me into a fucking cocker spaniel." More surprising is when a second-wave icon like Atkinson, onetime defender of Solanas, trots out TERF talking points at a Boston University conference in 2014: "There is a conflict around gender. That is, feminists are trying to get rid of gender. And transgendered [*sic*] reinforce gender." That Atkinson's remarks arrived at a conference whose theme was "Women's Liberation in the Late 1960s and Early 1970s" only encourages wholesale dismissals of the second wave as the Dark Ages of feminist history.

Yet consider the infamous West Coast Lesbian Conference of 1973. The first night of the conference, the transsexual folk singer Beth Elliott's scheduled performance was interrupted by protesters who tried to kick her off the stage. The following day, the radical feminist Robin Morgan, editor of the widely influential 1970 anthology *Sisterhood Is Powerful*, delivered a hastily rewritten keynote in which she unloaded on Elliott, calling her "an opportunist, an infiltrator, and a destroyer—with the mentality of a rapist." Morgan's remarks were soon printed in the short-lived underground newspaper *Lesbian Tide*, where they could enjoy a wider audience:

> I will not call a male "she"; thirty-two years of suffering in this androcentric society, and of surviving, have earned me the title "woman"; one walk down the street by a male transvestite, five minutes of his being hassled (which he may enjoy), and then he dares, he dares to think he understands our pain? No, in our mothers' names and in our own, we must not call him sister. We know what's at work when whites wear blackface; the same thing is at work when men wear drag.

This is where reports of the conference usually end, often with practiced sobriety about How Bad Shit Was. Yet as the historian Finn Enke argues in an excellent article in *Transgender Studies Quarterly*, many accounts leave out the fact that the San Francisco chapter of the national lesbian organization Daughters of Bilitis had welcomed a nineteen-year-old Beth Elliott in 1971 after her parents rejected her, that Elliott had been elected chapter vice president that same year, that she had been embraced by the Orange County Dyke Patrol at the Gay Women's Conference in Los Angeles, and that she had been *a member of the organizing committee* for the very conference where her presence was disputed by a vocal minority of attendees. As for the vitriolic keynote, Enke suggests that Morgan's attacks on Elliott were born of the former's insecurity over being invited to speak at a conference for lesbians despite her being shacked up with a man, whose effeminacy she often tried, unsuccessfully, to parlay into a basis for her own radical credentials.

This is to say two things. First, the radical feminism of the sixties and seventies was as mixed a bag as any political movement, from Occupy to the Bernie Sanders campaign. Second, at least in this case, feminist transphobia was not so much an expression of anti-trans animus as it was an indirect, even peripheral repercussion of a much larger crisis in the women's liberation movement over how people should go about feeling political. In expanding the scope of feminist critique to the terrain of everyday life—a move that produced a characteristically muscular brand of theory that rivaled any Marxist's notes on capitalism—the second wave had inadvertently painted itself into a corner. If, as radical feminist theories claimed, patriarchy had infested not just legal, cultural, and economic spheres but the psychic lives of *women themselves*, then feminist revolution could be achieved only by combing constantly through the fibrils of one's consciousness for every last trace of male supremacy—a kind of political nitpicking, as it were.

And nowhere was this more urgent, or more difficult, than the bedroom. Fighting tirelessly for the notion that sex was fair game for political critique, radical feminists were now faced with the prospect of putting their mouths where their money had been. Hence Atkinson's famous slogan: "Feminism is the theory, lesbianism is the practice." This was the political climate in which *both* Elliott and Morgan, as a transsexual woman and a suspected heterosexual woman, respectively, could find their statuses as legitimate subjects of feminist politics threatened by the incipient enshrining, among some radical feminists, of something called lesbianism as the preferred aesthetic form for mediating between individual subjects and the history they were supposed to be making— call these the personal and the political.

So while radical feminism as a whole saw its fair share of trans-loving lesbians and trans-hating heterosexuals alike, there *is* a historical line to be traced from political lesbianism, as a specific, by no means dominant tendency *within* radical feminism, to the contemporary phenomenon we've taken to calling trans-exclusionary radical feminism. Take Sheila Jeffreys, an English lesbian feminist recently retired from a professorship at the University of Melbourne in Australia. In her salad days, Jeffreys was a member of the Leeds Revolutionary Feminist Group, remembered for its fiery conference paper "Political Lesbianism: The Case Against Heterosexuality," published in 1979. The paper defined a political lesbian as "a woman-identified woman who does not fuck men" but stopped short of mandating homosexual sex. The paper also shared the *SCUM Manifesto*'s dead-serious sense of humor: "Being a heterosexual feminist is like being in the resistance in Nazi-occupied Europe where in the daytime you blow up a bridge, in the evening you rush to repair it."

These days, Jeffreys has made a business of abominating trans women, earning herself top billing on the TERF speaking circuit. Like many TERFs, she believes that trans women's cheap imitations of femininity (as she imagines them) reproduce the same harmful stereotypes through which women are subordinated in the first place. "Transgenderism on the part of men," Jeffreys writes in her 2014 book *Gender Hurts*, "can be seen as a ruthless appropriation of women's experience and existence." She is also fond of citing sexological literature that classifies transgenderism as a paraphilia. It is a favorite claim among TERFs like Jeffreys that transgender women are gropey interlopers, sick voyeurs conspiring to infiltrate women-only spaces and conduct the greatest panty raid in military history.

I happily consent to this description. Had I ever been so fortunate as to attend the legendarily clothing-optional Michigan Womyn's Music Festival before its demise at the hands of trans activists in 2015, you can bet your Birkenstocks it wouldn't have been for the music. Indeed, at least among lesbians, trans-exclusionary radical feminism might best be understood as gay panic, girl-on-girl edition. The point here is not that all TERFs are secretly attracted to trans women—though so delicious an irony undoubtedly happens more often than anyone would like to admit—but rather that trans-exclusionary feminism has inherited political lesbianism's dread of desire's ungovernability. The traditional subject of gay panic, be he a U.S. senator or just a member of the House, is a subject menaced by his own politically compromising desires: to preserve himself, he projects these desires onto another, whom he may now legislate or gay-bash out of existence.

The political lesbian, too, is a subject stuck between the rock of politics and desire's hard place. As Jeffreys put it in 2015, speaking to the

Lesbian History Group in London, political lesbianism was intended as a solution to the all-too-real cognitive dissonance produced by hetero-sexual feminism: "Why go to all these meetings where you're creating all this wonderful theory and politics, and then you go home to, in my case, Dave, and you're sitting there, you know, in front of the telly, and thinking, 'It's *weird*. This feels *weird*.'" But true separatism doesn't stop at leaving your husband. It proceeds, with paranoid rigor, to purge the apartments of the mind of anything remotely connected to patriarchy. Desire is no exception. Political lesbianism is founded on the belief that even desire becomes pliable at high enough temperatures. For Jeffreys and her comrades, lesbianism was not an innate identity, but an act of political will. This was a world in which biology was not destiny, a world where being a lesbian was about what got you woke, not wet.

Only heterosexuality might not have been doing it for Dave, either. It seems never to have occurred to Jeffreys that some of us "transgenders," as she likes to call us, might opt to transition precisely in order to escape from the penitentiary she takes heterosexuality to be. It is a supreme irony of feminist history that there is no woman more woman-identified than a gay trans girl like me, and that Beth Elliott and her sisters were the origi-nal political lesbians: women who had walked away from both the men in their lives and the men whose lives they'd been living. We are separatists from our own bodies. We are militants of so fine a caliber that we regu-larly take steps to poison the world's supply of male biology. To TERFs like Jeffreys, we say merely that imitation is the highest form of flattery. But let's keep things in perspective. Because of Jeffreys, a few women in the seventies got haircuts. Because of us, there are literally *fewer men on the planet*. Valerie, at least, would be proud. The Society for Cutting Up Men is a rather fabulous name for a transsexual book club.

But now I really am overreading. That trans lesbians should be pedes-taled as some kind of feminist vanguard is a notion as untenable as it is attractive. In defending it, I would be neglecting what I take to be the true lesson of political lesbianism as a failed project: that nothing good comes of forcing desire to conform to political principle. You could sooner give a cat a bath. This does not mean that politics has no part to play in desire. Solidarity, for instance, can be terribly arousing—this was no doubt one of the best things the consciousness-raising groups of the seventies had going for them. But you can't get aroused *as an act of* solidarity, the way you might stuff envelopes or march in the streets with your sisters-in-arms. Desire is, by nature, childlike and chary of government. The day we begin to qualify it by the righteousness of its political content is the day we begin to prescribe some desires and prohibit others. That way lies moralism only. Just try to imagine life as a feminist anemone, the tendrils of your desire withdrawing in an instant from patriarchy's every touch. There would be nothing to watch on TV.

It must be underscored how unpopular it is on the left today to countenance the notion that transition expresses not the truth of an identity but the force of a desire. This would require understanding transness as a matter not of who one *is*, but of what one *wants*. The primary function of gender identity as a political concept—and, increasingly, a legal one—is to bracket, if not to totally deny, the role of desire in the thing we call gender. Historically, this results from a wish among transgender advocates to quell fears that trans people, and trans women in particular, go through transition in order to *get stuff*: money, sex, legal privileges, little girls in public restrooms. As the political theorist Paisley Currah observes in his forthcoming book, the state has been far more willing to recognize sex reclassification when the reclassified individuals don't get anything out of it. In 2002, the Kansas Supreme Court voided the marriage of a transsexual woman and her then-deceased cisgender husband, whose $2.5 million estate she was poised to inherit, on the grounds that their union was invalid under Kansas's prohibition on same-sex marriage. The sex on the woman's Wisconsin birth certificate, which she had successfully changed from M to F years earlier, now proved worthless when she tried to cash it in.

Now I'm not saying I think that this woman transitioned to get rich quick. What I am saying is, *So what if she had?* I doubt that any of us transition because we want to "be" women, in some abstract, academic way. I certainly didn't. I transitioned for gossip and compliments, lipstick and mascara, for crying at the movies, for being someone's girlfriend, for letting her pay the check or carry my bags, for the benevolent chauvinism of bank tellers and cable guys, for the telephonic intimacy of long-distance female friendship, for fixing my makeup in the bathroom flanked like Christ by a sinner on each side, for sex toys, for feeling hot, for getting hit on by butches, for that secret knowledge of which dykes to watch out for, for Daisy Dukes, bikini tops, and all the dresses, and, my god, *for the breasts*. But now you begin to see the problem with desire: we rarely want the things we should. Any TERF will tell you that most of these items are just the traditional trappings of patriarchal femininity. She won't be wrong, either. Let's be clear: TERFs are gender abolitionists, even if that abolitionism is a shell corporation for garden-variety moral disgust. When it comes to the question of feminist revolution, TERFs leave trans girls like me in the dust, primping. In this respect, someone like Ti-Grace Atkinson, a self-described radical feminist committed to the revolutionary dismantling of gender as a system of oppression, is not the dinosaur; I, who get my eyebrows threaded every two weeks, am.

Perhaps my consciousness needs raising. I muster a shrug. When the airline loses your luggage, you are not making a principled political statement about the tyranny of private property; you just want your goddamn luggage back. This is most painfully evident in the case of bottom surgery, which continues to baffle a clique of queer theorists who, on the strength and happenstance of a shared prefix, have been all too ready to take transgender people as mascots for their politics of transgression. These days, the belief that getting a vagina will make you into a real woman is retrograde in the extreme. Many good feminists still only manage to understand bottom surgery by qualifying it as a personal aesthetic choice: *If that's what makes you feel more comfortable in your body, that's great.*

This is as wrongheaded as it is condescending. To be sure, gender confirmation surgeries are aesthetic practices, continuous with rather than distinct from the so-called cosmetic surgeries. (No one goes into the operating room asking for an ugly cooch.) So it's not that these aren't aesthetic decisions; it's that they're not *personal*. That's the basic paradox of aesthetic judgments: they are, simultaneously, subjective and universal. Transsexual women don't want bottom surgery because their personal opinion is that a vagina would look or feel better than a penis. Transsexual women want bottom surgery because *most women have vaginas*. Call that transphobic if you like—that's not going to keep me from Chili's-Awesome-Blossoming my dick.

I am being tendentious, dear reader, because I am trying to tell you something that few of us dare to talk about, especially in public, especially when we are trying to feel political: not the fact, boringly obvious to those of us living it, that many trans women wish they were cis women, but the darker, more difficult fact that many trans women *wish they were women, period.* This is most emphatically not something trans women are supposed to want. The grammar of contemporary trans activism does not brook the subjunctive. Trans women *are* women, we are chided with silky condescension, as if we have all confused ourselves with Chimamanda Ngozi Adichie, as if we were all simply trapped in the wrong politics, as if the cure for dysphoria were wokeness. How can you want to be something you already are? Desire implies deficiency; want implies want. To admit that what makes women like me transsexual is not identity but desire is to admit just how much of transition takes place in the waiting rooms of wanting things, to admit that your breasts may never come in, your voice may never pass, your parents may never call back.

Call this the romance of disappointment. You want something. You have found an object that will give you what you want. This object is a person, or a politics, or an art form, or a blouse that fits. You attach yourself to this object, follow it around, carry it with you, watch it on TV. One day, you tell yourself, it will give you what you want. Then, one day, it doesn't. Now it dawns on you that your object will probably never give you what you want. But this is not what's disappointing, not really. What's disappointing is what happens next: nothing. You keep your object. You continue to follow it around, stash it in a drawer, water it, tweet at it. It still doesn't give you what you want—but you knew that. You have had another realization: not getting what you want has very little to do with wanting it. Knowing better usually doesn't make it better. You don't want something because wanting it will lead to getting it. You want it because you want it. This is the zero-order disappointment that structures all desire and makes it possible. After all, if you could only want things you were guaranteed to get, you would never be able to want anything at all.

This is not to garner pity for sad trannies like me. We have enough roses by our beds. It is rather to say, minimally, that trans women want things too. The deposits of our desire run as deep and fine as any. The richness of our want is staggering. Perhaps this is why coming out can feel like crushing, why a first dress can feel like a first kiss, why dysphoria can feel like heartbreak. The other name for disappointment, after all, is love.

2018

This was the first proper essay I ever wrote for a general audience. The tremendous response it received (at least it seemed tremendous to me) enabled me to get an agent, score a small book deal, and ultimately quit my miserable graduate program. I am told that it is now regularly taught in gender studies courses across the country. Reading it today, I am irritated by the obscurity of the antagonists and the amateurish tone—that kind of bloggy "voiceyness" was dated even then—and I am amused by how little I understood about myself, including my own gender, which has in the intervening years tended toward female masculinity. But I was only twenty-four. It is probably the first and only thing I have ever written just for myself. It occurs to me now that I was writing without the benefit of a tradition; there were precedents, but they were few and mostly uninspiring. Today there is far more activity than there was even six years ago; nevertheless there is as yet no great trans literary tradition in this country, either in fiction or in nonfiction. This is hardly the fault of trans people: we are a small, young, marginalized, freshly self-conscious community who, when given the opportunity to write, are still overwhelmingly expected to write our memoirs. Even "On Liking Women" did not escape this mandate; I would not truly break free of it until after the pandemic.

Meanwhile, the religious right has drawn up a blood pact not just with TERFs, whose public profile has grown considerably, but also with a segment of the center-left that I have dubbed TARLs: trans-agnostic reactionary liberals. As I write this, they are engaged in a smiling campaign of medical delegitimation against trans kids. In this respect, if you gently sweep aside the self-pity and the melodrama, "On Liking Women" was quite prescient: it correctly identified the point of imminent collapse within the gender identity model and it proposed a radical model based on desire. I recently revisited these problems in a cover story for New York *about "the right to change sex," an idea which as of this writing continues to be unassimilable for great swaths of the population. I expect I shall revisit them again.*

Bad TV

The day the Kevin Spacey allegations broke, I was sitting with my girl-friend on our couch in Brooklyn. By accident, we found ourselves play-ing a dark game. One of us would name a male star, as if removing an article of clothing, and the other would respond on instinct—first, with the chances of his being outed as a sexual predator, then with how disap-pointed she would be in the event of his fall from grace. The goal was to pick men who scored high in both columns. The whole thing smacked of truth or dare, or spin the bottle: games of needless, voluntary exposure, games about the risk of being caught wanting things you shouldn't.

The secret, of course, was that the red-skied reckoning that had fol-lowed a blitz of sexual misconduct allegations against the film producer Harvey Weinstein in October 2017 could be, whatever else it was, fun. Out there, in the fields of something like history, women were talking, telling stories of rape and abuse and harassment and weird texts and constant gaslighting. Most of these stories weren't new. Those that were cleaved so tightly to the genre that they bore the seal of instant recogni-tion. Maybe nothing would change; maybe this was one of those *Matrix* things, where the system would just adjust and reboot. But there isn't anything especially feminist about being jaded. A world was ending, maybe. At any rate, the stars kept falling.

And then here we were, bae and I, kids playing hide-and-seek in a fallout shelter. We were enjoying it. Ours wasn't just the righteous satis-faction of justice finally served, or even the hot joy of revenge. For sure, there was real pleasure in the prospect of seeing bad men suffer. But there was also another, less flattering kind of enjoyment, floating right beneath the waterline of consciousness. For all the great to-do, all the scandal and vindication, there were certain stars of film and television—just a select few, we told ourselves, a special club—whom, in a week or month or two, once the fires were out, we would find it in our hearts to forgive. That's a lie, actually. We wouldn't forgive them. But we also wouldn't stop watching their shows.

Jeffrey Tambor hit particularly hard. I'd been avoiding starting the fourth season of *Transparent* on account of its multi-episode Israel arc, which filled me with the dread of Having to Have an Opinion. *Transparent*, for me, had never been about telegraphing a politics, as I imagine it had been for many cis people. (For that, I had *Orange Is the New Black*.) I had taken in the first two seasons with dumb luxuriance, as if ordering macaroni and cheese at a restaurant with three dollar signs on Yelp. The third I binged on a few months into transition, popping estrogen and waiting for the sadness to kick in. "I don't *wanna* be trans!" cried Tambor's character, in a bitter argument with her estranged sister. "I *am* trans!" Me neither; me too.

Then, shortly after the fourth season of *Transparent* went live on Amazon Prime, a former personal assistant of Tambor's alleged that the actor had engaged in what *Deadline Hollywood* was calling "inappropriate behavior." Tambor denied it and to my knowledge no legal action was ever taken against him. There was here, I knew, a brief window of plausible deniability: if I was going to binge with a clean conscience, it was now or never. But by the time *Transparent* actress Trace Lysette came forward with her own allegations—on set, she said, Tambor had told her he wanted to "attack [her] sexually" and mimed sex acts while pressed up against her—I still hadn't watched.

The irony was thick and frothy: the idea of a transgender actress having been sexually harassed by a cisgender actor who was playing a transgender woman, to tremendous critical acclaim, and with a winsome humility it was easy to slip your belief into, like a pair of comfortable shoes. Tambor was a good woman. Accepting his second consecutive Emmy for the role in 2016, Tambor thanked a team of trans media consultants and said the show had changed his life. When a piano tried to play him off, he shushed it, his face sad and urgent. "I'm not going to say this beautifully," he warned, "but to you people out there, you producers and you network owners and you agents and you creative sparks, please give trans"—his voice failed midword, his mouth still moving, then he rallied—"transgender talent a chance." The audience, warm and charmed, let the slip slide. "One more thing," Tambor continued over the cheers. "I would not be unhappy were I the last cisgender male to play a female transgender on television," he finished, awkwardly flipping the words *transgender* and *female*. More cheers, louder and looser. Sure, he hadn't quite stuck the landing—but that could be forgiven, couldn't it?

Television was never good for you. In 1950, there were, by some estimates, six million television sets in the United States; a decade later, something like sixty million—nine out of ten households. By the midsixties, Herbert Marcuse was suggesting that the masses would rather chance nuclear annihilation than be deprived of television. What postwar critics were talking about when they called it a technology of mass consumption was how television broadcast, on a historically massive scale, the helplessness of desire in the face of its object. TV didn't have to be good to be good: all viewers asked for was the possibility of returning, over and over, to the scene of enjoyment's crime—hence the episode, the serial, the sitcom. Trash just had to be reliable. Even contempt could breed familiarity. If the barrage of televisual garbage that Americans were willing to consume proved anything, it was that once hooked, desire is very hard to spoil. This was perhaps the ultimate spoiler.

Hence early critics' second objection to television: its inherent quashing of the instinct for political resistance, or even just public life. "Television atrophies consciousness," wrote Theodor Adorno. For him, television's danger was its capacity for producing in viewers a feeling of social belonging that was in fact ideological cover for their increasing alienation under capitalism. The warm togetherness of the average American family gathered around a little box in their living room was a lie fabricated to keep people off the streets where politics might happen. Even Marshall McLuhan, no one's idea of a Marxist, thought that television was too "cool," too sensorially engrossing to drive political change. The political effect of television on the average American was therefore the formal inverse of the fascism of the forties: Hitler's radio had uprooted one country; now, television was potatoing another. "The dreamless dream," Adorno called it, crowning it king of the culture industry. "The Timid Giant," McLuhan called it, quoting from *TV Guide*.

At some point, someone poked it. One will be forgiven for thinking that the current tenant of the White House represents a full-on invasion of the political by television. Even the popular fan theory that the president is secretly a Russian patsy, credible or not, feels ripped from the plotlines of some drama on the USA network. Equally, more than ever, television is political. "The Great Awakening," the writer Molly Fischer called this in *The Cut*, describing how wokeness—as in "stay woke," an exhortation to political awareness popularized by Black Lives Matter— has consolidated as a televisual aesthetic. Witness *Black-ish, Girls, Insecure, Louie, The Handmaid's Tale, I Love Dick, Transparent, Master of None*, even the rebooted *Will & Grace*. At worst, woke TV has all the moral subtlety of an after-school special. In one episode of *Master of None*, Aziz Ansari's character has sexism explained to him by his female friends. The tone is self-congratulating and anti-gallant, as if pointedly sparing a lady the chivalry of an opened door. Writes Fischer, "This is not a blow to the patriarchy; this is *Sesame Street*."

The promise of woke TV is that the naysayers of the sixties were wrong: watching television can be a kind of political act, if only minor and tenuous. If this sounds like wishful thinking, that's not just because wokeniks like Tambor and Ansari left themselves vulnerable to getting called on their shit. It's also because in the very act of delivering on its promise to make people feel political, woke TV accidentally proved that political was something you could be made to *feel*. That *Transparent* can make you feel political—the way, say, *This Is Us* can make you feel sad— implies that the political is essentially a special effect, a trick of the light, TV magic. The full discomfiture of this claim can be shrugged off as long as you maintain the fantasy that somewhere out there, in the bleeding wilds of the world, there exists a secret glade called Politics where the gods of history dance. This will let you cleanly cleave the world in two: true and pretend, genuine leftism and performative wokeness, real life and the stuff of television. In truth, you can't book a direct flight to the political. There are always layovers in aesthetic form: in tone, mood, shape, and everything else a work of art might employ to try to get you to feel part of something bigger than yourself.

The other way to say this is that politics is often just a very special episode of belonging—and belonging is TV's forte. Television was never just a box; it has always been primarily a social event. When Adorno complained that television was a "substitute for a social immediacy," he had forgotten that every public is a fantasy, projected by rituals and shibboleths that if held up to the light just so will, like the medallion in *Raiders of the Lost Ark*, point the way to God. This applied to the halo of national pride that in 1969 descended, like the lunar module, onto the rapt faces of viewers at home; it equally applies to the numberless moons of fandom now wandering the internet's night sky. Mediation, televisual or otherwise, has always been necessary to make the leap from me to you, individual to group. All communities are imagined, as Benedict Anderson taught, simply because they could not be otherwise.

But the fear of missing out is real. This is truer than ever today, when twenty-four-hour streaming services have succeeded in making live television live forever. Hence the recap: a new genre of internet writing that mixes summary with commentary while being neither, anchored by the gravity of a show's sacred lore but prone to flashes of passion and diaristic longing. More than reviewing plot or assessing style, the recap's first job is to record the achievement of holding a shared object. Here in the Golden Age of Television, the point is not just to watch but to *have* watched—to have been there, in a sense not wholly imaginary, for that twist, that fire, that wedding. Death emcees most of these ceremonies. (Jimmy Kimmel, the rest.) Take *Game of Thrones*, a high-fantasy program whose appeal rested in its defiance of the economy of celebrity. Central characters whom other shows would have clad in plot armor could be cut down with the ignominy of an extra. It could be anyone, at any time. They even had a saying in Braavos, the financial capital of the *Thrones* world: *Valar morghulis*, all men must die. And so the nation got hooked on a show about famous men falling when you'd least expect it.

As *Game of Thrones* sailed off toward its final season, a new show rose to fill its slot. #MeToo was another kind of fantasy drama, one that resuscitated the dream of seventies feminism: arrows dipped in anger, fletched with optimism. Time's up. Ban men. Burn it down. Only this time, the revolution would be televised. Allegations rolled out like your regularly scheduled programming. A political movement could be a form of entertainment; America had just learned this the hard way. Now justice was on prime time, and everyone was watching. In coffee shops, on public transit, all across social media, the whisper network was suddenly, shockingly loud, as if someone had forgotten to cut its mic. Soon, it was congressmen, journalists, professors, radio hosts, talking heads, celebrity chefs. The news reports popped up on our phones like recaps of a phantom show no one had ever seen. Even the hashtag was an impossibility, an improvised attempt to build a universal out of nothing but particulars. Me, too. The singular, multiplied.

Those who called it a witch hunt had clearly never watched the short-lived series *Salem*, whose premise was that the witches hunted you. But the backlash came all the same. Before long, the devil had enough advocates to hang a shingle. Could all women really be believed? That was a lot of women. Someone with money started calling in op-eds. The standing orders were clear: for every twisted panty, a wrung hand. There was bad sex, and then there was bad sex. The thing had degrees. It was complicated. Some, calling themselves allies, cautioned that sex panics are never good for queer people, people of color, sex workers. If it wasn't careful, they said, the movement would jump the shark.

For others, it was already too late. Aziz Ansari, who for years had played a failed pickup artist on NBC's *Parks and Recreation*, had finally persuaded a nerve into letting him touch it. A woman with the pseudonym Grace told the lifestyle site Babe that Ansari had pressured her into a blow job and kept wheeling her awkwardly around his apartment looking for a space to park his dick. Everything was consensual-ish. "You guys are all the same," she had told him. "You guys are all the fucking same." The internet went up in tiny flames. Harassment in the workplace was one thing, but a national referendum on heterosexuality? What were we supposed to do, *not have sex*? Bari Weiss, with *The New York Times* feeding quarters into the back of her head, figured that if Grace had been assaulted, so had every woman, including Bari Weiss, which obviously wasn't the case. Someone in *The Atlantic* compared Grace to the weak female protagonists of the moralizing chick lit of the seventies, at once slutty and hapless. Suck it up, honey. Spit it out. Call a cab.

What they were really saying was that Grace's story played like bad

TV. It was all too tropey: wine, tears, countertops. This wasn't real life; this was Shondaland. They shouldn't have described her outfit; they shouldn't have included that sex thing with the fingers. Grace needed a better editor. But it was quickly becoming clear that #MeToo could turn broadsheets to tabloids with a single, unwanted touch. The truth was, many of the allegations read like outlandish episode pitches. Even Frank Underwood of *House of Cards*, who once had a bisexual threesome involving a Secret Service agent and also, like, *murdered people*, didn't have a button under his desk that locked the door behind female colleagues he wanted to bone. At some point, the most unimpressed feminist could allow herself the trashy pleasure of disbelief briefly unsuspended. What do you mean, he masturbated into a potted plant? That was something out of *Quantico*, or *Billions*, or *Scandal*. It's a twist we could have seen from miles away. It turns out that the men on TV act like the men on TV.

Good television, of the longform narrative sort, is believable. Believability is never about reproducing reality. Time travel may be believable; a kitchen sink may not be. Believability is, essentially, an aesthetic of proportionality. It consists in the invention of an imaginary but plausible relationship between character and plot: that is, in negotiating some kind of correspondence between the squishy sentimentality of interiority and a few discrete, relatively high-impact events that interrupt, like meteors, the atmosphere of everyday life. In the land of television, critical acclaim is handed out to whichever shows manage to bridge these twin peaks most attractively. Usually, this means keeping the writing within a few standard deviations of the premise at hand: no secret clones, unless it's *Orphan Black*; no acts of God, except on *The Leftovers*.

Sexual violence is, however, notoriously difficult to portray realistically on television—hence its relegation to the fringes of good taste, from the family melodrama to the police procedural. Even HBO's female-driven *Big Little Lies*, which follows a clique of affluent women in airy California beach houses as each gets caught in a riptide of abuse, couldn't help draping rape in the lush folds of Emmy-nominated cinematography. The show's failure—and, equally, its success—was to have made abuse believable. In this way, *Big Little Lies* predicted, a little too well, how Harvey Weinstein would fall. *The New York Times'* Weinstein report was a believability project years in the making: it systematized abuse, turned it into a pattern your eye could follow. There were interviews, emails, audio recordings, legal documents; facts were double- and triple-checked. But the report's paradoxical consequence was to set the bar far too high for every subsequent story whose breaking it had made possible. What's a little masturbation between friends when the king of Hollywood kingmakers had employed former agents of Mossad to silence his accusers? In one final instance of gaslighting, the Weinstein story made all other allegations of abuse look not so bad and all other evidence look not so good.

But trauma rarely announces itself the way it does in *The New York Times* or on HBO, in the dramas that win big men statues of little women. In real life, trauma is soapy. The soap opera is distinguished not by the tremendous suffering borne by its characters but by the requirement that the *degree* of this suffering feel unwarranted. An unexpected death may be mourned in minutes; a personal slight can be grounds for arson. It's always too much, or not enough: despite all of *Big Little Lies*'s high production values and A-list stars, there were still critics who classified it as an "upscale soap." When *Vogue* asked Reese Witherspoon (who both acted and produced) for her response, she laughed at the question. "This is how women really speak to each other," she said. "There are a lot of dynamics where women are not telling each other the truth, and I think it's deeply relatable." *Big Little Lies* wanted to tell the truth about the truth about abuse, which is that the truth will always sound like a lie.

This is why the case against #MeToo rested, ironically, on charges of disproportionate response. Calm your tits, its critics said. Most men aren't monsters. Most things aren't rape. The thing about moral panics is that it takes one to know one. Women are panicking, they said, panicking. But it's genuinely worth considering whether panic is the only form of publicness available to the airing of sexual grief. Sexual harm is constituted by the impossibility of its being proven. Outside of statutory provisions around age, consent is basically immaterial. Rape and its cousins are ultimately determined not by the presence of physical violence but by the victim's mental state. Of the latter there can never be direct proof, only secondary indicators. Sexual assault is therefore, by definition, all in your head. Hence the slogan "yes means yes," a spell for conjuring a world where people always say what they mean and mean what they say. But usually, they don't—and usually, they can't, since people are rarely any more transparent to themselves than they are to others. Events are not self-narrating. Violence is rarely realistic. You're expecting a break, but instead you get weird, curved continuity. Someone missed their cue. That can't be the line. What did he just say? Where are we going? Did I ask for this? No one calls cut. No one checks the gate. Not knowing what happened becomes part of what happened.

It is impossible to have a proportionate response to something that never, strictly speaking, occurred. That's why the beautiful risk run by all the public blacklists, unchecked facts, and internet yelling that coalesced alongside the due-diligence journalism like #MeToo's evil Twitter twin was its wholesale refusal to play ball with believability's evidentiary regime. No smoking guns, no blue dresses. Saying so would be proof enough. This was breathtaking, the way the open maw of deep space is breathtaking: nothing, catching fire. Nuance exists, obviously. We're big girls. Women hoard subtlety in a world where belief is something you have to save up to buy. This is a secret of femininity: paying careful attention to the world's complexity can mean letting it walk all over you. But to admit this was to concede too much. We deserved some reckless-ness. It can look like violence when women afford themselves the luxury of generalization.

That's certainly how it went in *Big Little Lies*. Nicole Kidman's abusive husband cannot be defeated until he is revealed, in the season finale, to be Shailene Woodley's rapist. For a split second, two different women's experiences of abuse are perfectly aligned, like lenses in a camera, each bringing into focus the objective reality of the other. The monster must be shared to be slain. And he is—falling down a long staircase in what the show's women tell the police was an unfortunate accident. They're lying, obviously. Abuse's solution ends up as unspeakable as abuse itself. The season's final shots depict the women spending a day at the beach, touching each other affectionately and looking out onto the breaking waves. Among a group of women accustomed to wielding niceness like a telescopic baton for knocking out each other's kneecaps, it's a scene of genuine female solidarity.

The price of this was murder, of course. Maybe it always is. #MeToo never actually killed anyone, though that might have just been an accident of opportunity. The desire to kill was real enough. While sensible people, garden-party appalled, wondered aloud if important men should really lose their careers in the small of some woman's back, we sat at home knowing that getting fired was mercy, not vengeance. But the desire to punish, for better or worse, isn't the same thing as punishment. Unlike the women of *Big Little Lies*, most of us will never get the chance to watch our abusers die. That mass murder would be morally untenable, or at least practically tricky, only whets the poignancy of the thing. That is the dark comedy of the desire we call feminism: we are ethically compelled not only never to get what we want but never to stop wanting it, either. The only real justice would be unforgivable injustice. Separatism, the only answer, is also the wrong one. That fucking sucks. It suggests that justice is the biggest little lie of all.

The thing is, it's all of them. It's every single last one of them. Not just the famous ones. Not just the ones you don't personally know. Never let anyone persuade you otherwise, even if they write for a fancy magazine. But let us say, too, that it is a specious compassion that would make us reluctant to admit these things. Whether or not men deserve forgiveness—and if so, which ones—is not the question, much less the answer. In fact, there is no question. The reality is harder. What hurts isn't when the people we love do unlovable things. What hurts is when, afterward, we still love them. This goes as much for the neon of celebrity identification as it does for the quieter affections: friends, mentors, exes. What this means is that all of us will be caught wriggling on the flypaper of apologism before this thing is over. Lines in the sand blow away eventually.

No wonder, then, that the ninetieth Academy Awards, the first held after Harvey Weinstein's expulsion from the academy, passed largely without incident. The Oscars are prom for famous people. There is a white-people jazz band. The writing is cut from cardboard. The whole thing is equal parts ham and cheese—hardly the place to hold a protest. Viewers who had tuned in expecting *#MeToo Live!* were met with gentle ribbing. Host Jimmy Kimmel jokingly praised the male Oscar figurine for having "no penis at all." Emma Stone announced the Best Director nominees as "four men and Greta Gerwig." People said the word *women* a lot. The closest anyone got to the wrath of yesteryear was Best Actress Frances McDormand, butcher than usual and dependably electric, who ended her speech with the enigmatic phrase "inclusion rider," pronouncing it like code for something dangerous. Perplexed viewers scrambled to Google, whose guess was as good as theirs. The next day, the media clarified that an inclusion rider was a way for A-listers to stipulate diversity in casting and staffing as a condition of their fancy contracts. Oh, we said. That sounded like probably a good idea.

Like most finales, the Oscars were a disappointment, masquerading as a shock. If anything, they were a reminder that #MeToo never stood a chance. The celebrities were just doing what we've always wanted them to do: acting out our fantasies, not because we can't, but so we don't have to. Television is Westworld for people who can't afford to leave their living rooms. That its stars were all just trying to get paid made them no worse than those of us who were just trying to pay them. And just like them, at some point, we will cut to a commercial; at some point, we will change the channel. This could be an indictment, but it doesn't have to be. Politics, too, can be a guilty pleasure. A political movement is no more tarnished by its finitude than a romance, or a childhood, or a good TV show. Maybe it will be a relief to remember that #MeToo accomplished what every guilty pleasure accomplishes: itself. Weigh us; find us wanting. Wanting could be enough. Desire isn't revolution. But it might play one on TV.

2018

Pink

My cat was two the day I got my pussy. She had beaten me to it—
bottom surgery, I mean—by some twenty-one months. By the time I
found her, in a small shelter near the United Nations building in Manhattan, I had nearly thrown in the towel. Three days of leaving the house
in the freezing January rain, holding the cat carrier I'd purchased on
Amazon Prime; three days of returning after dark, damp and empty-
handed. Getting a pussy is harder than you'd think. Cats mate in spring
and summer, so adopting a kitten in the winter can be tricky. But on the
fourth day, at the fifth shelter, I met a tiny creature, silver and marbled
and three months old, freshly fixed by the vet upstairs. She clung to me
like a tree, or a hope. They told me she was a boy, but I'd heard that one
before.

It was winter when I got my pussy, too. By design, the weeks leading
up to surgery were a blur. I recolored my hair from metallic green to
silver-gray with a violet undertone. I staggered ridiculously to the end of
a book manuscript, tossing it to my editor as if finally clearing from my
fridge the bluing leftovers of something I'd always known I'd never eat.
I got new glasses. I saw a dentist.

I got my first tattoo, a geometric vulva, on my forearm. A friend
held my hand. It would be no novel observation to remark that getting
a tattoo is very painful, although it is a peculiar quality of pain that it
never really gets old. All bodily pain begins with shock at the audacity
of physical trespass, a kind of astonishment at the frankly unbelievable
insinuation that one is not, in fact, the center of the universe. I learned
this the electric way, during the yearlong depilation of my genital region,
as each follicle was individually targeted with several tiny, precise bursts

from a hair-thin probe. After months of struggle we reached a cautious détente, the pain and I, acknowledging each other's presence on the tacit condition of mutual noninterference, like exes swapping nods at a holiday party.

In truth, I was collecting pains, pinning them like insects to the corkboard of my brain, scribbling little labels below. Together I hoped they might testify to a deeper metamorphosis than the mere rearrangement of flesh. In vaginoplasty, the penis is not removed but delicately opened up and turned inside out—think slicing a mango. The scrotum, its tenants evicted, helps to line the vaginal wall and form the labia. I dutifully observed the garden-variety anxieties: that I would have a complication, that I would regain consciousness on the operating table. But really, I wanted to be cut, sawn in two like a lady in a magic show. I feared not that the degree of change would be catastrophic but that it wouldn't be catastrophic enough.

On the eve of the operation, I held a small celebration on the second floor of a Brooklyn pub. I'd spent weeks looking for a new dress. "Miss Andrea Long Chu asks that you join her and her loved ones at a funeral for her dick," read the invitations. Funeral attire was advised. When I arrived, I discovered that one guest had combed the party store for all the balloon letters needed to spell out HAPPY NEW VAGINA. They now adorned the wall in a lazy swoop, silver foil on exposed brick—the H a little out of place, as if huffy about its new employment. That night we pantomimed the death rites. "I'm sorry for your loss," said more than one friend, knitting their brow in mock sympathy. Someone gave me a pair of sexy underwear; someone else, a banana cut in half. At the evening's end a dear friend called me to the front of the room and presented me with a gender reveal cake, which she invited me to cut. It was pink. I was safe.

Nine hours later, I was trotting awkwardly down a hall with an OR nurse, hospital booties catching on the floor. I don't know why, but we were in a rush. I couldn't see anything without my glasses—I'd been told to leave them behind—so she had tucked my hand tightly under her arm like a football. Jogging, we chatted. She told me that she had recently gotten laser surgery to eliminate the need for prescription lenses. "It's more convenient for my job," she told me. "My family was worried about the risks, but it's what I wanted." And then we were there: a large door with a porthole, as if we were defectors about to board a submarine. Inside it looked like a film set, probably because the only operating rooms I'd ever seen had been in movies or on TV. They strapped me to the table. People in scrubs rushed to and fro, checking things, taking readings. One of them joked to me that the scene felt like a pit stop. In this analogy, I was the car. Someone went about finding a vein. "I've been told I have good veins," I bragged.

They say that when the anesthesiologist instructs you to count backward from ten, most people don't make it past nine. I don't remember counting.

It is difficult to explain why I wanted a vagina. There were technical concerns: tucking was a major inconvenience, and I was never any good at it. Sex, too, was a big motivator. Having sex with the body I had was like trying to write on a chalkboard with a lemon—and that was true even before I developed a painful tightness during arousal. The message boards said this was atrophy, a side effect of testosterone blockers. Evidently, your body turns off the gas if you stop paying your bills. But the simplest explanation was that I hoped a vagina would make me feel more like a woman. Unfortunately, this was also the most complicated answer.

The situation of the vagina in feminist politics today is, even by optimistic standards, hairy. One need look no further than the first Women's March on Washington in January 2017, one day after the inauguration. Two months before the march, inspired by the president-elect's having bragged about grabbing women "by the pussy," amateur knitters Krista Suh and Jayna Zweiman published a viral design for a simple rectangular beanie that, when placed on the head, buckled into the shape of a cat's ears. Zweiman has stated that the color pink was adopted in ironic citation of its girly, frivolous reputation. By the weekend, the pussyhat had become the unofficial uniform of the Women's March; aerial photos of the event, the largest single-day protest in the nation's history, show a sea of fuchsia dots.

The critique of the pussyhat came to be dominated by two slogans: not all pussies were pink, and not all women had pussies. The first objection, which amounted to an allegation of racism, seemed to turn on widespread but largely unremarked confusion about the multiple senses of the slang word *pussy*, which can refer either to the vagina, being the muscular birthing canal of the female mammal; to the vulva, which includes all the external genitalia (labia, clitoris, vaginal opening, even the mons); or to both taken together. Add to this the fact that the word *vagina* is often colloquially used to denote the vulva, and all bets are truly off. Vulvas do tend to reflect skin color, often having a darker hue; vaginas, however, are always pink, as sure as blood is always red. (The same is true of the vulvar vestibule, that little curtained foyer you or a loved one may discover by parting the inner labia with your fingers.) This is not to say that broader critiques of the whiteness of the Women's March were unfounded—quite the contrary. But when it came to the pussyhat itself, what felt like a pressing political question about coalition building, representation, and feminism's long love affair with racism could well have been put to bed with a simple hand mirror.

The second objection—that not all women had vaginas—was trickier to address. In the first place, it had the distinct advantage of being true: not all women *do* have vaginas, nor do all vaginas have women. Then again, the pussyhat was not an artistic rendering of the female genitalia but a simple bit of costuming. Its most literal suggestion was not that the wearer was a woman but that the wearer was a cat. This ensured that the relationship between the hat and the sex organ was, whatever else it was, figurative: a verbal and visual pun that afforded demonstrators a sly bit of plausible deniability in matters of bourgeois decency. After all, it was not as if attendees were required to flash their gash before gaining entry to the Women's March. The real question posed by the pussyhat was not whether women should be directly equated with an elastic muscle—a laughable notion, espoused by literally no one—but whether the refracted image of a vagina could be trusted to play the role of political symbol for a feminist movement that has largely denied itself the luxury of symbolism.

Doubtless there were transgender women who really did find the hats alienating. There were also those, including myself, who didn't. In fact, trans women as a demographic had a variety of opinions about the pussy-hat; some of us even had *two* opinions. Yet many cis women appeared to derive a disturbing sense of political satisfaction from projecting onto trans women their own ambivalence regarding the pussyhat (not to mention their actual canals) in the name of solidarity. In reassuring one another that the vagina must be prevented from circulating metaphorically, these women were effectively arrogating the disputed organ to themselves. After all, the pussyhat could be arraigned on charges of biological essentialism only if one had decided in advance that the only possible relationship to the vagina was having one. "Not all women have vaginas," our defenders seemed to say, "*but we do.*" At worst, this line of thinking served as cover for the same old transphobic obsessions with our genitalia. Somehow, under the guise of inclusivity, cis women had given themselves the responsibility of reminding us of our dicks. At best, it assumed, with marvelous ignorance, that trans women simply wouldn't be interested in a vaginal imaginary—as if our basic psychic integrity did not regularly rely, *like everyone else's,* on identification with things we do not, in the hollowest sense of reality, possess.

I'm getting worked up. Whatever. The pussyhats were silly and cutesy and looked like your mom made them. For some that was a deal-breaker; for others, a selling point—especially, it seemed, for the middle-aged suburban white women whom the defeat of Hillary Clinton had jolted into feminist consciousness. In this respect, the pussyhat came to signify youthfulness as distinct from biological age: a political youth whose identifying trait was a kind of embarrassing rhetorical childishness. The real problem with the pussyhats was that they offered up, with the winsome naïveté of the recently radicalized, the promise of a universal category of womanhood, which feminism has long made a cardinal virtue of forgoing. It would not be fantastic to suppose that those feminists who criticized the pussyhat most fiercely did so in part because they saw in its blithe adopters a younger, warmer version of themselves, still ugly-sweet on the romance of political consciousness, not yet having learned to be frugal with their hopes. Embarrassment is usually just pride, later.

Two months before my operation, I dreamed I was a character in a video game. As sometimes happens in video games, I died. When I respawned, I had a new face, the face of another woman altogether. Upon discovering this in the dream, I collapsed into my companion's arms and told her, through tears, that all I had ever wanted was to become unrecognizable to myself.

I woke up in the recovery room delirious. The general anesthetic was worming its way out of my system slowly, like a parasite that couldn't be bothered. The pain was intense and sharp, as if I needed to pee but had been forced to hold it for a week. Two rubber tubes slithered out of my bandaged pelvis. I eventually became coherent enough to grasp that one was a Foley catheter, to drain urine from my bladder, and the other something called a wound VAC, which was sucking out blood-red fluid and chunks of something dark. Me, presumably. But what slumbered then beneath those bandages, no one could have said. No one genital seemed more likely than any another—or, for that matter, than a new limb, or the face of the only beautiful woman in the world.

The doctors had assured me that I wouldn't be hungry after the operation, as anesthesia gives one out of three patients nausea, so of course I was ravenous. I began demanding food, petulant. The nurse coolly offered me a graham cracker; I ate it with a child's delight, letting the coarse wheat turn to pulp in my mouth. Soon I was visited by a small parliament of blue scrubs who double-checked with the nurse that I was on a strictly liquid diet. She confirmed this without missing a beat. "Thanks for not saying anything," she whispered after they left. Now we both had a secret.

I was in the hospital for another five days. My girlfriend slept on the couch in my room. I tried watching a cooking show on Netflix, but the glistening cuts of meat began to feel too close to home. On the third day,

I successfully staggered from my bed to a chair. I was immediately nauseated, vomiting athletically into the oncoming trash can in a smooth parabolic arc. Friends stopped by with flowers and gossip. One brought me a garland of construction-paper vulvas she had crafted after getting high in Seattle. Another brought me a pussyhat. The final morning, the surgeon arrived in high spirits to unbandage her creation, pulling a long bloody ribbon of gauze from my introitus like a magician showing off. With the canal clear of tubes and debris, she took out a teal rod lined with small white circles, gave it a dollop of thick lubricant, and slid it into me with the pomp of a woman at a gas station. It was a medical dilator, one of a set of three rigid polyurethane dildos. This was mama bear.

That night, in bed at my apartment, I wept. I wailed, actually, the way mothers do in ancient manuscripts. My voice, which I have over several years trained myself to lift and smooth, grew raw; at a certain point, it broke, like a woman's water, and something low and hoarse and full of legs crawled up my throat and out of my mouth. The truth was, I didn't feel any more like a woman. I felt exactly the same. The pitiless beauty of the operation is that it's all the same nerve endings, reclaimed like lumber from an old boat. This meant my vulva was alive, full of sensation, but it also meant that these sensations were the very ones I had gone under the knife to escape. The ship would always belong to Theseus, no matter how many parts I replaced. I guess I should have known this beforehand. I did, intellectually. You can stand on the beach and spy a sandbar across the water; if you swim, you can stand on the shoal and look back. Your location will have changed, but your position will be identical. You will always be Here, wherever Here happens to be. The tide goes in and out, but distance as such—that is the unswimmable. There, there is only drowning.

In the *Metamorphoses*, Ovid tells the story of Alcyone, queen of Trachis. When she finds her shipwrecked husband's corpse washed up on the shore, she attempts suicide by throwing herself into the sea. Moved to pity, the gods turn both of them into kingfishers—also called halcyons, after Alcyone. As birds, they stay together. An old man marvels at their love, watching the pair soar across the waves. This is a happy ending, I guess. Still, I wonder about Alcyone, about the theft of her death. Ovid says she tries to embrace the body in her arms as they turn to wings. With her new beak she prods her lover's lips, convinced she can kiss. What kind of bird knows only how to be human? What is it to be flying and yet unable to believe it?

Feminism has never succeeded in securing women as a collective subject of history, as the Marxist intellectual tradition once hoped to do with the working class. Contemporary feminism is arguably defined by its *refusal* of womanhood as a political category, on the grounds that this category has historically functioned as a cruel ruse for white supremacy, the gender binary, the economic interests of the American ruling class, and possibly patriarchy itself. This has put feminism in the unenviable position of being politically obligated to defend its own impossibility. In order to be *for* women, feminists must refrain from making any positive claims *about* women. The result is a kind of negative theology, dedicated to striking down the graven images of a god whose stated preference for remaining invisible has left the business of actually worshipping her somewhat up in the air.

Perhaps the simplest solution to this paradox has been to quietly shift the meaning of the word *feminism*. In popular culture and especially online, *feminism* has become the go-to signifier for what the legal scholar Janet Halley calls convergentism: the belief that justice projects with different constituencies have a moral duty to converge, like lines stretching toward a vanishing point. Once the name of a single plank in a hypothetical program of universal justice, *feminism* now refers, increasingly, to the whole platform—hence the so-called Unity Principles put forward on the Women's March website, which include calls for migrant rights, a living wage, and clean air as well as the familiar demands for reproductive freedom and an end to sexual violence. "It ain't feminism if it ain't intersectional," tweeted Ariana Grande in March 2019, echoing a viral 2011 blog post by the writer Flavia Dzodan. Dzodan's original phrasing was "my feminism will be intersectional or it will be bullshit"; popular variations now include the formula "if your feminism doesn't include *x*, then it's not feminism," where *x* might be trans women, women of color, fat women, sex workers, nonbinary people, or any number of other groups. The idea is not that feminists, being desirous of justice, should also commit to anti-racism, anti-imperialism, and all the rest; it's that feminism *by definition* consists in the making of extrafeminist commitments, such that without them, it would not be feminism at all. This is odd. It is as if, having guiltily assimilated the impossibility of speaking on behalf of all women, feminism has resigned itself to the modest virtues of playing hostess for other, frankly more persuasive political discourses—most of whose constituencies *are composed of* women, of course, but never *as* women. In this arrangement, feminism describes not a concrete political project but the moral imperative to do politics in the first place.

In other words, a feminist is a *good person*. If that sounds cliché, that's kind of the point. The conviction that it is both possible and desirable to *be* a feminist, in an ontologically thick way, has no parallel in any other left political discourse, and a wide array of digital media has arisen to guide and instruct initiates: just as *Better Homes & Gardens* once taught its readership how to cook and decorate like good women, so do *Teen Vogue* and *The Cut* offer tips on how to be a good feminist while getting dressed in the morning. The irony is that feminism, having some fifty years ago introduced the radical idea that the personal was political, has today ended up with the laborious task of making politics feel personal. Hence the possessive pronoun—*my* feminism, *your* feminism. It's easy, and foolish, to dismiss this as neoliberalism or corporate co-optation. Digital slogans like Dzodan's, regardless of their original intention, find popularity not because they are true (even when they are) but because their repetition across social media helps people achieve feelings of belonging, purpose, and importance that allow them to bridge the yawning gap between their individual everyday lives and the grand narrative of political universality. This is, as it were, the women's work of the political imagination; it is thankless, sentimental, and impossible to do without.

I suppose what I'm saying is not that the desire for a universal is politically defensible but, more simply, that the desire for a universal is synonymous with having a politics at all. In a punishing twist, feminism has become both the preferred name for this desire and the very politics that must not claim it. Indeed, the minimal definition of a feminist might be a person who, affirming that women will never constitute a political class, privately hopes it might happen anyway. Can you really blame the Women's March for wanting a symbol for universal womanhood, if symbolism was all it could ever have? In anticipation of the march, the Twitter account for *The Washington Post*'s free daily newspaper, the *Express*, tweeted an illustration of a crowd in the shape of a circle with an arrow on one side. This was the wrong gender symbol—Mars, not Venus—an eminently avoidable gaffe whose ridiculousness multiplied in proportion to the number of editors whose desks one imagines it must have passed over. But the error was easy to miss if you weren't looking for it. This may have been thanks to the illustration's color, a radiant peach pink, or to the fact that it wasn't even a conventional Mars symbol, the arrow boasting a full triangle reminiscent of the Clinton campaign's rightward barb. But the mistake may have also owed its endurance to an unconscious editorial assumption that desperation for a political sym-bol—*any* symbol—was a condition so persuasively female as to render the specifics of that symbol irrelevant.

In April 2018, Janelle Monáe released the music video for "Pynk," the third single from her studio album *Dirty Computer*, to wide critical and popular acclaim. The video features Monáe dancing in magnificent vulva-shaped pants and frequently alludes, both lyrically and visually, to cunnilingus and fingering. (The actress Tessa Thompson, long rumored to be the artist's girlfriend, features prominently.) Monáe was praised for her inclusivity—some of her backup dancers didn't wear pussy pants—but there was no denying that she, too, was in hot-pink pursuit of some kind of universal. "Pynk, like the inside of your . . ." begins the song's first line, trailing off before resuming, coyly, on the word *baby*. For all its visual frankness, "Pynk" is essentially a song about withholding: all the pink things implied by the singer—not just her lover's pussy, but her tongue, her brain, the quick under her nails—are partially or entirely hidden by flesh, keratin, or bone. "Deep inside, we're all just pynk," Monáe purrs during the outro, and she's right: pinks, the family of flow-ers from which the color takes its name, are also called carnations, after the Latin *caro*, meaning a cut of flesh. In the end, "Pynk" may have suggested once again what the pussyhat had proved, if only by accident of controversy: that the universal can be glimpsed only by being cut into. This is the substance of any politics with a hole in it—a pink universal, invisible except where the skin breaks or opens blindly on its own onto risk, or sunlight, or someone else's tongue.

Women explain things to me. They tell me that no woman feels good about herself; that no one's actually good at makeup; that it's very difficult for all women to find clothes that suit their body types; that everyone's breasts are hung a little off; that everyone's hormones are a little out of whack; that all women envy other women. They tell me that sex hurts; that orgasms are nothing special; that everyone was ugly in high school; that teenage girls don't have the kind of slumber parties they appear to have in films, or when they do, they don't paint their toenails, and if they did, the polish would stick to the bedsheets. They tell me that there is no universal experience of being a woman, except that no woman actually feels like a woman; they tell me that in fact, being a woman feels like nothing at all.

I think they think they are being kind. They aren't, but that's kindness for you. This is the germ of feminist consciousness, I suppose: women telling women that no one's normal, no one gets it right. But my friends don't know the cruelty of their confidence, the bladed irony of the implication that anyone who believes that being a woman is possible couldn't possibly be a woman. They don't know how much it hurts to watch the object of your desire broken into pieces just because you wanted it. There's an old story about two women who come before Solomon the Wise, each claiming to be the mother of the same baby. When the king proposes cutting the baby in half, the first woman agrees, but the second woman, the true mother, pleads with him to give the baby to the first. She would rather lose the thing she loves than see it come to harm. I am the second woman. Maybe I will always be.

Cis women hate when trans women envy them, perhaps because they cannot imagine that they are in possession of anything worth envying. We have this, at least, in common: two kinds of women, with two kinds of self-loathing, locked in adjacent rooms, each pressing her ear up against the wall to listen for the other's presence, fearing a rival but terrified to be alone. For my part, cousin: I don't want what you have; I want the way in which you don't have it. I don't envy your plenitude; I envy your void. Now I've got the hole to prove it. I would give anything to hate myself the way you do, assuming it's different from the way I hate myself—which, who knows. The thing about vaginas is you can never get a good look at them.

2019

Given the extent to which the public has been invited to consider my genital configuration over the years, I am pleased to report an error that was not brought to my attention until several years after the publication of this essay. It turns out I am the first woman after all.

China Brain

She gets there and it's like someone's aunt has decorated the place. Big block colors and weird expressionist paintings, limbs and tits hanging out of color fields, but also an oriental rug on the wall, zigzag throw pillows, boho-Bauhaus. Orange, red, orange, orange. And then just attic crap: old chairs, audio cables, yellowing books, jigsaw puzzles, a Rubik's Cube. In the bathroom, she finds a porcelain replica of Fowler's phrenology head resting above the toilet. From where she's sitting now, in a big blue chair purchased at a discount from a folded dental practice, she spots a large model of a human ear covered in small Chinese characters, for acupuncture training. Her *hanzi* are poor, but she knows a few. Heart, eyes. 心, 目.

It's her shrink who first recommends it to her. *Transcranial magnetic stimulation*, she says with her throaty uvular *R*s. Her psychiatrist is literally German. Frau Doktor explains that TMS is relatively new, a bit experimental, but the idea is to provide a noninvasive alternative to electroshock for patients whose depression has resisted medication, which hers has. But the procedure sounds like something out of science fiction. What they will do, her psychiatrist tells her, is put a big magnet on her head and shoot electricity into her brain. Like jump-starting a car.

She will try anything at this point. It's been two years since her first depressive episode and nothing feels good anymore. She doesn't want to have sex or see anyone. Her girlfriend takes care of her, and that's basically their whole relationship now. She can't write. She backed out of a bunch of gigs a few months ago; gradually, editors have stopped asking her to do things. When they ask, she doesn't know how to say no. She hates to say she's sick, like she's trying to skip school. She eventually settles on the word *sabbatical*, because it sounds like a vacation. She is terrified of vacation.

The slightly nutty psychiatrist who runs this place goes by Dr. L. She is Italian, not German, but really Dr. L inhabits a tiny nation of one, her own private Monaco, from which she communicates by long-distance telephone. Despite appearances, it's a real clinic, at least in the sense that Dr. L is board-certified, and the bald, sarcastic technologist who runs the machines with his small team of graduate students claims to be among the most experienced TMS practitioners in the city. This man, it turns out, is Dr. L's husband, Dennis. The two make a strange pair, bright and gloomy, talkative and laconic; she stands like a bird in his crocodile mouth. Together they decide where to put the magnets. Opposites, something something.

They did an EEG last week, an electroencephalogram, to listen to her brain. The technician was a sweet pudgy man named Timothy who stuck electrodes onto her scalp with conductive gel. She had to scrub her hair hard to get it out, like bad sex. Today they give her the results: two sets of sine waves, one recorded with her eyes closed and the other with them open. "You have a high alpha peak frequency," says Dr. L. She compares this to the sampling rate of an audio recording. Her husband grunts from his terminal, "It means you're smart."

Above her head she can see the magnet itself, a large figure-eight coil attached to a posable black tube, which runs behind her chair into a generator with a display screen. When Dennis lowers it onto her scalp for the first time, it looks like a giant black butterfly has died on her forehead. Dr. L is busy explaining what an alpha wave is. "They're in the less-active range frequency-wise, between eight and twelve hertz," she says, unconsciously lifting her arm and resting it on her motor cortex. "Your neurons oscillate in an alpha rhythm when you're relaxed, or when you close your eyes." The magnet is heavy but not uncomfortable, and the machine chirps behind her as Dennis fiddles with its settings. Dr. L stares up at the ceiling. "Now alpha waves are perfectly normal," she says, "but in the case of a depressed patient like you, there's an increase in alpha band coherence in the left dorsolateral prefrontal cortex, which has to do with executive function—decision-making, planning, et cetera. And what we think is that this alpha coherence inhibits executive function." So that's what it is: her brain is walking around with its eyes closed. "It's like a tumor, but it's not made of tissue. It's a pattern of concentrated wave activity with a two-centimeter radius, give or take." Dr. L touches her pointer to her thumb. "About the size of a golf ball. That's what we're targeting."

Once the machine is ready, the first thing Dennis does is determine her motor threshold, which means he gradually increases the power until her hand twitches, like he's tapping her brain with a little hammer to see if it kicks. They run this test to make sure they don't give her a seizure. When her hand finally shudders like a dying spider, what's strange is that it feels like a choice. "Now what we're going to do," says Dr. L, "is send an envelope of electromagnetic waves into that golf ball at regular intervals, to try and break up the alpha coherence." It's like radio interference, she thinks; it's like in science fiction when they get in a space battle and somebody yells, *Jamming their comms!* so the bad guys can't talk to one another.

Dennis fires up the magnet. It shoots seven pulses of electricity into her brain, then pauses, then sends another packet, then another. It sounds like the igniter on a faulty gas burner. It feels like getting flicked in the head with a pencil.

For a while, that's all it is. The machine keeps the minutes. Sunlight gently pushes through the blinds. Outside, summer is ending.

"So what do you do?" asks Dennis.

"I'm a writer," she answers.

"A writer?" He smirks, turning back to the glow of his computer. "Are you gonna write about this?"

"Maybe," she replies. "Probably a little fictionalized, some first-person stuff."

"First person? What, like you'll be the narrator?"

"No," she says. "The narrator will be my brain."

Hello.

Sorry for the runaround. I just wanted to make sure we could talk in private, you and me. Brain to brain, if that's okay. It's your brain that's reading this right now on your computer or your phone, or bless you, maybe in print, feeling the coarse weight of the paper stock under your fingers, which are your brain's fingers, with their thousands of nerve endings. The truth is it's always the brain, reading or writing. It's always the brain talking or eating, having sex, not having sex, lying about why, apologizing for earlier, walking around the apartment wondering where did I leave that thing, saying how could you do this to me, asking is this really happening, asking what will I do without you. Brains softly crying together. Brains kissing brains goodbye.

Now I've forgotten what I was going to ask you. Maybe it's, Have you ever been sick? I had this teacher in middle school, I can't remember her name. I can't even remember what she taught. History? She had this bit she would do where she would say something like, "And the Puritans said to themselves, *Self? Let us cross the Atlantic in search of religious freedom!*" That was so funny to us, the idea of someone addressing their own self. She was young and alarmingly bony, and she had this long, curly brown hair she wore in a homely ponytail. She had a piano in her classroom and a beautiful operatic voice. She loved music. Did she teach music? I don't know. Anyway, she died. Brain hemorrhage.

That's not what I meant, though—sick like that. I mean, I do mean that. That was the first funeral I ever went to. But I also mean my English teacher, who threw himself off an overpass a few years after I graduated. He was a bad English teacher. I don't know what his brain was like, if it was depressed or manic or just tired. He was young and energetic, and he was bald with a short beard, and he had a frenzy behind his eyes and a guitar behind his desk. He loved music too. He would bring in songs from rock bands and we would analyze them like literature. We did "Hallelujah" once. What he didn't love was English. He gave us vocabulary words: *harbinger*, noun, a sign that something's coming. But he pronounced it *har-binger*, like it rhymed with *folk singer*, which is what he should have been instead. I whispered to the other brains, it's a *juh* sound not a *guh* sound. *Harbinger*. Like *injure*. Like *jump off a bridge*.

Then there was my old crush's older sister. She said the word *fuck* like it wasn't anything, like she was flicking a ladybug off her arm, and she loved long words and *Star Trek*. I don't remember how she died, only that she posted a note to Facebook, which I guess is the world we live in, though she doesn't anymore. They say it's ruining us, the internet, melting us down until we drip out of our ears. We say it too, don't we? There goes our last brain cell, we tweet; this is what finally broke our brain. She has brain worms, we say, or we get our hands to tell our fingers to type out *G-A-L-A-X-Y B-R-A-I-N* when someone posts something so magnificently stupid it's like their brain has engulfed an entire star system.

Is that where they all went, brain? Where no brain had gone before?

Almost immediately she notices the effects: a jolt of energy in the afternoon accompanied by trembling agitation, like she's holding a hornet's nest in her cheek. This doesn't feel good, but it feels like something, which is more than she can say of the past two years. She goes in for half-hour sessions four, sometimes five days a week at first. They tell her this is normal; that once they've established a baseline, it'll be more like two or three days a week, until they hit remission—maybe eight to twelve weeks total if all goes well. She tells Dr. L about the buzzing in her mouth and Dr. L confers with Dennis, who adjusts the protocol to include something called a theta burst. To supplement, they decide to give her a ketamine nasal spray right before treatment. Horse tranquilizers. They tell her it's not to anesthetize her, just to make her brain more pliant, more plastic. The brain, like a horse, can sleep standing up.

She has never done ketamine before, or any drugs really. Does ibuprofen count? She's done a lot of ibuprofen. In high school she started to get debilitating migraines, especially after staying up late. It got to where she was popping a few ibuprofens before bed out of habit. Eventually her pediatrician wrote her a prescription for sumatriptan. At the appointment he joked—it must have been a joke—that maybe her brain was too big for her head. Now, when she's on the ketamine, it's the world that's too big for her brain. Her field of vision acquires a kind of curvature; the carpet curls up toward the wall, which is buckling into the ceiling. No hallucinations or anything, though. Beyond, you know, consciousness.

Dennis hates Donald Trump. He hates him rapturously. On the wall he has hung a bizarre plaque featuring a brass relief sculpture of the president's face and engraved below it the notorious lines about grabbing things. She would be able to see it from where she sits, this seditious monument, if it weren't for the fact that turning her head would allow the magnet to reach its fingers into her motor cortex and make her dance like a marionette.

Sometimes she argues with Dennis about Bernie Sanders, whom he also hates. This is a bad idea, but she can't help herself. Other times they discuss the science of the treatment. Dennis comes alive talking about the brain. He tells her that TMS requires you to think in terms of electromagnetic events, to treat the brain less like a computer and more like the weather. The target area, that two-centimeter golf ball? It *moves*, says Dennis. The golf ball moves around. Not far, just a few millimeters usually, fidgeting around in her head thanks to minute variations in alpha activity. Waiting impatiently for someone to drive it down the fairway.

Dennis refers to this book a lot, *Rhythms of the Brain*, by a neuroscientist named György Buzsáki. Later she will flip through the busted copy that he leaves for her in the waiting room. The cover has this big gray brain on it, plopped down in a desert of red cortical folds; it reminds her of the evangelical space fantasy novels she was given as a child. The book is very technical, way over her head, but she gets the thesis from the introduction. "Most of the brain's activity is generated from within," she reads, "and perturbation of this default pattern by external inputs at any given time often causes only a minor departure from its robust, internally controlled program." She mentions this to Dennis, as he once again positions the magnet on her scalp, this idea that most of what the brain does is, as it were, business-facing. His eyes light up. "The brain is intelligence!" he says, and he says it in this booming, revelatory voice, and the thing is, for her it is a revelation somehow, to realize that the same intelligence that builds cathedrals and invents gunpowder is also, and in fact primarily, responsible for itself.

In 1978, the philosopher Ned Block put forward a thought experiment called the China Brain. Block was trying to settle a debate in analytic philosophy over the relationship between the brain and the mind. The dominant cluster of thought at the time was called functionalism; generally speaking, functionalists argued that mental states like perceptions or emotions could be understood purely in terms of sensory inputs and behavioral outputs. In theory, this meant that minds were "multiply realizable": mental states could be realized not just by the human brain but by *anything* capable of matching outputs to inputs—for instance, a silicone-based Martian brain, or a computer.

Block disagreed and proposed the following scenario: Let every person in China be given a two-way radio. Then let massive satellites be shot into space that can be seen from anywhere in the country. The purpose? For each comrade to function like a neuron: a billion identical Chinese in their little Mao suits radioing each other in response to the signals beamed down from the people's satellites in the sky. In theory, China would now be functionally equivalent to a brain if it were hooked up to a human body. Yet surely this strange dictatorship of the proletariat could not be said to have mental states, Block argued; hence, functionalism was false. Surely China could not, for instance, feel pain, or fall in love, or taste the sting of alcohol on someone's lips. Surely it could not wallow in resentment, or beg for another chance, or get a horrible sinking feeling way down in its Yellow River heart.

A few years later another philosopher, John Searle, put forward a similar thought experiment called the Chinese Room. (Analytic philosophy is nothing but this kind of stuff, brain.) Searle set out to disprove the functionalist view, popular among some researchers in artificial intelligence at the time, that the brain functions like a computer program. Here was his scenario: a hypothetical version of Searle finds himself sitting in a room, where he has been provided with several packets of symbols, as well as a set of instructions in English for how to relate the symbols to one another. A new packet of symbols is slid under the door by his faceless handlers, and by following the English instructions, Searle is able to produce his own packet of symbols in response, which he slides back out. The process repeats.

Now here is the trick: unbeknownst to the man in the room, the first symbols form a story, the second symbols form questions about that story, and the symbols he sends out form thoughtful answers to those questions—all in Chinese characters. Searle argued that to an observer outside the room, the room's occupant would appear to be a fluent Chinese speaker answering questions in Chinese, thus passing the Turing test—Alan Turing's test of a machine's ability to imitate human language—all without the man inside understanding a word of Chinese. Hence, he concluded, the brain must not function like a program, precisely because a program can function like the brain without having any idea what it's doing. Interestingly, Searle was not arguing in favor of some kind of metaphysical consciousness, just for a biological explanation for intelligence. "Can a machine think?" he asked. "My own view is that *only* a machine could think, and indeed only very special kinds of machines, namely brains."

But why Chinese? Why China? It's a curious coincidence, which is to say, probably not one. Block said he chose China because the brain had about a billion neurons and China had about a billion people. I don't know if he knew about Lenin's definition of communism: soviet power plus electrification. I do know that Mao Zedong had been dead only two years in 1978; by the time Searle was writing in 1980, Deng Xiaoping had opened the country to foreign capital. Was communist China the closest Block could get to a red planet without leaving the atmosphere, its citizens as alien as the Martians in his colleagues' papers? The Chinese were already ideal for experimenting on. In the first place, they had that air of oriental mystery, just like the Mechanical Turk, the turbaned automaton that played chess for the Habsburgs until it was revealed to be operated by a chess master hiding inside. But they were also socialists, cogs in a giant organized machine that nevertheless could not yield a single blossom of intelligence. Did you know that the word *brainwash* comes directly from Chinese? 洗腦.

That's you, brain. That little *x* floating inside your skull, like John Searle locked inside his room. Searle, for his part, chose Chinese because it was all Greek to him, though he didn't use Greek, did he? "I'm not even confident that I could recognize Chinese writing as Chinese writing distinct from, say, Japanese writing or meaningless squiggles," he wrote. "To me, Chinese writing is just so many meaningless squiggles." A language with an alphabet would still have been too close to his native English, a code he might have accidentally cracked. But Chinese "symbols," as he called them, were perfectly cryptic, impossible to parse. Not true, in fact, since most characters are phono-semantic, connected by a loose threadwork of indices and rhymes. But true enough for Searle, for whom every word in the Chinese language could symbolize the same thing: the brain, the brain. Intelligence uncomprehending itself.

Let's try a different thought experiment. Suppose the year is 1900. Empress Dowager Cixi has just dispatched Manchu troops to support the Boxers' violent campaign against foreign missionaries. In Jiangsu province, my grandfather's grandmother is sitting in a room. In it, she finds several stacks of symbols. Thanks to her gentry family, she is literate. She reads the first stack, which turns out to be a story. She reads the second stack, which turns out to be questions about the story. She thinks for a minute, then writes down some answers and slides them under the door. She receives more questions; she sends out more answers. The third and tallest stack sits undisturbed on the table next to her, covered in strange squiggles. She wonders, with a growing sense of dread, what they could possibly mean.

She asks the kid running the machine today if he believes in Chinese medicine. He's one of Dennis's master's students, early twenties maybe. He has one of those names, like Kyle or something. They struggle to relate to each other. He is from the Midwest. He plays fantasy football.

Kyle says he doesn't believe in alternative medicine. "Or," he qualifies, "like obviously if it works, it works, but I just think there's always going to be some kind of scientific explanation for it." This is the easy answer; she knows because she's often used it herself. Her ex's mother had trained in traditional medicine back in Beijing, so her ex grew up drinking these teas made with bark and herbs, which her ex always hated. This was the Chinese mother she never had, the woman whose *jiaozi* recipe she still uses. They are still friendly. Sometimes they text in squiggles.

"But that's the thing," she says to Kyle. "The whole 'if it works, it works' thing, that's how Western medicine works too." She once talked about this with the Chinese father she does actually have, that doctors like him mostly don't know what the drugs they use do. "They just make sure they do what they want them to do without doing anything bad," she says.

Kyle angles his chin toward Wisconsin.

"Also," she presses on. "These fields, like medicine or biology or whatever, they're historically located. Like the phrenology bust in the bathroom. The only reason we say phrenology is a pseudoscience is because it fell out of favor and got replaced by something else. Don't you think neuroscience is gonna get replaced by something one day?"

The magnet ticks away like a bomb.

"Maybe," Kyle says slowly.

"Science is just pseudoscience with a bigger budget," she finishes triumphantly. She prewrote this line in the notes app on her phone.

Kyle frowns. "Not necessarily," he says. "Take evolutionary psychology. They get tons of money, but it's all bullshit."

I have been thinking about the mad German scientist Mel Brooks plays in *The Muppet Movie*. Brooks does this zany caricature of a Nazi doctor, though that was lost on me as a small child. He has arrived to perform an "electronic cerebrectomy" on Kermit the Frog, whom the movie's villain has been trying to secure as the spokesman for his tacky chain of frog-leg restaurants. The doctor wheels in a sinister machine with a small chrome seat, above which hangs the tiny, electrified dome that will be lowered onto Kermit's head. The villain asks what the machine does. "Vat does it do? Vat does it *do*?" scoffs Brooks. "It turns ze brains into *guacamole*."

I will tell you a secret: Kermit the Frog doesn't have a brain. Kermit the Frog has a *hand*—specifically, Jim Henson's hand, one of the greatest hands of his generation, which was his brain's hand, with its thousands of nerve endings. Go watch Jim Henson on Johnny Carson in 1975, operating Kermit in plain view of the studio audience, no camera tricks, no hiding that it's just his arm wrapped in some felt. "I got a bad throat," Kermit tells Carson glumly, "I got a person in my throat." That's frog humor, Kermit clarifies over the audience's laughter. Later Johnny ponders the experience: "It's funny the way that the fantasy starts, and you get so caught up—I'm sitting here talking to a frog!" He puts his index finger to his temple and twists it like a corkscrew. "You must know when you're ready for the home," he quips, as if talking to someone without a brain has made him question the integrity of his own.

It always terrified me to see Kermit clamped into that electric chair, the little transparent dome descending onto his ping-pong eyes. Brooks calls it an electronic yarmulke. It did put the fear of heaven in me, brain. I would cover my ears or leave the room until it was over, like the electricity might leap from the cathodes straight into my skull, and in a few irreversible seconds there would be nothing left of me, the only part of my body I had ever been taught to love. Each time, there was a chance, a real chance, that Kermit might not make it out, that he might finally become what he already was: a puppet, with someone else's hand up his brain.

They say we're muscles, you and I. It's not true; we're mostly fat. We think we're the ones pulling the strings, but if all it takes is a couple of strings, what's the point of having a brain at all? No heart, no eyes, no little calculi, just five fingers, a song, and a dance.

She is sitting in a noodle shop with a friend. They are talking about the philosophy of mind. She is saying something about how she doesn't want to believe that how she feels is just an effect of neurons firing or whatever. She tells her friend that she is trying to work out an ontology where everything is equally real.

"Let's say objects only exist within their own systems," she says, crunching black fungus between her teeth. "Like, alpha waves do exist, but only as objects inside of neurobiology."

"Right," says her friend.

"But at the same time, a catatonic episode is also a real object, but its reality is located within psychiatry."

"Right."

"So then it's like oil and water. Objects in the same metaphysics can act on one another, but not on other kinds of objects. Like, an antidepressant can block a serotonin transporter because they inhabit the same biochemical reality, but neither of them can interface with intrusive thoughts, which are psychological objects. And nothing is an 'effect'"—she does the air quotes with her chopsticks—"of anything else, there's just a massive number of these object systems superimposed on each other acting in parallel, and they're all completely blind to each other."

"Right," says the friend. "You can't drive a train through a field."

"Right."

They finish their noodles. 拉麵.

Later, she thinks things can't be that simple. Objects get lost or misplaced all the time. They wander, migrate from one reality to another, visit one another's dimensions. Isn't that what depression is? Electricity flaring into consciousness.

You *can* drive a train through a field, after all. It's called a train wreck.

If you are considering trying transcranial magnetic stimulation for yourself, I think you'll find that its appeal lies in treating your depression not as a psychological disorder, or even a chemical imbalance, but as a basically electrical problem. Sure, you can talk to a therapist or a psychoanalyst about all the things that make you want to die. They will help you narrativize your pain, or the jagged border around your pain; if they cannot stitch the hole inside you, then at least they can help you hem the edges. Or you can get a psychiatrist, and they will write you a prescription for an antidepressant, and you can spend months or years negotiating a dose with the animalcules who operate your cells. But the magnets are different, brain. They promise direct manipulation of the voltages inside you, much closer to physical therapy than to an SSRI. The magnets say, it's just physics, dummy. The magnets say, what you need is a good kick in the head.

Of course, if it's direct intervention you're after, you could always get electroshock, like a sad lady in a movie, which could be fun. Electroconvulsive therapy is considered no riskier than general anesthesia, but the brochure points out that they anesthetize you because, no joke, they are literally going to give you a seizure. And so you settle on TMS, which is much less invasive and nominally cheaper, though that's just a nice bit of advertising, because who knows how long you'll be doing this. And I hope you have insurance, brain, because I know I just said it's cheaper than ECT but it's still a bitch, and honestly it helps maybe 60 percent of people. But here you are now, in the big blue chair, and while the magnet pecks away at your skull like a bird looking for worms, they're just gonna ask you some questions about how you've been feeling. But don't worry: they just want feedback so they can adjust the machine. They don't really *care*.

But you care. You care a lot. Way too much, actually. I know you feel like life is meaningless, but that meaninglessness is saturated with meaning. Nothing has ever felt more important to you than the waxing conviction, as the afternoon sun moves across your motionless body, that nothing fucking matters. So that's the promise of TMS: less meaning. The magnet will come for you with its little chisel, and bit by bit, if you're lucky enough to be 60 percent of a person, it will carve away the existential meaninglessness of your depression until all that's left is the electromagnetic meaninglessness of static on the radio. Whether this is something gained, or something horribly, terribly lost, will be up to you.

When I was a kid, my parents were regular listeners of *A Prairie Home Companion*, the variety show on public radio. My favorite bit was this fictitious sponsorship by the Ketchup Advisory Board. "These are the good years for Barb and me," a man named Jim would say, describing their mild suburban lives. But then Jim would find Barb softly crying in the garden or staring blankly at the wallpaper. And it was always something small at first—a rescheduled vacation, a misplaced pen—but really she was consumed with middle-aged malaise, middle-class void. So they would talk or bicker, getting nowhere, until finally a new thought would occur to him. "Barb," Jim would say, "I wonder if you're getting enough ketchup."

A reader once wrote to tell me that they'd been depressed for seven years when they discovered that they had a food allergy. They cut the offending item out of their diet—I think it was gluten—and just like that, the depression stopped. Seven years of suffering, from a protein.

I told my therapist about this, and she asked me well didn't I think they might be exaggerating. Maybe, I said. But what an idea, brain, to reach down through that stack of needles and find a tiny piece of wheat.

"I always think of the Tacoma Narrows Bridge."

It's Timothy on the machine today. They are a little acquainted now. Timothy knows the Latin roots of things. She likes Timothy.

"That's how I think of thalamocortical dysrhythmia," he says. Timothy explains that this is an abnormal kind of brain wave oscillation that some researchers have proposed as a key element of depression, plus Parkinson's, tinnitus, and other disorders. There are these columns of electromagnetic resonance in her brain, he says—thalamocortical columns they're called, on account of they run from the cortex down into the thalamus, which as Timothy can tell her is the Greek word for chamber, and well especially a marriage bed, she says, because she knows the roots of things too. But sometimes the thalamus says, Do it this way, I like it this way, and the cortex says, I just don't know what you want from me anymore, and suddenly the columns start to vibrate all wrong, and now the whole house is quivering all the way up to the eaves because that's what columns do: they hold things up.

Treatment is not going well. It's exhausting coming in day after day. She can't take two days off without pitching back into despair. It's so imprecise; each session, the magnet wanders around her head like a cheap contractor, banging on the drywall. She begins to have these trepanation fantasies. Of taking a power drill to her temple and releasing all the spirit or phlogiston or whatever. Of a metal bar passing into one ear and cleanly emerging from the other, like the tamping iron that blasted through that railroad worker's skull during the gold rush. Meanwhile, Dennis grows more truculent with each passing primary debate on TV. "You can't do anything to me," he cries during one of their arguments. "I'm threatening my wife with retirement!" Autumn is waning, and the trees in the park outside are giving up their leaves like joss paper. One day, Dr. L abruptly takes her off the ketamine, without explanation; somewhere, a horse gets its wings.

Timothy pulls up a black-and-white video on the big monitor across the room and hits play. She remembers the Tacoma Narrows Bridge now, from some physics textbook. What had happened was, to save money, the state of Washington hired a big-time civil engineer from New York who promised a sleeker design at a lower cost. The resulting structure was especially vulnerable to what the textbook had called mechanical resonance; when the wind was right, the deck would oscillate at one of its natural frequencies, like a musical instrument, producing visible undulations that led the construction workers to nickname the bridge Galloping Gertie. One day in 1940, a strong wind induced a new kind of motion in the bridge, which began twisting back and forth in increasingly violent waves. "Until it collapsed," says Timothy, which is what it's doing now in the video, drowning itself in Puget Sound along with a journalist's daughter's doomed cocker spaniel.

Curious, she looks it up on her phone. The internet tells them that despite what they may have learned in high school, the Tacoma Narrows Bridge actually collapsed as a result of a much more complicated phenomenon known as aeroelastic flutter, not mechanical resonance. Less wineglass, more plane crash. They agree this is a less romantic explanation.

The magnet on her head is making her eye twitch. Timothy restarts the video. Without speaking they watch the bridge writhe in the wind. Silently singing itself to death.

I just want to check in, brain. How are you feeling? Do you need some water? You always need some water. You know that thing about how you only use 10 percent of yourself? That's because the other 75 percent is water. I know that's only 85 percent. The last 15 we set aside, like the last yarrow stalk in an *I Ching* reading. We reserve it for the Infinite. 無極.

Brains are so fragile, brain. How easily we break. China brains, like china dolls, balanced on the shelf. One little bump and there we go.

We're almost done now. I believe in you.

It's bitter cold. Timothy does a second EEG to see if the treatment has had any lasting effects. More crusted gel in her hair. Good news: she isn't pregnant. But the golf ball is still there. The trees outside are empty now. They reach their dendrites toward one another, trying to synapse.

They are going to put the EEG results up on the big screen. Her girlfriend is here today, come to witness the science of her suffering. They are both suffering, and whenever she has pictured the bottle of bleach under their bathroom sink, holding it in her mind for a few seconds like hot toast, her girlfriend has pulled her close and rocked her away into the dark early night, but has she ever really done the same when her girlfriend was staring deep down into the down deep, and how long have they been doing this, loving each other away?

She's in the big blue chair. Her girlfriend is next to her. Dennis is on the machine. Dr. L is leaning back against the windowsill. Timothy is at the computer bank. Kyle is at home, dreaming of the open sky. The whole coast vibrates.

Timothy jumps the data to the television. This time they show her something new, topographic maps. There are these circles, like diving helmets viewed from above: little rectangular ears, little triangle noses pointing north. Inside them are the waves, which means the divers are dead. These bands of color in her head, they look like rain on the weather channel, going from blue to green to yellow to red, increasing in intensity. Dr. L points up at the circle labeled *10–12 Hz*, which is within the alpha range. The top of the circle is fully engulfed in red, radiant burning red, and in the middle of all the red, a little to the left—right where they put the magnet—there's this prominent magenta spot, like a fire pit, or a volcanic crater, or a cyclone on a distant moon.

"That's it," Dr. L says. "That's it."

She looks up at the moon. What she's thinking is, she wrote this book last winter, and it's coming out soon. Actually, I'm mixed up. Her book came out already, and what she's thinking is, she has this book tour coming up, and she's leaving tomorrow on a plane for Los Angeles, or maybe San Francisco, I forget which, and she's been trying to pretend it's not happening, the book or the tour or any of it. She's sitting in this sky-blue vintage Thunderbird of a chair and staring up at that big fucking hole in her brain, and what she's thinking is that she didn't even know she had anything left to give, but she's giving it up now, she's giving it all up, she's pouring it into that two-centimeter hole, and that night she cancels everything, she eats the plane ticket and digs herself a two-hundred-centimeter hole in the middle of her living room that goes all the way to Wuxi, where her ancestors were scholars for a thousand years, all those brains one after another, strung out in a line like paper lanterns across the sky, and then seven million centimeters away, in Wuhan, people start getting sick, and suddenly it's like somebody blew a hole in the entire world, the whole big China brain of the world, and TMS is done, the clinic goes quiet, she hears nothing from them, nothing, not so much as a postcard, and then everything just fucking stops.

It's okay, brain. We're okay.

The stupid end to this stupid story is that the magnets didn't help because what we didn't know then is that I am bipolar. Evidence for the success of transcranial magnetic stimulation in bipolar patients is partial at best, since excitation of the prefrontal cortex, like antidepressants, can trigger hypomania. A patient is considered to have bipolar II disorder when their psychiatric history includes at least one hypomanic episode lasting four days or longer, as well as at least one depressive episode lasting two weeks or longer, often much longer. The symptoms of depression are common knowledge: low mood, little pleasure or interest in doing things, lying on the couch like your entire body is an anvil, crying a lot. Hypomania, by contrast, is like mania without the psychosis. Symptoms include excessive goal-oriented activity, racing thoughts, not shutting up, and euphoria. That's me: up and down, positive and negative. You know, like a magnet.

Now my psychiatrist has me on lithium, a mood stabilizer, like she's shipped me back home to a sanatorium in the Alps. It means I shouldn't take ibuprofen if I can help it; nonsteroidal anti-inflammatory drugs can make it harder for your body to pass lithium, potentially leading to toxic levels of the metal in your blood. And lithium really is a metal: unlike most drugs, lithium carbonate occurs in nature. They discovered it at an alkaline lake in Tibet in the eighties, and later in a little town called Kings Mountain in North Carolina, not far from where I grew up. But most of the world's supply of lithium carbonate is synthesized from brine water in Chile and Argentina by people who know how to do that sort of thing. Then they sell it to other people, and those people use it to make batteries and heat-resistant glass, and to make tile mortar set faster, and to make fireworks red, and to keep china from cracking when you glaze it.

Brain, how's your chemistry? My chemistry teacher was young and handsome in a wiry way, and he wore his dirty blond hair short. He had sunglasses on his forehead and tenth-grade girls wrapped around his finger. He probably liked music, I don't know. He was a decent chemistry teacher too, though sometimes he would start working a problem on the whiteboard and get lost in his own hieroglyphs. Which, right—lithium carbonate. The molecule is simple: two lithium ions and one carbonate ion, consisting of one carbon atom and three oxygens. If you want, you can synthesize lithium carbonate through what's known as a salt metathesis reaction. You just take lithium chloride from a salt flat in Chile, a salt of equal parts lithium and chlorine, and you treat it with another salt, sodium carbonate, also called soda ash, which you probably got from a mine in Wyoming. In the reaction that follows, the sodium ions will give up their carbonate ion and receive the chlorine, leaving the lithium ions free to bond with the carbonate. Now you've got two new salts: NaCl, which you may recognize as table salt, and Li_2CO_3, the lithium salt of carbonate.

And you know what, brain? Maybe I just wasn't getting enough salt.

2021

III

Psycho Analysis

"I never pretended to be an expert on millennials," writes Bret Easton Ellis halfway through *White*, and the reader desperately wishes this were true. Ellis is best known for *American Psycho*, the controversial 1991 cult novel about an image-obsessed Wall Street serial killer; the film adaptation would star Christian Bale as the psychotic investment banker Patrick Bateman. Following several increasingly metafictional novels and a few bad screenplays, *White* is Ellis's first foray into nonfiction, and the result is less a series of glorified, padded-out blog posts than a series of regular, normal-size blog posts. Mostly, Ellis hates social media and wishes millennials would stop whining and "pull on their big boy pants"—an actual quote from this deeply needless book, whose existence one assumes we could have all been spared if Ellis's millennial boyfriend had simply shown the famous man how to use the mute feature on Twitter.

White makes a few gestures at the memoir genre: passages about Ellis's childhood as a rich, unsupervised white kid growing up in 1970s Sherman Oaks, where he developed a taste for gruesome horror flicks; the surprise success of his debut novel, *Less Than Zero*, which Ellis started writing when he was a teenager and saw published while a junior at Bennington; the cocaine-hazed Manhattan where Ellis, a member of the literary Brat Pack, wrote *American Psycho* between benders in the late eighties. These sections—I cannot call them essays—are serviceable and of mild interest, I suppose, to fans who might wish to know what went wrong with the film adaptation of *Less Than Zero*, or how it feels to do a lot of drugs.

But Ellis's true purpose in the remaining two hundred pages of *White*, a rambling mess of cultural commentary and self-aggrandizement, is to offend young, progressive readers while giving everyone else the delight of watching. Bret Easton Ellis would like you to know that he thinks "boys will be boys." He thinks #MeToo is pathetic. He thinks *La La Land* should have won Best Picture instead of *Moonlight*. He thinks HBO should make that Confederacy show. He thinks Tyler Clementi, the gay college student who jumped off a bridge after his roommate secretly taped him making out, got too worked up over a "harmless freshman dorm-room prank." He misses Milo Yiannopoulos, alt-right gadfly, and he calls Leslie Jones "a middle-aged comedienne who couldn't handle a vicious yet typical Twitter trolling." Even the title *White* is a provocation, designed to simultaneously anticipate, incur, and mock accusations of white privilege.

Ellis feigns ignorance of all of this. "I was never good at realizing what might offend someone," he shrugs, unconvincingly. "I've been rated and reviewed since I became a published author at the age of twenty-one, and I've grown entirely comfortable in being both liked and disliked, adored and despised." Like much of *White*, this is disingenuous. People who do not care what other people think do not waste their time telling other people this, and they certainly don't write books about it.

This presents a problem for the reviewer in my position: namely, whether to take the bait. I could write an incensed review that fiercely rebuts *White*'s many inflammatory claims, thus giving the impression that they should be taken seriously; if my review were to go viral, it would likely trigger more negative coverage on pop-culture websites like *Vulture* and *Vice*; Bret Easton Ellis might trend for a bit on Twitter, where we would all take our best shots at dunking on this dude; and at the end of it all, the author would get to feel relevant again, and maybe finally write a movie that people actually liked. But why bother? For years now, Bret Easton Ellis has been accused of being a racist and a misogynist, and these things are true; but like most things that are true of Bret Easton Ellis, they are also very boring.

The thesis of *White* is that American culture has entered a period of steep, perhaps irreversible decline, and social media and millennials are to blame. This is ridiculous, not because social media hasn't changed things tremendously, but because such claims are invariably rooted in a childish nostalgia for an uncomplicated mode of human communication that has never, in fact, existed. One supposes that the last freethinking men of ancient Sumer, lamenting that cuneiform had ruined their political discourse, must have longed for the good old days of throwing rocks at each other's heads.

"Somewhere in the last few years—and I can't pinpoint exactly when—a vague yet almost overwhelming and irrational annoyance started tearing through me maybe up to a dozen times a day," Ellis writes on the first page of *White*. By this, he just means Twitter, which he believes to be governed by an authoritarian conformism out to suppress true free speech. He has gotten this impression, it seems, from some mean things that people said to him online in response to a few harmless tweets. "That a gay man can't tell a joke equating AIDS with Grindr (something my boyfriend and I had used a number of times) without being scorned as self-loathing is indicative of a new fascism," Ellis announces. Readers may wonder what kids in cages are indicative of.

It is perfectly acceptable to bitch and moan about how the mean people didn't like your good tweets, but there is a time and a place for such behavior, and it is not the offices of Alfred A. Knopf, publisher. Surely someone will let Bret Easton Ellis into their group chat. "Twitter encouraged the bad boy in me," he admits, the first man to whom this has ever happened. Yet if you feel you must spend pages clarifying what you meant when you tweeted, in 2012, that *Zero Dark Thirty* director Kathryn Bigelow was overrated because she was "a very hot woman," then not only are you a bland sexist, but also, and much more importantly, you kind of suck at Twitter. In this regard, *White* is a simple case of illiteracy. Indeed, one begins to question if Ellis, who cannot stop bragging about his Gen-Xer negativity, has ever taken a good look at Twitter, the most inventively negative cultural institution of the twenty-first century, whose *own users* regularly call it "this hell site."

Ellis refers to millennials as Generation Wuss, which sounds like something your dad made up. Lots of *White* is given to this kind of feeble bullying. The first mention of safe spaces is on page 9; helicopter parents, also page 9; participation trophies, page 17. Everyone is coddled, everyone is a whiny baby. Ellis sympathizes with millennials' economic precariousness—his own college-educated millennial boyfriend spent a "hellish year" looking for a job—but the brutal truth is that life is disappointing, cruel, and frequently unfair. "Shit happens," Ellis barks, a football coach who just wants the best for his boys. "Deal with it, stop whining, take your medicine, grow the fuck up." He approvingly cites the Trump campaign's theme song "You Can't Always Get What You Want." One longs to tell him what the Rolling Stones told Trump: Please stop.

This amounts to a lecture on kettles from one of our leading pots. It is, of course, Ellis who won't stop whining; Ellis who can't handle being trolled; Ellis who calls criticism "oppression"; Ellis who manically describes the tendency of people online to react disproportionately to things as a "vast epidemic of alarmist and catastrophic drama." "When did people start identifying so relentlessly with victims, and when did the victim's worldview become the lens through which we began to look at everything?" asks the true victim, a rich writer who lives in Los Angeles. It is a curious thing that makes one generation project onto the next everything it hates most about itself. It suggests that age, far from embittering the individual, awakens in him a fresh stage of naïveté. Having never grown up himself, he clings to the hope that someone else will grow up in his place. When the young fail as he did, he becomes petulant, contemptuous, and easily offended—in short, a child again.

The prose in *White* is shapeless, roving, and aggressively unedited. One waits in vain for an arresting image. Several passages recycle or embellish material from the past few years, including a baffling 2011 essay for *Newsweek* on the difference between "Empire" and "post-Empire" celebrity that reads like Marshall McLuhan without the rigor. For a man who prides himself on roguish individuality, Ellis uses a laughably derivative vocabulary, a mélange of *Breitbart* talking points and weirdly apolitical anti-establishment ideas, as if he has just discovered Nietzsche on his older brother's bookshelf. He bemoans "the democratization of culture," he calls social media "Orwellian," and he regularly tosses off words like "groupthink," "corporate," and the dreaded "status quo." The Man, man. "Social-justice warriors never think like artists," Ellis declares, as if this is a sentence. Like his hero Joan Didion, Ellis believes that style is everything; what a shame he has written a book with so little of it.

Then again, it is impossible to write without style, just as it is impossible to cook without flavor, and yet this is exactly what Ellis insists has happened to American culture: political correctness has muzzled all artistic freedom, and Hollywood has been sapped of all aesthetics and turned into a puppet for "ideology," by which he means Black people. For years, Ellis has perseverated about "ideology versus aesthetics" on *The Bret Easton Ellis Podcast*, where he plays the thinking man's shock jock, talking about movies with that lush transcendence that enters a man's voice when he is no longer forced to endure the inconvenience of talking over someone else. Cinephilia, as we know from science, is a progressive disease for which there is no cure, but Bret Easton Ellis is taking it like a champ.

On the episode I listened to, posted in February just a few days before the Oscars, Ellis rants for almost half an hour about how Best Picture nominee *Black Panther* received its nod only because the Academy, succumbing to a "diversity push," has been "shoveling" hundreds of unqualified young women and people of color into its ranks. After the break, Ellis asks his guest, the writer Dennis Cooper, a "stupid question [that] has been nagging me for the last few years"—that is, if growing up white, wealthy, and comfortable in Southern California has influenced Ellis's work. "Though, of course, I guess, I mean, I don't know, class doesn't necessarily affect what you write," he ventures, "but I wonder if it *does*."

Cooper bypasses the question, but we all know the answer. One cannot read *White* as anything but a book about being rich and bored. *White* becomes nearly unreadable when Ellis finally reaches the rise of Donald Trump, whose freewheeling amorality Ellis compares, favorably, to Heath Ledger's Joker in *The Dark Knight*. Ellis didn't bother voting; he claims to be neither a conservative nor a liberal. "Sometime during that year and a half I had come to understand that I was many different things," he writes; if anything, he is a "romantic." "I'd never been a true believer that politics can solve the dark heart of humanity's problems and the lawlessness of our sexuality," Ellis muses, going full eighth-grader. The romance crumbles in the wake of the election, when he must attend dinner after dinner with shell-shocked liberal friends whose "hysterical" refusal to accept the results drives him up a wall. "My first reaction was always, *You need to be sedated, you need to see a shrink, you need to stop letting the 'bad man' help you in the process of victimizing your whole life*," Ellis writes.

Ellis has dinner at the Polo Lounge in Beverly Hills; he has dinner at a West Hollywood restaurant. In fact, in the span of seventeen pages, Ellis describes attending no fewer than *eight* dinners with friends of his, including a well-known writer, a commercial director, and a liberal Jewish woman in her fifties with a penthouse overlooking Central Park and a net worth of more than ten million dollars. At a restaurant on Beverly Boulevard, this woman explodes "into a spastic rage" and accuses Ellis of "white male privilege" when he casually suggests that Black Lives Matter has a PR problem. "We finally calmed her down," he reports, "but our dinner had already been ruined." Dinner, it seems, is the greatest casualty of liberal fascism. "Who you supported politically would determine if you were invited (or not) to a party or a dinner table," Ellis complains. (He really feels for White House press secretary Sarah Huckabee Sanders, who was asked to leave a restaurant in Virginia last summer.) Yet it never occurs to Ellis, a man who is surely 70 percent dinner, that his friends are annoying the shit out of him not because they hold left-wing political views but because, like him, they are rich, and rich people are universally horrible.

At some point, one must ask if a man who sees *1984* all around him is really just stuck in the eighties. The comparison between *American Psycho*'s serial-killer protagonist and its controversial author is easily made. Patrick Bateman and Bret Easton Ellis are both rich. They both attend a lot of dinners. They both admire Donald Trump. Ellis himself makes the comparison at the end of *White*, recalling how he poured all his frustration—"what seemed expected of me and other male members of Gen X, including millions of dollars, six-pack abs, and a cold amorality"—directly into Bateman, "a fictional figure who was my own worst version of myself, the nightmarish me, someone I loathed but also considered, in his helpless floundering, sympathetic as often as not." To Ellis, who describes himself as an "outsider" and a "freak" since childhood, Bateman's social criticism sounded "almost entirely correct."

Like *The Catcher in the Rye* before it and *Fight Club* after it, *American Psycho* was a book designed to convince comfortable white men that they were, in fact, "outsiders and monsters and freaks." Its critique was never just that the shallow consumerism of the Reagan years held, caged beneath it, the bloodthirsty, animal rage of the suppressed individual, but also that even when this rage was unleashed—in *American Psycho*, through murder, rape, cannibalism, necrophilia—everyone would be too self-absorbed to care. When Bateman tells a model he's interested in "murders and executions," she hears "mergers and acquisitions." When he confesses to his lawyer that he's murdered his work rival, the man laughs it off as a joke. This was Bateman's "greatest fear," Ellis writes in *White*. "What if no one was paying him any attention?" Ellis does not realize he is talking about himself, an angry, uninteresting man who has just written a very needy book.

2019

Shortly before this review appeared, I was persuaded to purge the original final paragraph. I personally felt that its Bateman-like nonchalance was a clever way to preempt the author's inevitable claim (which did in fact materialize) that I myself had been "triggered." I reproduce it here for posterity:

> *So if it's late at night, and you hear a noise in your building, do not be alarmed. It's just Bret Easton Ellis again, stabbing your dog and raping your neighbors. Feel free to ignore him. Or if you must, just tell him what we say on Twitter: Go home, Bret. You're drunk.*

No One Wants It

As a lightweight behind-the-scenes look at a critically acclaimed television series, Joey Soloway's new memoir *She Wants It: Desire, Power, and Toppling the Patriarchy* is just south of worth purchasing at the airport. As a book about desire, power, or toppling the patriarchy, it is incompetent, defensive, and astonishingly clueless.

This is a story about someone who responds to criticisms of their TV show by taking "a glamping writers' retreat" to El Capitan: "We had a shaman come. She did magic incantations as we lay on the floor of a yurt." It is an unwitting portrait of a rich Los Angeles creative type with a child's knack for exploiting the sympathies of others, a person whose deep fear of doing the wrong thing was regularly outmatched by an even deeper distaste for doing the right thing. The nicest thing that can be said of this oblivious, self-absorbed, unimportant book is that it proves, once and for all, that trans people are fully, regrettably human.

The substance of *She Wants It*, such as it is, concerns the author's time working on the show *Transparent*, whose premise—a Jewish transgender woman comes out late in life to her adult children, throwing the whole Pfefferman family into disarray—was drawn from Soloway's own experience as the child of a late-transitioning trans woman. In 2014, back when the words "Amazon original series" made as much sense as the words "Jim Carrey solo exhibition," Soloway, then a married mother of two, could believably protest to *Rolling Stone* that the show's explorations of gender and sexuality were "not really autobiographical." But as this book confirms, Soloway's life has rapidly imitated their art. Like Sarah Pfefferman, they would leave their husband for a woman; like Josh Pfefferman, they would become a successful entertainment industry player, in douchebag shades and trousers with kicks; like Ali Pfefferman, they would date a celebrated lesbian poet and experiment with a nonbinary gender.

The truth is, Soloway appears to know little more about trans people now than when they began production on *Transparent*. The memoir suggests that when they wrote the show's pilot, Soloway thought of trans women like their parent as little more than cross-dressing men, and the lessons conducted by the writer and series consultant Jennifer Finney Boylan (and subsequently trotted out by Soloway on their book tour) are appallingly basic:

> The word "trans" is Latin for "bridge," she taught us next. Then she wrote the word "transbrella" on the whiteboard. "Not everyone is at one end of the spectrum or the other," she explained. People use the word "trans" to refer to all kinds of people, including drag queens, butch lesbians, and genderqueer folks, who metaphorically stand *on* the bridge, in the middle, rather than using it to cross from one side to the other.

As far as I can tell, the hideous portmanteau *transbrella* is of Soloway's own inventing. (Boylan likely used the usual term *trans umbrella*.) "Bridge," meanwhile, is a spurious translation of the Latin word *trans*, which is a common preposition meaning "across." Evidently no one at Random House could be bothered to crack open the old Wheelock. Do bridges go across things? They do. May one go across a bridge? Reader, this cannot be denied. But I hope, for Boylan's sake at least, that the *Transparent* team was told that *trans* may be thought of as being *like* a bridge, for pedagogical purposes. This would have been a metaphor, a word which comes from the Greek *metapherō*, meaning "I carry across"—for instance, across a bridge.

None of this matters, because Joey Soloway lives in a world where the words *radical trans* can be followed, without a hint of irony, by the word *content*. Their production company Topple, which featured prominently in a recent, glowing *New York Times* profile, models its core tenets after Amazon's corporate leadership principles. (Number two is "Be Chill.") In Soloway's voice, one finds the worst of grandiose seventies-era conceits about the transformative power of the avant-garde guiltlessly hitched to a yogic West Coast startup mindset that speaks in terms of "holding space" and "heart-connection." It's like if Peter Thiel were gay.

But self-importance alone could never guarantee writing this atrocious. Narcissism can be wildly compelling in the hands of a professional. That this is the prose of a celebrated television auteur may be explained only if one recalls that TV writing, unlike the art of memoir, is a group effort. The narrator of *She Wants It* is a Gen-Xer in millennial drag: precious, out of touch, and exceedingly prone to bathos. Without a second thought, they rattle off lines like "I woke up with a Zen koan in my head" and "I decided I would have to have an interesting life if I ever wanted to be like Jack Kerouac." The following is an actual sentence: "As we all took over the bowling alley, the sheer variety of the ways to be queer and alive in Los Angeles in 2014 exploded my mind."

Soloway introduces deep-sounding quotes from other authors like a middle schooler phoning in a Kate Chopin paper. They mix metaphors like a bartender in a recording studio. An urge to break up becomes "that anxiety snowball racing down the mountain at my back that I inherited from my mom." Can snow be bequeathed? They lovingly refer to their sister Faith as "actual liquid faith," a figure of speech that, being presumably analogous to the common nickname for alcohol, would make sense only if their sister were in fact a beverage. Also, fragments.

Throughout *She Wants It*, Soloway alternates, confusingly, between contradictory sites of gender enunciation. One moment, they will wax poetic about "not having to choose" a binary identity ("How would it be if everybody saw pure soul before gender?"); the next, they will breezily reference "our lives," "our bodies," "our interests" as women. There exist intelligent attempts to think through contradictions like these (Laurie Penny's work comes to mind), but this is not one of them. Readers would be forgiven for thinking Soloway a fairweather woman: female when it's culturally advantageous to be female, and not, when it's not.

The ethics of gender recognition, now more than ever, compel us to accept without contest or prejudice the self-identification of all people. They do not, however, compel us to find those identities likable, interesting, or worth writing a book about. Soloway certainly makes it easy to believe the long-standing charge that they see trans people as creative oil to be fracked. "Something about my parent coming out immediately shattered a wall," Soloway writes early on in *She Wants It*. "She was being her true self, a woman. Now I could be my true self, a director." If the circumstances of their shiny new gender are, shall we say, suspect—the cisgender creator of a television show about trans issues, long criticized for presuming to speak for trans people, comes out as trans themselves— all we need remember is that being trans because you want the attention doesn't make you "not really" trans; it just makes you annoying.

Over and over, Soloway worries if they have made a wrong turn, before plowing ahead regardless. Over and over, they anxiously seek the counsel of others, only to blithely ignore it. They have regrets, but never remorse: the problem is not that they have made a poor decision, but that someone else has gotten offended. Before *Transparent* goes to series, Jenny Boylan warns that Soloway will face "a fair amount of blowback" for casting Jeffrey Tambor as a transgender woman. When an audience member raises this very objection at a festival, Soloway cries. "My God," they write, "I hadn't been expecting this." (Boylan has called *She Wants It* "provocative, generous, and inspiring.")

When Soloway gets a Zionist itch to film season four of *Transparent* in Israel—"I don't have a lot of things in common with Jared Kushner, but low-grade Jerusalem Syndrome might be one"—the writer Sarah Schulman cautions that breaking with the Palestinian-led boycott movement will put the show in hot water with many queer activists. "Ugh," writes Soloway. "I was so annoyed. How did I get stuck in this very narrow place of being forced to choose?" (Bafflingly, this is a callback to Soloway's description of being nonbinary.) Eventually, they buckle, filming the season on the Paramount lot—before taking a small crew to Israel to shoot B-roll. Soloway will later refer to this solution, incredibly, as "our Israel compromise." (Schulman has called *She Wants It* "a rollicking tale of how an enmeshed family sometimes brings out the best.")

But nothing is more cringeworthy than Soloway's account of the #MeToo movement, with which the book concludes. "Two years after I'd yelled 'Topple the patriarchy!' onstage, it all indeed came tumbling down," marvels Soloway, breathlessly equating the firing of several famous men with the end of a regime as old as history itself. Our author apparently believes that they can take history's pulse by glancing at their own Fitbit. Here they are reeling from the 2016 election: "We thought we had power, but no, actually, we were this thing—this Other Thing called Women, and we could be silenced, disregarded, with a vote." (Never mind that for every nine women who voted for Clinton, there were seven who voted for Trump.) Now here they are attending early Time's Up meetings with Reese Witherspoon, Ava DuVernay, and other celebrities: "I went home overflowing. The revolution was happening." Soloway never suspects that they might be conflating global upheaval with a sudden influx of rich and famous friends.

All this is damage control, of course, for Soloway's own scandal. If *She Wants It* has any purpose, it is to exculpate its author in the matter of Jeffrey Tambor, who in November 2017 was accused by his former personal assistant Van Barnes and his ex-costar Trace Lysette—both trans women—of on-set sexual harassment. At this, it fails miserably. It comes as no surprise that Soloway's leap into *Transparent* was "powered by a wild jealousy of Louis C.K. and Lena Dunham," both acclaimed creators of television shows in which they played unlikable, narcissistic versions of themselves, only to be revealed as unlikable narcissists in real life.

Neither escaped #MeToo unscathed. The same month as the allegations about Tambor (who denied them), the *Times* reported on C.K.'s penchant for jacking off in front of female coworkers. Days later, when the actress Aurora Perrineau accused *Girls* writer Murray Miller of rape, Dunham issued a confident statement of support—for Miller. On Twitter, she appeared to defend herself: "I believe in a lot of things but the first tenet of my politics is to hold up the people who have held me up, who have filled my world with love." This is what omertà would sound like if you bought it for $8.99 on Etsy. (Dunham later apologized for the statement.)

If a Mafia analogy seems crude to you, hold that thought. "I needed to find out why she was going straight to the press with her story, to understand why she hadn't come to us," Soloway writes of Lysette. "We could handle this, I wanted to tell her, but let us do it internally, inside the family." Soloway is never so sulky as in these pages, pouting about their "legacy" and losing any lingering ability to complete sentences: "If Trace released a statement, it would be over for Jeffrey. And that meant Maura.

The show. Our TV family. Everything." In a climactic, chapter-ending scene, Soloway parlays with Lysette at a Coffee Bean picnic table. "I can't believe you're doing this," they tell the actress. "Well, it happened to me," Lysette coolly replies. What happens next is so incredible that I must quote it at length:

> "I had to tell my story," she said. "But I said in my statement that I wanted the show to continue."
>
> "But the idea of the show will be tarnished now in everyone's minds," I said. "In Middle America when people think of trans people there's still so much suspicion, and Maura became this beautiful symbol of transness and now you're laying this imagery out there of her being a predator."
>
> Suddenly, I started crying.
>
> She was horrified.
>
> "I'm the victim here and YOU'RE crying?" she demanded.
>
> She was right. I was sitting across from her, frozen with fear. I tried to stop myself from crying. Like Michael in *The Godfather*, I tried to play it stoic and cool. I didn't say, *Fredo, after all I've done for you*. I said, "I wish you luck."
>
> And then I walked away.
>
> An hour later the article came out.

Set aside the fact that Trace Lysette, a former sex worker whose pampered male costar gleefully told her he wanted to "attack [her] sexually," is obviously a much more fitting symbol of transness than wealthy professor emerita Maura Pfefferman ever was. What's truly shocking is that, presented with the opportunity, and I'm being completely serious here, *to lie*, or at least fudge the truth, Soloway once again nukes themselves without even noticing, gravely comparing a sexual harassment victim to the fictional character Fredo Corleone from *The Godfather Part II*, the Oscar-winning 1974 crime film at the end of which, if you'll recall, Fredo was literally *executed* for betraying Al Pacino.

The only conclusion to be drawn from this very bad book, which puts the "self" in "self-aware," is that Joey Soloway has an unstoppable, pathological urge to tell on themselves. In fact, it's all they've ever done.

If autofiction like *Girls*, *Louie*, or *Transparent* teaches us anything, it's that there is no better disguise than one's own face. Midway through *She Wants It*, while prepping three different Emmy acceptance speeches, Soloway wonders if they suffer from a "delusion of grandeur," before dismissing the phrase as a diagnosis for "cis white guys." "Is it delusional to try to suggest to yourself that it is okay to believe you might be magnificent when the world raised you to mostly admire men, to reserve grandiosity or genius only for them?" they ask.

If the question is whether queer people can be pretentious assholes, *She Wants It* holds the answer.

2018

When this essay was published, Soloway was answering to both she *and* they, *telling* Good Morning America, *"'She' is fine; when people say 'she' and 'her,' I don't correct them, but when people say 'they' and 'them,' it's like frosting." At the time, it felt appropriate to me to deny Soloway the latter indulgence—I wrote that my review was a "muffin"—given what I considered their disingenuous approach to womanhood as a political category. Since Soloway now exclusively uses gender-neutral pronouns, I have updated the essay accordingly. Cake it is.*

This essay was the first of what are sometimes referred to as my "take-downs" of famous writers, and its untidiness and generally jeering tone reflect this. In truth, it was not about Soloway at all; it was about a similarly irritating person of my own acquaintance who was not famous enough to be worth writing about. It strikes me today as a vicious piece, but not a very cruel one. Viciousness is the attack dog who has not eaten in three days; cruelty is the person calmly holding the leash. These days I aim for cruelty.

Metro-Goldwyn-Myra

One learns very quickly that Myra Breckinridge is an unreliable narrator. Her writerly voice—for we are reading her diary entries, composed for the benefit of her psychoanalyst—is foxy, cerebral, with the bombast of an unpublished academic, as well as a nearly cosmic narcissism into whose delusional gravity you cannot (and by *you*, I mean *me*, which could be a slogan for narcissism) help but be sucked. Myra's a liar. This is redundant, because Myra is a transsexual, and in the medical literature the transsexual is, invariably, a deceiver. None is more famous in this regard than the woman known to posterity as Agnes, who posed as intersex in order to secure treatment at UCLA in the late fifties.

It's an old phobic premise: the transsexual lies, because the transsexual *is* a lie, a fiction, a fantasy. *Myra Breckinridge*, which Gore Vidal is supposed to have written in a matter of weeks in Rome, does not do away with this premise so much as displace it from the doctor's office to the acting school. After the death of her husband, Myra comes to Los Angeles, nominally, to claim her inheritance: a onetime orange grove in Westwood where her weaselly uncle now runs the fictional Academy of Drama and Modeling, just down the street from the very real UCLA Gender Identity Research Clinic, where Agnes scored her vagina in 1959. Myra quickly hustles her way into a position at the academy, teaching empathy and posture. The only surgical procedure Myra Breckinridge is after is a realignment of the world's mythic spine, sans anesthetic. Like anyone who's ever moved to LA, Myra dreams of becoming a god, but the price of her ascension will be the ritual humiliation of the male sex, beginning with her own students—a violent deposition of the usurper Priapus and a restoration of the ancient feminine principle.

Myra sees this principle incarnated in the giant, spangled mechanical girl that turns hypnotically outside her window in the room, across the street from the Chateau Marmont hotel, where she has installed herself. The Sahara Girl, as she was known to drivers on the Sunset Strip, is to Myra what the eyes of Doctor T. J. Eckleburg were to Gatsby: a piece of the divine, smuggled to an atheist earth in the form of commercial advertisement. Myra adores her. A photo of the spinning showgirl was even included in *Myra Breckinridge*'s original cover art; the poster for the 1970 film adaptation, which *Time* magazine called "about as funny as a child molester," featured Raquel Welch as Myra herself in the same pose. The Sahara Girl is an avatar of the 1940s, whose films constitute not just the golden age of Hollywood but, if you ask Myra, the apex of human civilization—an opinion she shares with her late husband, Myron Breckinridge, film critic, whose unfinished manuscript *Parker Tyler and the Films of the Forties; or, the Transcendental Pantheon* advances the thesis that "this century's only *living* art form is the movies."

That's no figure of speech. Myra *is* Myron, of course—a spoiler that Vidal and his publishers impishly hoped to protect by refusing to provide advance copies to reviewers, but which comes as no surprise to any reader half paying attention. ("Did Myron take his own life, you will ask? Yes and no is my answer. Beyond that my lips are sealed. . . .") Myra is a film critic who, having peered too far over the brim of her object of inquiry, lost her balance and fell in. She has succumbed, in other words, to the deadly temptation, faced at one time or another by every critic, to become the thing one studies. This makes Myra Breckinridge a male-to-film transsexual, a being of pure celluloid cut together from references to the starlets of the forties. She rasps in a low voice "modeled on that of the late Ann Sheridan (fifth reel of *Doughgirls*)," with notes of Jean Arthur, Margaret Sullavan, and "a sweet tone not unlike Irene Dunne in *The White Cliffs of Dover*." When she chooses, she wears a "beautiful yet knowing smile like Ann Sothern in the first of the Maisie films." Her superb breasts are "reminiscent of those sported by Jean Harlow in *Hell's Angels* and seen at their best four minutes after the start of the second reel." She is, in a word, "a dish, and never forget it, you motherfuckers, as the children say nowadays."

A male writer's fantasy, one could protest, but it's fantasy Myra wants. Certainly her expectations are no more unrealistic than those of your average transsexual. At any rate, it never occurs to Myra that being a male director's wet dream should disqualify her from her mission to destroy "the last vestigial traces of traditional manhood." The two go, on the contrary, hand in hand. Myra considers herself a New Woman in every sense: confident, sexual, dominating, yes, but also literally new, assembled just two years prior in Copenhagen by, readers could assume, the same studio that put Christine Jorgensen on the front page of the *New York Daily News* in 1952. Myra tears through Los Angeles with the frivolity of a vacationing god, and about the same regard for what mortals call consent. The brutal justice of her self-appointed task—to rape the men of Hollywood—needs no further comment today. Myra intends her infamous molestation of Rusty Godowsky, a dumb blond stud from her posture class, as an act of revenge, not just against the men who fucked her as a self-described fag in New York City, but against Myron himself, a bloody sacrifice that, by symbolically repeating her surgical castration, is supposed to transform Myra into "the eternal feminine made flesh, the source of life and its destroyer."

Not a few reviewers were repulsed. "Is the Olympia Press alive and publishing in Boston?" asked *Time*, referring to the earthy small press that first published *Lolita*, *Naked Lunch*, and, in 1968, the take-no-prisoners manifesto of a sex worker and sometime-lesbian playwright named Valerie Solanas, another famous man-hater. With a little artistic license, it is tempting to imagine the dildo of Myra Breckinridge sliding past the rosy rear lips of her sideburned Hollywood hunk just as, on the opposite coast, a bullet is exiting the chamber of the .32 Beretta automatic pistol that Solanas has just pointed at her friend Andy Warhol in the latter's Manhattan studio. Two women, a whole America between them, one fictional and one who might as well have been, each with a deep desire to break into show business and a funny way of showing it; and two wanton acts of humorlessness, two Very Bad Jokes, personal vendettas raised to a biblical power: rape and murder, Sodom and Gomorrah, rites for summoning sex apocalypse.

It's no wonder those critics not left clutching their pearls and clucking their tongues imagined that *Myra Breckinridge* had crushed sex roles like grapes and gotten drunk on the wine. "Today," mused *The Times Literary Supplement*, "sex is metamorphosed as easily as fancy dress," while for *The New York Review of Books*, the novel had invoked nothing short of "the ultimate shared fantasy of the age—a future of androgynous independence." This is a very ordinary, if tedious, view of transsexuality, often encountered within that pretty pie-slice of the population that goes about its daily activities trapped in the right body; its counterpart today is the blithe assumption, among cis and trans alike, that the manifest goal of the current wave of transgender identity politics is to slay an invisible two-headed monster called the gender binary, a beast that everyone knows but no one can describe.

True, Myra does at times suspect "a polymorphic sexual abandon in which the lines between the sexes dissolve . . . may be the only workable pattern for the future"; in this, she is a mouthpiece for Vidal himself, whom the conservative William F. Buckley Jr. would call a "queer" on live national television later that year. And to back this up, there is indeed no shortage of perverse personae among the novel's supporting cast: Myra's uncle Buck Loner, a former horse-opera star whose spooneristic *nom de cowboy* belies a low-budget machismo reduced to picking up groceries for his wife and sneaking happy endings from his masseuse; the self-styled analyst Dr. Randolph Spenser Montag, in fact just a closeted dentist with a love of ice-cream sundaes; the agent Letitia Van Allen, a ball-busting cougar who day-drinks martinis and likes to be thrown down the stairs during sex.

But this is something of a front, I suspect. *Myra Breckinridge*'s bite, like that of all satire, is sharpest when sincere. All the bluster about end-times can conceal the fact that the mystic twisting anima for which Myra is but a vessel is really just that old god they call Desire, whose psychedelic mysteries are kept in every kitchen in America. Myra wants, but like any of us, she cannot say why, or where wanting will take her. "I have no clear idea as to my ultimate identity once every fantasy has been acted out with living flesh," she admits, in a brief seizure of self-awareness. The discovery that fantasies, like novels, have to have an ending, or at least a fraying edge disguised as an ending, is something you must never forget to keep forgetting, over and over again, if you are to last very long in this world. This is especially true if you, like Myra or me, are transsexual. Maybe that is why some people go to the movies the way other people go to church: to have their faith in the infinite restored. Take it from Myra, on her way to visit the back lots at Metro-Goldwyn-Mayer: "I feel better already. Fantasy has that effect on me."

2018

Join the Club

Ziggy Klein has no boobs. The only thing growing on her chest is anxiety. Fifteen years old, Jewish, and hesitant, with an interior life like a hoarder's apartment, Ziggy has just transferred to Kandara, an all-girls preparatory school in the glossy Sydney suburbs, where she promptly begins studying the dense hierarchical ecology. At the top are the Cates, old-money girls with hyphenated surnames and pearlescent Instagrams. At the bottom are the ugly, the suspected lesbians, and, Ziggy assumes, herself.

Before long, she has fallen in with the feminists. They indoctrinate her immediately. Has she read "A Cyborg Manifesto"?

> "I'll send you a link to the essay," says Tessa. "It talks about how we're all transhuman because of our dependence on technology, which is good because it means you don't have to totally submit to the patriarchy. Cyborgs are part machine, part organism, so they don't have dads."
>
> "She was basically writing about iPhones in 1984," Lex adds, her voice sparkly.
>
> "Who was?"
>
> "Donna Haraway," says Tessa. "She's cool. She really hates hot girls."

Tessa, who explains to Ziggy that cyborgs identify as "women of color" because they're the most excluded, is a bossy redhead with a prosthetic arm whose Anglo grandmother once lived in Cairo. Lex, an edgy music producer whose parents adopted her from Bangladesh, is an actual woman of color. She is also gorgeous, stirring something in Ziggy that feels like racist misogynistic objectification, or failing that, a crush.

In Lexi Freiman's *Inappropriation*, feminism is a club. Ziggy's new friends collect traumas like comic books, sheathing their precious wounds in fantasy's protective plastic sleeves. They comb their classmates' Instagrams for heteronormativity. They attend pool parties at the popular girls' gated mansions in hopes of getting harassed. Ziggy lunges along excitedly, unsure what is cool and what is ableist, but eager to fit in. On the weekends, Tessa and Lex take her to the mall, where they imagine all the men with boners and fantasize about getting catcalled. Tessa, an aspiring movie star, calls this "method acting." These games make sense to Ziggy. They are the millennial version of the workshops her mother, Ruth, runs out of their living room, New Age group-therapy sessions in which women séance each other's relatives, then break to decorate throw pillows. Like her friends' games, these workshops teach Ziggy that the gap between the self and historical pain can only be bridged by make-believe.

This is satire, but it is not sarcasm. A lesser novel than *Inappropriation* would pick on what the book's jacket copy calls "PC culture," a fruit that hangs so low it might as well be a vegetable. It is easy, and always flattering, to condemn performative wokeness. It is harder, and smarter, to ask if politics *ever* transcends adolescent fantasy. Ziggy uses the political as an excuse for belonging. Are you telling me you don't? Freiman suspects you do, and she has the same thick, buttermilky compassion for her readers as she does for her characters, sour and full of saggy lumps. She burlesques them—and you—but only because she identifies.

The results are darkly funny. It's always nice to read a book with the right number of Holocaust jokes. Ziggy regularly shuts herself in a closet with "an onion, a bottle of vinegar, and a sympathetic Nazi," reenacting a close call her perennially sequined grandmother Twinkles once had with some SS officers. Then, not long after she begins at Kandara, Ziggy fancies that a troupe of alt-right trolls named Hitler Youth has annexed her mind like Austria, mostly just to neg her. The Aryan ephebes drop thought bombs in Ziggy's ears, telling her to drink soy milk so her breasts will grow, then calling her a misogynist softcock when her consensual sex fantasy about Rolfe and Liesl from *The Sound of Music* threatens to escalate from "brown paper packages" to "tied up with strings." In fact, most of Ziggy's erotic life involves Nazis. She blames her mother.

But the issue isn't generational trauma so much as how trauma gets scrambled, like a code or an egg, en route from one generation to the next. As with feminism, Ziggy's sense of the Shoah is a patchwork of personal anecdotes and erotic fanfiction; it has all the narrative consistency of a cosmic game of Telephone. It's mostly an excuse to feel things: horny, gassy. Her grandmother, a retired gastroenterologist, explains this to Ziggy at a food court through an accidental koan.

> "In her womb the baby get it mother bacteria, which stay in the stomach for the rest of it life. That mean you fart smell like you mummy's. And that—"
> "Okay."
> "—Mummy fart like mine."
> Ziggy nudges her plate away.
> "And it not just mummies. We get the germ from everyone. Our gut is full of other people. Some bacteria make us happy, some angry. Explain why so much irritable bowel syndrome."
> "What has this got to do with God?"
> "The stomach like a universe."

Ziggy really is a gastric mess, vacuuming up little crumbs of self from everything she touches. She bluffs her way through every conversation, like an AI in the early stages, recycling Tessa's buzzwords and Lex's brooding and the jokes from her mother's guru's YouTube channel. When her friends ditch her for boyfriends, Ziggy spends an awful amount of time online, a pubescent Dante wandering Virgil-less through the decreasingly cuck-friendly circles of the internet. She reads *Teen Vogue* and Wikipedia and Tumblr. She learns the difference between homoromantic and homosexual. Eventually she finds Reddit, where she shuttles back and forth between a queer POC forum and an alt-right group called Red Pill, internalizing the lingo of each. The technical term for this kind of behavior, on the internet at least, is *lurking*. Ziggy is a lurker; Ziggy lurks.

If it would be banal today to say that social media has made cyborgs of everyone at Ziggy's school, it was already banal in the eighties when Haraway said the same thing about silicon chips and handheld camcorders. The big mistake of "A Cyborg Manifesto" (though it is hard to pick just one) was its assumption that human enmeshment with tech was, taken on its own, politically interesting. Freiman's acknowledgment of this is, as always, gently cruel. When Ziggy invokes the manifesto as justification for being permitted to wear a GoPro on her head at school, coming out to her headmistress as transhuman—"Donna Haraway says we're all augmented by technology, which makes us inorganic orphans beyond the gender binary"—readers familiar with the essay's academic legacy will recognize this as one of its less ridiculous uses.

But Freiman also respects the real, energizing thrill of discovering theory for the first time, the way you just *assume*, with the faith of the freshly deflowered, that these imposing new tools of critique are diamond cutters, when in fact they are baseball bats. Ziggy doesn't really get the manifesto, but she "really likes the gist." Theory is always gisty; its primary function is to produce in the reader neither knowledge nor political action, but rather what on Twitter we call a "big mood."

Freiman's style, meanwhile, is nimble and pert, parkouring disrespectfully across the suburban mall of the English language with little regard for its more bipedal shoppers. *Inappropriation* doesn't have that full-Brazilian look sometimes favored by the New York literati, but something bushier. When Ziggy gets her period, the blood leaves stains under her fingernails "like the dark veins of prawn shit." When holding in a sob, Ziggy's body gets as "tight and steamy as a wonton." Horny teenage boys "unfurl" in Lex's presence, "pink and willing like well-walked dog tongues." A running gag about a vertically challenged American action hero delights at every resurfacing, as Freiman provides a string of ever more creative epithets for the technically nameless celebrity, who may or may not have a film opening in the summer. The author has a particular love of verbing, and she tucks her coinages into paragraphs like tiny, spiky gifts. A lit joint "jewels"; pubic mounds "cauliflower"; a tiny boy "turtles" from his ill-fitting formal wear. For a moment, your eyes are teenagers again, groping inexpertly at the sentence's bra clasp. Reading rebecomes gawky. The eye trips. The mind chrysanthemums.

Along the way, *Inappropriation* manages to hit many of the familiar beats of the coming-of-age novel. It begins on a first day of school; it closes with a formal dance. In between, the plot meanders from scene to scene, mimicking Ziggy's own shifting interests as she drifts, like a bit of plankton, through the ambient jellyfish bloom that is the tenth grade. Like high school itself, it drags in the middle. But things tighten up in time for the finale, as Ziggy plots the humiliation of a rich douchebag from the neighboring boys' prep school. Even there, Freiman keeps a wry eye on the weird billiard-ball mechanics of teenage alliance, the conspiracy deflating into something oddly touching, in an indie-movie sort of way. Maybe Ziggy grows up; maybe the novel just happens to be over.

The philosopher Gilles Deleuze once observed of becoming, before this became the noodly mantra of his disciples, that it pulls in both directions: one cannot become taller than one was without, simultaneously, becoming shorter than one will be. Becoming is therefore a kind of backhanded compliment—an intuitive claim for anyone who's ever felt the flattering smack of a "Most Improved" award. This is the paradox of the coming-of-age story: growing up is always, at the same time, a regression. Only the immature mature, and even then, they don't. That's why adults do not, as every adult knows, exist.

2018

Angel in the Wings

"All women are lesbians," the writer Jill Johnston told a packed house of rowdy New York literati in the spring of 1971, two years and forty blocks removed from the violent queer riots that consecrated the Mafia-owned Stonewall Inn as Ground Zero of gay liberation. Johnston was fighting the same war in a different theater—the Town Hall theater on West Forty-Third Street, to be exact, now bristling with cultural elites who had paid twenty-five dollars a head to hear a debate on the women's movement. "All women are lesbians," Johnston told them, "except those who don't know it, naturally."

Johnston—dungarees and all, the token degenerate on a panel on women's liberation headlined by noted man-fucker Germaine Greer and moderated by noted man Norman Mailer—was one of the ones who knew it. Over dinner in Chinatown, the Theater for Ideas organizer had advised the panelists, among them the literary critic Diana Trilling and National Organization for Women (NOW) chapter president Jacqueline Ceballos, to craft their remarks in response to Mailer's controversial "The Prisoner of Sex," recently published in *Harper's Magazine*. The book-length essay had commandeered most of the issue, ending with a smug parenthetical in which the author boasted of ending the piece with a parenthetical. Johnston couldn't get through the thing.

Now, in bell-bottoms and a rose-trimmed denim jacket, Johnston read in the limber, free-associative style she had been honing in her weekly dance and art column in *The Village Voice*, which Mailer himself had cofounded in 1955. She ended up somewhere between a Beat poem and a tight five. "Who vants the Moon ven ve can land on Venus?" Johnston asked the raucous crowd. (Mailer had written 115,000 words about the moon landing for *Life*.) Soon, another coup: "He said, 'I want your body.' She said, 'You can have it when I'm through with it.'" Howls of laughter filled the auditorium.

It was here, in the penumbra of someone else's star, that Mailer decided to interrupt, claiming that Johnston had had "fifteen minutes already" and that it wasn't fair to the other panelists. (In the 1979 documentary *Town Bloody Hall*, shot that evening by D. A. Pennebaker, Johnston would appear to speak for about eight minutes before Mailer stuck in his oar—the same amount of time taken by Ceballos and Greer.) Suddenly, mistaking Johnston's stunned pause for her cue, a long-haired woman in shiny brown pants slipped swiftly out of the wings and began necking with Johnston onstage; a second confederate soon joined them, the three women collapsing into a sapphic pile behind the rostrum.

Flustered and flush with anger, Mailer got mean. "Now come on, either play with the team or pick up your marbles and get lost," he spat into the mic. "Come on, Jill, be a lady." Later, Susan Sontag would ask him from the front row why he kept using that word, *lady*. Some members of the audience, whose constituents were already confabulating wildly with one another, urged Mailer to let Johnston continue. "What's the matter, Mailer?" a woman shouted. "You threatened 'cause you found a woman you can't fuck?"

As she would reflect two years later in her memoir *Lesbian Nation: The Feminist Solution*, now a canonical text of lesbian separatism, Johnston had agreed to take part in the debate against her better judgment. In retrospect, the affair had clearly been engineered to promote Mailer's new book. The *New York Times* critic Anatole Broyard, present that evening, would declare it Mailer's best. As the male moderator of a dialogue on women's lib, the forty-eight-year-old novelist and failed mayoral candidate had deposited himself at the center of attention, flanked on either side by two "ladies of the Liberation," as he called them in *Harper's*. "Better to expire as a devil in the fire than an angel in the wings," he wrote there, expressing the sentiment of a man who had burned through so many wives by this point that it was getting hard to remember which one of them he'd stabbed.

Things were only made worse by the presence of Greer, who would, the next month, grace the cover of *Life* magazine under the caption

"Saucy Feminist That Even Men Like"—a "giant godiva rising out of the celtic mists," Johnston calls her. "Many people although nobody actually said it were looking forward to the town hall affair as the great matchmaking epithalamium of the century," quips an irritated Johnston, who suspected that Greer "wouldn't mind fucking" their esteemed moderator. (Greer was hot in the 1970s, but that was nothing time and transphobia couldn't fix.) Greer's very person—to the Town Hall she had worn a sleeveless black dress and a fox stole ("cost a pound she said afterwards")—seemed to prove that, when you got right down to it, heterosexual feminism was nothing less than an elaborate mating ritual.

This was Johnston's diagnosis, but it was also, interestingly, Mailer's. "The angry feminists after all all they needed was a good fuck might be a line you'd expect to find in the very article that brought us all together," Johnston writes of his *Harper's* piece. The two species of chauvinist—male and lesbian—could find in this intuition their common ancestral bone: namely, contempt for the weak-willed heterosexual woman who couldn't follow the logic of women's liberation all the way to the end. The idea tickled the novelist but radicalized the dance critic. "The lesbian is *the* revolutionary feminist," Johnston declares in *Lesbian Nation*, "and every other feminist is a woman who wants a better deal from her old man."

And so it fell to Johnston to holler out one last nuptial objection from the back of the church. The brief, amorous zap, for which the writer had enlisted two of her friends, was in her estimation "the most satisfactory plan short of bombing the place." A self-described exhibitionist, Johnston rarely passed up an opportunity to stick her tongue in someone else's cheek. The summer prior, the *Voice* had dispatched her to a Women's Strike for Equality lawn party at the art collectors Ethel and Robert Scull's chic monochrome bungalow in East Hampton—"the ultimate sort of party where nobody shows up except the people who write about it." Accosting the organizer Betty Friedan, the cofounder of NOW, Johnston asked her point-blank if she thought gay liberation and women's liberation were connected. "Her eyes went big 'n bulgy and her lipstick leered crimson and she said crisply enunciating each word that 'it' is not an issue." Later, as Friedan addressed the assembled guests in a polka-dot dress that slipped off her shoulders as she spoke, Johnston ditched her pants and dove into the Sculls' swimming pool, removing her top after the second length. "I always say if you have a pool, you have a pool," said a resigned Ethel Scull to the *Times*.

The lesbian question had by then been roiling women's lib for months. That spring in New York, the Lavender Menace, so named for a disparaging phrase of Friedan's, had hijacked the Second Congress to Unite Women to protest the exclusion of lesbians from the movement. Heterosexual feminists alleged that lesbians were imitating male chauvinism and using the movement as a louche excuse to pick up chicks; the lesbians shot back that heterosexual feminism was plainly a contradiction in terms. (No one liked the bisexuals.) In short, everyone was busy accusing everyone else of trying to get laid. This was the hairy, horned heart of it, a generalized anxiety that women's liberation would be unmasked as sexual politics in the worst sense of Kate Millett's famous phrase: sex transvested as politics, a Russian doll of policy proposals and radical protests that nevertheless housed at its center a single four-letter word.

That was the needle that Johnston would try to thread in *Lesbian Nation*, asserting that revolutionary lesbianism wasn't just about who you balled, but that it wasn't *not* about that either. "Feminists who still sleep with the man are delivering their most vital energies to the oppressor," she writes more than once. Like heterosexual feminists, Johnston was duly suspicious of butch-femme role-playing, which she saw as a survival tactic that developed among half-closeted, politically unconscious lesbians in the fifties. But no diesel dyke was half as embarrassing as a boyfriend. "If radical feminism is addressing itself to the 'total elimination of sex roles' while still talking sex in relation to the man who defines these roles in the sex act by a certain historical biological-cultural imperative," she writes, "they are going in circles of unadulterated contradictory bullshit."

No one was more vulnerable to charges of ulterior motives, however, than Johnston herself. If she was less of a lothario than Mailer, it wasn't for lack of trying. "Until all women are lesbians there will be no true political revolution," Johnston declares—a battle-ax of an idea that, when brandished in one hand, left the other one free to wander up the movement's skirt. No reader of *Lesbian Nation* will emerge without the impression that Jill Johnston, bless her, was one frisky motherfucker. At the Sculls', she requests a dance with Gloria Steinem, who evidently told a mutual acquaintance that Johnston was the first woman who had ever made a pass at her. ("It sort of threw me. But on the other hand I really liked her.") She feels up Ti-Grace Atkinson through a bulky sweater on New Year's Day before the latter loses her nerve. "I liked her below the chin," she writes of Friedan. And that's to say nothing of all the broads she actually beds in *Lesbian Nation*, from an heiress named Polly to the pair of women she spotted one evening necking in a Volkswagen. So what if this wasn't the revolution? Then again, so what if it was?

As for separatism, well, nice work if you can get it. Johnston plays the militant, but the "fugitive Lesbian Nation" of the title is a flying castle, not a political program. "I mean the man is paying me to write this book," she concedes in parentheses. Of her impromptu dip in the Hamptons, Johnston protests that she was merely "hot and drunk." Of the Town Hall affair, she writes, "I dunno. People will do anything for excitement. Rent a big hall and invite your friends." Than this, one will not find a finer description of what really goes on in New York literary circles, and *Lesbian Nation* is a sober reminder that much of what we remember as women's liberation was just some stuff that happened at some parties, etc., in that city's greater metropolitan area. Don't get me wrong, Johnston was right—about women and men and sex and the rest of it. The thing was always doing something about it. (I mean the man is paying me to write this essay.)

2019

Votes for Woman

The year is 1971. Hillary is a second-year law student at Yale, where she meets a charismatic classmate from Arkansas. Bill is leonine, voracious, a Rhodes scholar. "I have found a man who loves my brain," she confides to a friend from Wellesley. For months, the two devour each other. The conversation is as vigorous as the sex. That summer, while interning at an Oakland firm specializing in civil liberties, she discovers him kissing her boss's daughter. She forgives him, but she does not forget.

A few years pass. Hillary works as an attorney on the Nixon impeachment inquiry. Bill teaches law at the University of Arkansas and prepares to run for Congress. Three times he proposes to her; three times she hesitates. Then a former campaign volunteer approaches her in a grocery store parking lot, claiming that Bill raped her. "You shouldn't marry me," Bill confesses one night. "You should leave."

It is here that *Rodham*, the new novel from Curtis Sittenfeld fictionalizing the life of Hillary Clinton makes its first major departure from the historical record. Hillary Rodham takes a good long look at her life—and packs her things. The next morning, she loads up her car, hugs Bill Clinton goodbye, and drives north out of Fayetteville on Interstate 49. She is crossing the Missouri border, tears welling in her eyes, when a blazing tanker truck jumps the median and strikes her used 1968 Buick head-on, killing her instantly.

I lied. But that's fiction for you. From a falsehood, anything follows; in logic this is known as the principle of explosion. No, there is no fiery car crash in *Rodham*, nor does its eponymous heroine move to Maine, get a dog, and solve a string of cozy murders. This is a shame; if an author is just going to make things up, they might as well be interesting. Instead, the novel obeys what we might call the caterpillar effect: the principle that an apparently major change in the initial conditions of a complex system may, many iterations later, make almost no difference at all.

Here's what actually happens: Hillary Rodham doesn't marry Bill Clinton. Brokenhearted but determined, she moves to Chicago to teach law at Northwestern. In 1992, incensed by the treatment of Anita Hill during Clarence Thomas's Supreme Court nomination, Hillary decides to run for Senate; without the sex-addicted Bill to drag her down, she wins. That same year, without Hillary's guiding hand, Bill's presidential campaign quickly flames out following allegations of an affair with a cabaret singer. Over the next twenty-odd years, which Sittenfeld largely elides, Senator Rodham develops a reputation as a pragmatic Midwestern centrist and mounts two unsuccessful bids for the Democratic presidential nomination. During her second rodeo, in 2008, she loses the primary to Barack Obama; as in real life, he goes on to serve as president for two terms. By 2016, when Sittenfeld's Hillary runs for a third time, she is indistinguishable from the actual Hillary in all but circumstance: she is married to no one; she is a senator from Illinois, rather than New York; and—oh yes—she wins.

To call this speculative fiction would be an insult to that fine genre. *Rodham*, which seemed to top every must-read summer book list even after Covid-19 threw a wrench into Random House's trusty hype machine, began life as a short story commissioned by *Esquire*. Published in May 2016, on the eve of Clinton's real-life nomination, "The Nominee" found a fictionalized Hillary reflecting with patrician distaste on her unfair treatment by the press. For all Sittenfeld's pretensions at alternate history, *Rodham* is an unabashed continuation of that project; it imagines the world not differently but rather, with smug admiration for its subject, exactly as it always was. The resulting book is nothing but a large commemorative stamp, dependent wholly in use and function on the reader's willingness to lick it.

Rodham, which Hillary narrates, is actually the author's second first-person foray into the lives of presidents' wives. Her first was *American Wife*, a warmly received 2008 novel that fictionalized Laura Bush's journey from librarian to presidential spouse with undisguised sympathy. That book, too, had its roots in a magazine piece, an unctuous 2004 *Salon* essay that Sittenfeld—a self-described "staunch liberal"—had penned in praise of the first lady's quiet integrity and enjoyment of novels. "Laura Bush is a voracious reader of fiction," she explained. "It's the reason I believe she's smart: For one thing, her favorite book is *The Brothers Karamazov.*" Incuriosity, disguised as its opposite, already shone through here, with Sittenfeld attributing her interest in Bush to her own artistic sensitivity rather than, as is more likely, the efficacy of the first lady as a political prop. "I *love* Laura Bush," she wrote, too naïve to grasp that she was supposed to.

You will therefore not be surprised to learn that Sittenfeld is one of those writers who think they have discovered, always freshly and for the first time, that women are people. They are, obviously; the error resides in the belief that humanity—the sheer fact of someone's having it—is grounds for a novel. Case in point: much has already been made of the graphic sex scenes in *Rodham*, which invite readers to imagine, among other things, Bill fingering Hillary to orgasm while driving on the highway. But this is not juice; it is sugar in water. Such scenes represent only the affectation of candor, carefully calculated to bamboozle reviewers into thinking that the author, like Bill Clinton's penis, has adequately plumbed her subject's depths.

In fact, *Rodham* is a work of maddening prudishness, unwilling at every turn to flash its protagonist's motivations above the ankle. "I'd never had difficulty understanding why someone would run for office," Hillary blandly observes when weighing her first Senate campaign. "Changing legislation, improving people's lives—both were hugely, indisputably important." That's it: as close as Sittenfeld ever comes to laying bare her heroine's deepest desires. In an airport memoir, this would be mere pablum; in a novel, it amounts to dereliction of duty.

One might object that *Rodham*'s prose is meant to recall the clerical, laborious manner of speaking for which Hillary is known in real life. Whether this is a literary accomplishment or not hinges on how well-written you think books should be. I know that only so much may be expected of a book whose epigraph is taken—as God is my witness—from the libretto of Lin-Manuel Miranda's *Hamilton*. Yet this is an issue of characterization, not just style. Of her Senate days, Hillary recalls, "I loved being able to tangibly and directly take on the problems I had spent my adult life thinking about." How strange that readers, being trapped inside Hillary's brain for four hundred pages, should never encounter any of these adult thoughts. If only there were a way for a narrator to communicate directly with a reader! Alas, the plot of this book presumes at every point the reader's acceptance of the idea, often touted by the protagonist, that Hillary Rodham is a woman of dazzling, breathtaking intelligence. Why, then, does she sound like Hillary Clinton?

It's worth pausing to acknowledge that the real Hillary Rodham Clinton is a charming person of moderate intellect and ability whose true talent lies in persuading college-educated people that her ambition, and by extension *theirs*, is a genuine expression of competence. Among the striving professional classes there is no greater analogy for career advancement than the presidency, and Clinton's bitter defeat at the hands of a mad pretender has only deepened their conviction, successfully branded as feminist, that the height of injustice consists in the withholding of privileges owed. There is no question that Sittenfeld's Hillary, like our own, believes that she deserves to be president. During her first run in 2004, after finishing at the back of the pack in New Hampshire, she snaps at a male TV reporter who questions why she's running. "Why do you think it is you ask that of me but not of my opponents?" she retorts. "Why *wouldn't* I run for president? I've been a senator for two terms." Then she makes that unfortunate remark about how she could have been baking cookies; the media roasts her for hating other women.

Which brings us to the fictitious Hillary's other reason for running. "I liked doing things I was good at, and I liked being recognized for doing things I was good at," she admits. "But as much as I wanted to be president, I wanted a woman to be president." That simple image—a triangle in the Oval—composes the entirety of Hillary's vision for America in *Rodham*. Her platform is like one of Jay Gatsby's unopened books: one must be satisfied simply to know that it exists. Late in the novel, while prepping for a debate, Hillary complains that her detractors don't know the first thing about her voting record. Neither does the reader.

What readers do know is that in the 1992 Senate race, Hillary Rodham ousts former Illinois state legislator Carol Moseley Braun in the primary. In real life, Moseley Braun became the first Black woman elected to the United States Senate, where she served from 1993 to 1999; in *Rodham*, however, she exits public life after her loss, reappearing only in Hillary's guilty conscience. When Carol calls to concede the race, Hillary assures her that she was only doing what she felt was best for the state of Illinois. "For goodness' sake, Hillary," Carol tartly responds. "Let's not pretend that either of us really believes it."

This is a decisive moment in the novel. Sittenfeld clearly intends to show that Hillary has done something ethically compromising, even racist, in her pursuit of political office. The reader is asked to form this moral judgment not on the basis of the two candidates' political platforms or values—they have none—but because the prospect of the first Black female senator is *more historic* than that of the third white female senator.

Hillary's comeuppance for this sin will take three forms. First, her mentor and mother figure, a fictionalized version of children's rights advocate Marian Wright Edelman, coldly withdraws from their relationship; it is only two decades later, after police shoot a Black teenager in Chicago, that Hillary will send her a tepid apology. "I considered myself almost immune to racism, in part due to my work with you, and I thought that my dismissal of Carol's candidacy was wholly unrelated to race," she writes. "I have come to see that almost nothing is wholly unrelated to race."

Second, she has the misfortune of running against fellow Illinois senator Barack Obama in the 2008 Democratic primary, during which media coverage of her campaign becomes more vicious than ever. As in real life, she loses, and Obama ascends. That November, as Hillary watches the returns come in from a donor's twenty-thousand-acre Taos ranch, a friend muses, "All these years I believed Americans were more racist than sexist." "Did you really?" Hillary replies, wineglass in hand. "Given when the Fifteenth Amendment passed and when the Nineteenth did?" You may decide for yourself if that is supposed to be ironic.

Finally, in 2015, Hillary receives a phone call from an old flame. Bill—now a tech billionaire rumored to take part in Silicon Valley orgies—is calling to let her know he'll be competing against her in the coming Democratic primary. She is filled with fury but keeps her tone calm. "If you actually care about your legacy, help put the first woman president in office," she tells him. "Don't stand in my way." Bill fires back, "Says the woman who started her political career by cockblocking Carol Moseley Braun."

This heavy-handed analogy between what Hillary does to Carol and what Bill does to Hillary forms the closest thing to a moral spine in *Rodham*. But the suggestion here—that it's sexist to run against a woman, just as it's racist to run against a Black person—is ridiculous, and frankly offensive. This is public relations, not intersectionality. It insultingly implies that such candidates are progressive without even trying, while also being so devoid of actual political content as to be interchangeable. Worse, it obscures the obvious fact that political contests are, by nature, exercises in exclusion. The day when the first woman becomes president will also be the day, and you may quote me on this, when every other woman in America doesn't.

In real life, politicians are just that: politicians. Apropos of nothing, it may interest you to know that the real Carol Moseley Braun endorsed Joe Biden early in the Democratic primaries last year. Weeks after her election in 1992, Biden showed up unannounced at Moseley Braun's Chicago apartment to recruit her for the Senate Judiciary Committee. As that body's chairman, Biden had allowed Republicans to vilify Anita Hill the year before; now, he was looking to rehabilitate the committee, and himself. Moseley Braun warily accepted. Today, she's a surrogate for Biden's flaccid presidential campaign—her first time stumping in twenty years. This May, a day after Minneapolis protesters heroically burned down a police precinct, she told *The New York Times*, "I just need voters to see the Joe Biden I know, who is very clear on race and racism." And so he is: Biden opposed busing as a tool of desegregation, drafted the notorious crime bill that Bill Clinton signed into law, and has rejected the idea of defunding the police.

Then again, in order to care about any of that, you would first need to care about politics. *Rodham* does not; it is an unpolitical book by an unpolitical author about—for all her ambition—an unpolitical person, one who is manifestly uninterested in justice beyond her own professional rewards. This is, against all odds, the book's single insight into Hillary Clinton: she knew nothing of power except that she wanted it. Sittenfeld is fine with this. Her Hillary never promotes her husband's crime bill or votes for the Iraq War—she is conveniently spared the opportunity—but the one thing you must understand about this book is that it was written by and for someone who doesn't care that the real Hillary did.

The truth is, presidents are small potatoes in the larder of history. We can say with reasonable certainty that, were Hillary Rodham Clinton now president, millionaires and billionaires would still hold Washington in a death grip. The health-care industry would still be bleeding millions of people dry. ICE would still be terrorizing immigrants. The novel coronavirus would still have struck the planet; the response would still have been grossly mishandled by officials local, state, and federal. Police would still be murdering Black people with the approval and encouragement of the state. The current abolitionist uprising, decades in the making, would likely still be underway. We would still have misery; we would still have hope. The only thing we wouldn't have is this book.

2020

Oh No

The protagonist of Alex Norris's *Webcomic Name*, hosted on Tumblr since July 2016, is a simple pink cartoon blob with four pseudopods, two dots for eyes, and a single line for a mouth, which Norris tends to draw just shy of an em dash. The result is that its owner often reads as both a little happy and a little sad—or maybe just one of those, or maybe neither. In every strip, the blob wants something. It tries on a bra or gets a new job or has a fling. It overeats and oversleeps and underprepares. It looks in the mirror, tells a secret, has a sex dream, takes public transit; it flirts, paints, texts, drinks, binge-watches. Someone takes its picture. Someone asks its gender. No matter the setup, though, every episode ends the same way. The bra doesn't fit. The job is stupid. The blob makes accidental eye contact with a stranger. It gets in a codependent relationship. The nice thing it orders online finally arrives in a parcel labeled NOCE THUNG. "Oh no," says the blob, all lowercase, no punctuation.

This is a comic about disappointment. This is a tautology, because optimism and disappointment are the same thing. The blob never breaks down or cracks up; it suffers no traumatic cut. Hence *Webcomic Name*'s bland nonspecificity—a parody of the internet's love of relatable content—from its generic title and genderless everyperson protagonist to its unassuming, my-kid-could-do-that house style. Disappointment isn't some big production: it's a bit of a letdown, actually. Turns out not getting what you want doesn't make you not want it. Your desires are rarely brittle enough to break. This is a blob, after all, a kind of shock absorber for life's hard knocks. This is why one easily becomes disappointed with the comic itself: the gags are mostly small, dumb, flat. Desire is a bad joke. You can always guess the punch line.

Norris knows this. He knows you know it, too, and he's fond of displacing this knowledge you both share to the level of formal self-awareness. "Optimistic expectations," says the blob in one strip. The speech bubble pops, leaving the words *disappointing outcome* behind. "Generic lament," says the blob. In another strip, in each of the first two panels, the blob stares up at the phrase RUNNING GAG, spelled out in green bubble letters. In the third panel, the phrase turns orange and a single letter has been swapped out: RUINING GAG, it reads. "Oh no," says the blob. Knowledge is what happens in the gap between what you want and wanting it. "Oh no" is a stooge's eureka. No means know. In a rare six-panel strip, an "oh no" speech bubble floats aimlessly through the sky, as if having wandered off from some other comic. "I wish I could find a place of joy," it sighs, "but I make every moment despair." It comes across a couple in a park: an orange blob has just proposed to a pink blob. The bubble slides over the pink blob's head. "Oh no," says the blob. "Oh no," echoes the speech bubble.

What Norris suggests is that the knowledge disappointment brings arrives at the precise moment of knowledge's exhaustion. Knowledge is a loser's trophy. "Good game," etc. This makes knowledge a form of mourning—or better, a form of melancholy, a refusal to acknowledge defeat's receipt, a locket full of loss. Like everyone, the blob is a critic and, like every critic, a con. Reflexivity is such a gag. Analysis is just denial with more words. This doesn't mean that knowing better is any worse than not knowing at all. It just means that neither condition will rescue you from wanting things. At best, you may find a quantum of dumb relief in desire's never letting up. There is comfort in repetition. In a strip titled "Repetition," the blob gets an update on its phone from a content creator it likes. A THING YOU HAVE SEEN BEFORE, reads the phone's screen. Norris has posted this strip three times. There is comfort in repetition. Repetition is all comfort is, maybe.

This is not a political comic, but it does have something to say about the comedy that politics is. Radical politics since at least Marx has staked itself on the wager of self-consciousness. The meat of this fantasy is that "knowing will lead to knowing what to do." (The phrase is Robyn Wiegman's.) Such an outcome was the putative goal of the consciousness-raising feminist groups of the 1970s; it remains the aim of woke TV, woke Twitter. Now a fantasy doesn't have to be a lie. It's just something you'd believe even if it were a lie. The strength of your belief expresses the force of a desire. This is disappointment's upside, if you want to call it that, in a political landscape sucked dry by disappointments, electoral and otherwise. You'll keep on blobbing, all evidence to the contrary. You'll wake up, go on dates, feed your pets; organize and phone-bank and read things. The struggle is indeed real. But maybe it will get better. You never know. "Running gag," says the blob in one strip. "That wasn't funny," says its friend. "Just you wait," says the blob.

2018

IV

Authority

1.

Why do we ask the critic to have authority? We do not ask this of a painter or a short-story writer, although an authoritative tone may be found in particular cases—the majesty of Rothko, the erudition of Borges. We likewise do not require the memoirist to be an authority on herself; more often we wish her to be honest about the fact that she is not one. The same goes for the essayist, who may cover all manner of worldly topics with conversance and poise but must thread each of them, as Joan Didion did with California, through the fragile eye of her own ego. We certainly do ask for authority from a historian or sociologist, by which we mean that the scholar should *know what he's talking about*, in the sense of having mastered the existing literature, and that he should be *good at talking about it*, in the sense of having an effortless command of rhetoric, style, and the rest. But crucially, we also ask that scholarship be accurate, or at least committed to increasing the treasury of human knowledge. We also ask this of the journalist, whose dispatches must be not only authoritative but actually factual. Even from the opinion columnist, who we know is trying to lead us by the nose, we nonetheless expect the acknowledgment of a shared reality. We might conclude, then, that when we do ask for authority from a writer (which is hardly all of the time), we never ask for authority in isolation. Indeed, authority without a corresponding basis in some kind of *good reason*—the kind of authority that answers "Why?" with "Because I said so"—strikes us as false, or even dangerous.

But the critic is a curious case. She too must boast a firm command of the relevant tradition or tools of analysis: we appreciate it if she is acquainted with Chilean political history before pronouncing on Bolaño, just as we hope she will not attempt Sondheim without knowing an arpeggio from an appoggiatura. We may also ask the critic for charisma, for sophistication, for a fine way with words, and above all for the ability to make the work of art intelligible while preserving its integrity. She must be able to turn the meaning of a whole Hitchcock picture into a tiny reel of microfilm that we may slip furtively into our pockets. At the same time, we are not content to let the critic offer her mere *opinion*, since we are perfectly capable of those ourselves, nor do we wish for her to reminisce, however artfully, on her impressions of the work. We are not asking for another aesthetic experience; we are asking for a *judgment*. Here is where the trouble starts. For the critic may be witty or insightful or engaging or well-read or widely admired or a true virtuoso—but what she will never be is decidedly *right*. It is not possible, we are forced to admit, to prove the excellence of a novel or a painting through empirical evidence or logical argument; if it were, we could leave the business of evaluating art to the art historians and neuroscientists and politicians. (God knows they are eager to weigh in!)

This leaves the critic in the unhappy place of declaring that a given work of art is beautiful while being unable to provide a definitive reason why. He occupies, in other words, that terrifying position of *pure authority* which in most other cases we so ardently oppose: we are meant to take him at his word, and nothing more. What sort of strange job is this? We may be tempted to compare him to the priest, who guides by faith alone—or to the televangelist, who asks us to trust him on the authority of a god in which we do not yet believe (while also telling us what to do with our money). But the critic's authority is perhaps most like that of a king: his words have the force of law *simply because he is king*. We may find this sort of authority, which finds its source in nothing but itself, to be barely distinguishable from the abuse of authority, if not actual authoritarianism. In fact, it may be tantamount to the absence of any legitimate authority altogether.

This is probably why, since the birth of modern literary criticism in eighteenth-century Europe, critics have tended to speak of their chosen profession in the language of political crisis. The English critic Samuel Johnson, writing in the 1750s, complained of a dearth of "lawful authority" within his profession, whose sorry state he illustrated by way of allegory. Long ago, he wrote, the goddess of criticism bore a royal scepter with two ends—one perfumed with ambrosia, the other bringing mildew—which she used to immortalize some works of art and consign others to oblivion. But wearied by her duties, the queen broke her scepter into pieces, leaving these "fragments of authority" to be scooped up by the servants of flattery and malevolence. The result was that criticism had "lost her throne vacant to her slaves"—those whom Johnson derogatorily referred to as "modern critics," who were reducing the art of criticism to the "arbitrary edicts of legislators authorized only by themselves." The young empire of criticism, to hear the good doctor tell it, already stood on the brink of collapse.

How then was the critic's authority to be restored? Johnson wrote of his desire to "improve opinion into knowledge," thus establishing an authoritative body of principles to shape the vagaries of the critic's feelings. He imagined this process as a kind of political centralization, much as the first King of the English had united the Anglo-Saxons, the Vikings, and the Danes. In the name of beauty, Johnson hoped to bring the barbarian tribes of modern criticism, which had "hitherto known only the anarchy of ignorance, the caprices of fancy, and the tyranny of prescription," out of the bloody state of nature and into the civilized domain of science. (This was, after all, a man who believed that he could have been appointed Lord High Chancellor of Great Britain.) The improvement of opinion into knowledge would allow the critic to distinguish the kind of beauty that depended on rational bases from what Johnson called "the nameless and inexplicable elegancies" that delighted the critic's fancy but stymied all reasoning. It would equally cut out the "thousand extrinsic and accidental causes" that may lead any critic into prejudice—things like personal friendship with the author or prejudice against all Italians.

The problem with Johnson's plan was that whenever a critic appeared to have succeeded in getting beauty down to a science—for instance, Aristotle's theory of tragedy in the *Poetics*—these principles had soon atrophied into a set of decrepit precepts inherited, like hemophilia, from some "despotic antiquity." The law, by gaining a letter, had lost its spirit. It would be surely absurd, Johnson wrote, to declare that the English drama should never have more than three characters onstage simply because it had worked for Sophocles. Principles alone would not be sufficient; a rule was a scientific instrument that would "assist our faculties when properly used" but "produce confusion and obscurity by unskillful application." But here Johnson himself fell into confusion. If the correct application of the rules could not be fully inferred from the rules themselves, then how was the critic able to apply it at all without appealing to something "extrinsic" like common sense or personal preference? And if the laws of criticism were meant to change over time, where did the critic derive his authority to decide on the new laws, if not from the very laws he was meant to change?

2.

In three centuries of trying, no critic has managed to give a coherent account of his own authority without running into the same paradox: Where does authority come from? It is an ancient political question. The concept of authority first emerged in the Roman Republic, where the Latin word *auctoritas* had the basic sense of an opinion or judgment, and by extension, an ability to influence others. It was also another name for a *senatus consultum*—a written opinion of the Roman Senate, a body of elders from prestigious families. Importantly, the Senate's opinions were legally nonbinding, instead taking the form of advice to the magistrates that the latter nonetheless rarely ignored. Hannah Arendt would argue that the Senate drew its authority from the pedigree of its members, whose ancestors were supposed to have been present at the founding of Rome. Cicero wrote in *On the Laws* that while power lay with the people, authority belonged to the Senate, whose decrees every citizen had a customary obligation to defend as if they were law. Tacit here was the idea that authority, unlike power, had no inherent force of its own; it commanded not through threats of violence, as the Romans did with their slaves, but by appealing to a tradition that was both above the law and, as Arendt put it, "curiously elusive and intangible." True authority was nothing less—or more—than the opinion of one party effortlessly translated into the actions of another.

The question was whether such a thing could exist anywhere but in theory. The Roman foundation myth, after all, famously involved rape and murder. Cicero believed that the authority of the Senate should ideally be ratified into an actual lawmaking power—an unsurprising position to take during the collapse of the Republic. It was a special *auctoritas* of the Senate that Julius Caesar was to defy when he crossed the Rubicon soon after, launching civil war and helping to usher in the Roman Empire, where the Senate would diminish into a bureaucratic organ whose primary purpose was to rubber-stamp the emperor's absolute power. Arendt claimed that, after the fall of the empire in the fifth century, the ghost of the Senate arose again in the form of the Roman Catholic Church, which exerted great influence in the Middle Ages both directly and through the idea of divine right of kings. Yet even the church's authority rested on more than just tradition: to compel obedience, it needed an "elaborate system of rewards and punishments for deeds and misdeeds that did not find their just retribution on earth"—in a word, hell—which bore a terrifying threat of violence, excommunication being worse than execution. (The same could be said for the kings, who were generally satisfied with executing people.)

It was not until the Protestant Reformation that the idea of traditional authority began to break down in earnest. Martin Luther, writing in the years following his own excommunication in 1521 by Pope Leo X, drew a sharp distinction between the Christian's earthly subjection to the "temporal authorities" and his absolute freedom in the spiritual realm, which lay beyond the reach of any feudal or ecclesiastical power. "Among Christians there shall and can be no authority," Luther wrote—a radical idea that he immediately sought to contain. He had no desire to subvert the authority of worldly princes, maintaining that the Christian "submits most willingly to the rule of the sword." As Herbert Marcuse observed in an excellent little study on the topic, Luther wished to *rescue* the idea of authority by building the idea of freedom into it: in place of the passive model of obedience as surrender to a dominating force, Luther proposed an active model of obedience as the exercise of individual spiritual freedom. This implied that the Christian obeyed the temporal authority because he freely chose to; but it was also taken to mean, by the more anti-authoritarian currents within the Reformation, that Christians had the freedom to *disobey* a prince who had abused his office. Luther condemned the widespread peasant revolts put down in 1525, which he regarded as reducing all authority to "murder and bloodshed." Yet it was Luther himself who had already described the temporal authorities as mere "executioners and hangmen"—appointed by God but lacking any lawful authority over the "secret, spiritual, hidden matter" of the freedom of the soul.

From the Reformation onward, it became increasingly difficult to speak of authority without also speaking of freedom. In fact, the political thought of seventeenth-century Europe was characterized by a feverish dialectic of authority and freedom, with each term simultaneously fortifying and threatening to destroy the other. The great question was how to reconcile them. "Beset with those that contend on one side for too great liberty, and on the other side for too much authority, 'tis hard to pass between the points of both unwounded," wrote Thomas Hobbes in 1651. His own strategy was to posit the existence of a "covenant of every man with every man," in which the people collectively authorized a single person to rule over the rest as sovereign. Hobbes, who was always flirting with atheism, suggested that this commonwealth of men was a kind of "mortal god" that could neatly secularize the old system of divine right while continuing to justify absolute monarchy. It was clear that Hobbes had erred on the side of authority; John Locke, the more sanguine of the two, threw his lot in with liberty. It was impossible, he wrote, to derive "the least shadow of authority" from inherited tradition or divine right. The king's authority was delegated solely by the "constitutions and laws of the government," as established through the freely given consent of the people. "Against the laws there can be no authority," wrote Locke, echoing Luther. But the former arrived at a more revolutionary conclusion: any king who claimed such an authority was by definition a tyrant and hence had turned liberty back to the people, who could now justly oppose him by force.

At their most groundbreaking moments, the early thinkers of classical liberalism were essentially proposing that authority could be constructed entirely *out of* freedom. This reflected a larger historical shift currently underway in seventeenth-century Europe: a slow transition from the older model of authority as rooted in tradition or religion to what the sociologist Max Weber would later call *rational authority*, in which obedience is owed directly to the law itself, as established through mutual agreement. The new model was almost impossible to imagine in practice, but the old model was becoming insupportable. Hobbes had written the *Leviathan* during the English Civil War of the 1640s; Locke had published his treatises in the wake of the Glorious Revolution of 1688, ostensibly with the hope of legitimating the rule of the invading Protestant king. Of course, the real result of the Glorious Revolution was the ascendancy of Parliament as the true authority in England, which quickly declared that the suspension of law "by regal authority without consent of Parliament" was illegal. This did not mean doing away with the hereditary monarchy, as was currently the case in the Dutch Republic. (The English have yet to rid themselves of that particular habit.) But even a dedicated monarchist like Hobbes had already shifted the locus of authority from the literal person of the king to an impersonal legal order of which the king was the sovereign executor. Into this tiny gap between the king and the crown, the republican spirit began to drive a powerful wedge. For if authority rightly belonged with the law and not the king himself, what good—the philosophers began to whisper—was a king?

It is here on the cusp of the eighteenth century, amid the decline of one model of authority (traditional, religious) and the rise of another kind (rational, legal), that criticism as a literary genre first took shape. The judging of art is probably as old as civilization, if not consciousness itself—the Athenians, for instance, held contests to award the best new play—but criticism in the modern sense developed two important features, one inward and one outward. First, criticism shared with enlightened political thought the aim of establishing authority through agreed-upon rational principles, rather than relying on tradition or succumbing to arbitrary fiat. When Locke wrote that men freely entered into the social contract out of their need for a "known and indifferent judge" with the authority to sort out their differences, he sounded as if he was describing a critic. Second, modern criticism was intended for consumption by a *reading public*, and especially that informal community of European intellectuals known to itself as the Republic of Letters. In this sense, criticism was an unmistakable child of the periodical; the critic wrote not for himself, his friends, or his patron, but on the assumption that his handiwork would be circulated among his fellow men of letters, most of whom he would never meet.

From the beginning, then, criticism had to reckon with two interlocking problems of authority, one literary, the other political. In order to criticize well, the critic would need *both* the critical authority that derived from his own free use of reason *and* the freedom to publish his criticism without being suspected of posing a threat to the actual authorities. This reflected a strong post-Reformation association between faith and reading: Luther had written that while the prince had every right to put down a rebellion, he lacked all authority to force the Christian to "get rid of certain books." The first periodical dedicated solely to literary criticism, *Nouvelles de la république des lettres*, first appeared in Amsterdam in 1684. Its editor, Pierre Bayle, was a Huguenot refugee whose book on freedom of conscience had been burned in Paris the year before. (The French authorities had also imprisoned his brother, who died in his cell.) Emboldened by the relative liberality of his Dutch publishers, Bayle would write extensively on the subject of religious toleration, which he argued could be a "source of infinite public blessings" provided that the prince gave every man's beliefs equal protection under law. Likewise, Bayle promised not to set up his new literary journal as a "clearinghouse for gossip," promising to always seek the "reasonable middle-ground" between favoritism and censure. "We do not mean to establish any prejudice either for or against the author," he wrote. "It would take ridiculous vanity to lay claim to an authority so sublime."

In this way, early literary criticism served as a laboratory for testing out a central political question of the Enlightenment: if it really was possible for the critic to draw his authority purely from his own rational freedom, then perhaps it was also possible for a king to derive his authority entirely from the collective will of his subjects. Eighteenth-century criticism was strongly intertwined with the liberal political project that would find success in Great Britain, the Dutch Republic, and the Thirteen Colonies. Naturally, not all critics were actual liberals. When Johnson, a lifelong Tory, wrote in 1751 that the crude authority claimed by modern critics could be "justly opposed," he had in mind something like restoration, not revolution. (On the eve of the American War of Independence, he would similarly accuse the upstart colonists of reducing English

sovereignty to "dominion without authority.") Yet Johnson, too, understood that criticism could never attain the "stability of a science" without
some appeal to the universal laws written on the soul of every man. Indeed, criticism presented such an irresistible metaphor for rational-legal
authority that many critics began to regard it as the herald of some political utopia—assuming, that is, that criticism could first prove *itself.*

3.

Having set before themselves such a lofty task, the early critics quickly
ran aground. As Johnson discovered, critical authority could not be
secured through the blind application of principle. For all its talk of science, the criticism of the eighteenth century remained mostly unformal-
ized, defaulting instead to the received wisdom of the ancients and moral
character of the critic himself. Inevitably, the critics succumbed to the
impulse to list one another's many failings: their pride, their susceptibil-
ity to bias, their slavish adherence to arbitrary rules concerning, say, the
proper number of syllables in a line of poetry. "Some beauties yet, no
precepts can declare," wrote Alexander Pope in 1711, observing that the
great poets had often broken the rules, just as a king might suspend his
own laws. Pope meant this as a rebuke of empty legalism in favor of
what he called "true taste," but he was really articulating an impasse that
confronted criticism in general. For if beauty could not exist within the
confines of the law, how did the critic know it existed at all?

What the early critics lacked, in other words, was a good explanation
for why taste, of all things, provoked such an acute crisis of authority.
Common sense provided two contradictory rules of thumb: first, that
there was no accounting for taste, since one critic might find beautiful
what another found ugly; second, that taste must have some universal
standard, since one critic often tried to persuade the rest to agree with
him. The easiest solution to this knot was to cut it in half and throw
away the less persuasive string. In 1757, two philosophical treatments of
the subject appeared, one by David Hume, another by Edmund Burke.
Hume, always the skeptic, argued that any supposed laws of taste were,
at best, no more than "general observations" inferred from everyday

life by especially sensitive critics, who were rare and did not always feel the same. Burke, by contrast, maintained that beauty was so affecting that it must "depend upon some positive qualities"—he dogmatically asserted, for instance, that beautiful objects were consistently smooth, pale, delicate, and on the small side. But neither of these accounts was satisfying. Burke often seemed to be describing his rather narrow taste in women, rather than making a rational argument, while even Hume admitted that the search for authoritative principles of taste was only "natural," if largely fruitless in practice.

These questions stalled out in the British Isles. It was Prussia, then under absolute monarchy, that would provide probably the single most influential theory of taste in the history of criticism. It would come not from a literary critic but from a philosopher: Immanuel Kant. In his youth, Kant had been raised in Pietism, a reformist movement advocating a return to Luther's emphasis on personal faith over church orthodoxy. Even as an adult, Kant remained deeply concerned with how to reconcile human freedom with the existence of certain necessary laws of nature, morality, and thought. His strategy was to posit that such laws were *internal* to reason, which he defined as the cognitive power to arrive at universal principles without having to consult one's sensory experiences. Instead, reason could deduce these laws simply by examining its own inner workings—a process that Kant called *Kritik*, a word that may be rendered in English as both "critique" and "criticism." This was at once conservative and deeply revolutionary: it reaffirmed the law by removing it from the outside world and transforming it into a private feature of cognition. Like Luther before him, Kant wished not to undermine authority but to "institute a court of justice, by which reason may secure its rightful claims" in accordance with "its own eternal and unchangeable laws." "Our age is the genuine age of criticism, to which everything must submit," Kant wrote in 1781—including the law itself.

In the 1780s, Kant would apply his method of *Kritik* to the laws of nature and morality. With the appearance of his *Critique of Judgment* in 1790, also called the Third Critique, Kant turned at last to the laws of taste. He was influenced not just by Hume and Burke, whose theories struck him as skeptical and dogmatic, respectively, but also by his countryman Alexander Gottlieb Baumgarten, who had recently coined

the term *aesthetics* to refer to the "science of beauty." As Terry Eagleton
has observed, it was no accident that aesthetics as we understand it today first took root in the soil of enlightened absolutism, which could
not be truly absolute without reaching down into the sensory lives of its
subjects and bringing them "within the majestic scope of reason." This
was quite explicit in the case of Prussia: Frederick the Great, an aspiring
philosopher-king, advised his subjects—in a preface to a translation of
Bayle's writings, of all things—that "mankind's most important task is
to acquire judgment." Baumgarten's new science reflected this desire for
a rational account of sensation—he even defined beauty, curiously, as the
"perfection of sensible cognition." In the First Critique, Kant expressed
his admiration for Baumgarten's scientific ambitions without endorsing
them. "That endeavor is futile," he wrote—probably reminded of his
own earlier work on the beautiful, which had not progressed beyond a
naïve heap of empirical examples, including hedges, blue eyes, and pleasure palaces. By the Third Critique, Kant was even clearer on the subject:
"There is no science of the beautiful, only criticism."

Kant now advanced a theory of his own. If taste was to have any true
authority, he proposed, then it must be governed by the *idea* of a law—
and only the idea of one. It was clear to Kant, as it had been to Baumgarten, that a law was somehow involved in aesthetic judgments; yet it was
also clear that whenever the critic tried to determine the specific content
of this law, he inevitably found himself *interested* in the content—either
in the form of sensory gratification, as when sampling a fine wine, or in
the form of moral approval, as when witnessing an act of charity. But for
Kant, this did not imply that such a law did not exist; it meant only that,
while the critic had every right to *assume* the existence of such a law, he
had no right to know what was in it. In one of the most consequential
moves in the history of criticism, Kant took the futility of aesthetic science and reframed it as a maxim for the critic: *Always assume that beauty
has a rational explanation, but never pretend to know what it is.*

It is worth pausing to note the elegance of this argument. In his First
Critique, Kant had described cognition as the industrious collaboration
of several faculties: the senses, a small cohort of scribes who took in the
raw data of an experience (*red, circle, bright, far*); the imagination, a nimble clerk who organized this data into a brief (*a ruby spot in the morn-*

ing sky); and the understanding, a sober judge who provided a ruling in the form of a concept (*sunrise*). But in the case of aesthetic judgment, the process transpired differently. The senses still diligently transcribed the data of experience, this time focusing on feelings of pleasure (*warm, poignant, hopeful*); and the imagination still prepared a report (*a rousing vision of natural beauty*); but the understanding, usually so confident, now faltered. To its surprise, it could find no rule in the concept of a sunrise to explain why anyone should find one beautiful. Unable to proceed without falling into error, the understanding would judiciously shelve the case indefinitely and turn the brief over to its lively clerk, which it authorized to speculate freely on the matter provided the imagination did not try to slip on the wig and make a ruling of its own. Kant referred to this compromise as the "free play" of imagination and the understanding, in which the imagination was delegated a kind of authority he called "free lawfulness."

One of the unexpected advantages of this theory was that it relieved the critic from having to prove that beauty actually existed; in fact, it prohibited him from doing so. It was perfectly rational, Kant wrote, for critics to "quarrel" over why a work of art was beautiful; in fact it was inevitable, insofar as beauty consisted of nothing but the free lawfulness of the imagination. But what the critic could *not* do, at least not without abusing his authority, was to proceed beyond argument to a definitive answer. Any critic who apparently succeeded in doing so was not making an aesthetic judgment at all but a *practical* one: he was assessing how useful the work of art was for achieving a desired end, or else he was appraising its inherent moral value. This too was perfectly rational, so long as the critic did not forget—as he often did—that this determination had nothing to do with the aesthetic value of the thing in question. A hedge, for instance, might be very good for protecting one's garden from soil erosion, but this did not make it beautiful, nor could the beauty of a church be measured by the righteousness of the doctrines preached within. In solving one paradox, Kant had created another. On the one hand, the critic's authority originated in human reason, and hence was free of any external power; on the other hand, this kind of authority was *so* pure that the reasons behind it could not be grasped, only "pointed at."

Now if Kant pictured the art critic as exercising free lawfulness in the face of an unknowable law, he believed something very similar of the royal subject, whose political rights he both defended and undermined. At once a committed republican and a humble servant of the Prussian crown, Kant maintained that the public must be free to write and publish works of criticism, including criticism of the actual laws. (He himself would run afoul of the royal censors after Frederick the Great's death.) But he also insisted that the people had absolutely no right to "inquire with any practical aim in view into the origin of the supreme authority to which it is subject." The people had to behave as if all authority came from God, even if the government had come to power through deceit or bloodshed. Hence the curious motto that appeared in Kant's essay on enlightenment: "Argue as much as you want and about what you want, but obey!" There was no greater crime, he believed, than a violent attempt to overthrow the state, regardless of its failings; any people that did so was subverting not only the existing legal order but the very idea of law as such. Kant condemned, for instance, what he saw as the "misery and atrocities" of the French Revolution, even as he expressed deep sympathies with its rationalist values. What truly inspired Kant had not been the storming of the Bastille or the bloody spectacle of the guillotine—these appalled him—but the cohort of enlightened intellectuals who had engaged in spirited debate about it from the sidelines.

It is strikingly easy to draw an analogy between what Kant thought of the Revolution and what he thought of a beautiful sunrise. The sansculottes, he believed, had been well within their rights to ask why Louis XVI deserved to be king; they had erred, disastrously, by daring to answer their own question. But this is more than an analogy. Even as he barred all practical interest from entering into the critic's judgments about the beautiful, Kant postulated that the cultivation of good taste would help mankind improve its moral habits without making "too violent a leap." This, in turn, was part of Kant's broader political vision, in which the peoples of the earth, at first compelled by the physical might of a despot, could gradually be persuaded to respect the "mere idea of the authority of law," thus enabling a transition to representative government and world peace. The critic's task was therefore to keep taste free of any practical interests that would reduce it to usefulness or morality—but he would do this in the (all too practical) interest of ushering in some future republic. As the nineteenth century dawned, the critic was no longer just a metaphorical stand-in for the king. He was becoming a very real example of something else: a citizen.

4.

Kant's aesthetics found their way to England in the person of Samuel Taylor Coleridge, the Romantic poet. In 1814, Coleridge published a trio of essays in a Bristol newspaper outlining his own theory of criticism, which he grounded in a disinterested feeling of "immediate and absolute complacency." This passive turn of phrase was telling. Coleridge was writing just after the apparent end of the bloody Napoleonic Wars, which had by then consumed Europe for over a decade, and he saw the "tranquility of nations" as a perfect opportunity to make critics out of his fellow citizens, whom a pressing interest in world events had habituated to daily paper-reading. "We are now allowed to think and feel as men," Coleridge wrote, urging each reader to examine his own mind in order to discover the principles of criticism for himself. This vision of readerly equality was clearly influenced by the republican principles of the French Revolution, which had set a young Coleridge's heart aflame. (The same influence could be felt in Coleridge's mystical definition of beauty as "multëity in unity.") By the time of Napoleon's coup d'état in 1799, however, Coleridge had recanted his support, believing he had mistaken the dark and sensual motivations of the poor for the "spirit of divinest Liberty." The fraternity of critics he now proposed was far removed from the *fraternité* that had led to so much tyranny and war; it drew its authority not from hunger or violence but from the egalitarian nature of beauty itself.

Like all authority, the authority of the citizen-critic could be abused. The Republic of Letters was coming to an end; it was soon to be the age of the newspaper, and the new "mass of readers" frightened Coleridge as much as it cheered him. As Benedict Anderson observed in 1983, the nineteenth-century newspaper was the great canvas of the nation-state, combining all the varied, unrelated events of the day into a single cheap, mass-produced item to be consumed in the "lair of the skull." Every time the citizen opened the paper, he could feel the rest of the nation reading alongside him; this is how he knew the nation existed. Yet in Coleridge's opinion, the nationwide circulation of literature had turned criticism into a "barrel organ" that even a deaf man could crank. In ancient times, he wrote, books had been handled like religious oracles; now they were treated as criminals at the mercy of "every self-elected, yet not the less peremptory, judge." At the same time, Coleridge resented those popular but mediocre authors who considered even the faintest reproach to be "violent and undisciplined abuse." Properly practiced, he argued, criticism was "no giant but a windmill": it attacked no one, favored no man's grain over another's, answered to no wind but harnessed them all into a single perfect arc through the sky. "But this space must be left free and unimpeded," Coleridge warned. Gnats and wasps could pass through unharmed and ignored, but any self-styled Quixote who found himself slung aloft by criticism's "remorseless arm" had only himself to blame.

For the nineteenth-century critic, the question of authority would be a matter of distinguishing the tyranny of the mob from the equality of free citizens. Here we find a renewed emphasis on the *disinterestedness* of criticism. Where the eighteenth century had striven to make criticism into an objective science, the nineteenth century began to think of criticism as a kind of *mission*, one whose goal was to improve society by refining its members. In this context the critic's disinterest took on the character of a civic virtue: it prepared the citizen to evenly receive "the best that is thought and known in the world," as Matthew Arnold famously put it in his 1864 lecture "The Function of Criticism at the Present Time." An unabashed moralist, Arnold wrote the "bane of criticism" in England was its subservience to "the rush and roar of practical life." He specifically had in mind the many political and religious factions in Victorian England, each of which appeared to have its own magazine: *The Edinburgh Review* for the Whigs, *The Quarterly Review* for the Tories, and so on. This quagmire of political bias—not to mention physical print—made it difficult for critics to engage in what Arnold, paraphrasing Kant, called the "free disinterested play of mind." "There should be a criticism, not the minister of these interests, not their enemy, but absolutely and entirely independent of them," Arnold argued. "No other criticism will ever attain any real authority or make any real way towards its end—the creating of a current of true and fresh ideas."

We may note the two-step: Arnold was saying that criticism should be free of political interest in the interest of political freedom. For him, this was no contradiction. Arnold, like Kant, never denied that the critic's current of fresh ideas might one day make its benefits felt in the social and political sphere; in fact, he would later claim in no uncertain terms that "culture suggests the idea of the State." Nevertheless, it was crucial that the critic limit himself to the "slow and obscure work" of ideas. Arnold, too, was thinking of the French Revolution, which he believed had sent the ideas of liberty and equality "rushing furiously into the political sphere" and, in so doing, destroy it. Hence the subtle, indirect function of criticism, which Arnold imagined as both headwater and dike, with the current of fresh ideas entering the practical world as if by gentle evaporation. "If we look at the world outside us we find a disquieting absence of sure authority," he wrote. "We discover that only in right reason can we get a source of sure authority, and culture brings us towards right reason." For Arnold, it was the critics, and not the Jacobins, who were the "true apostles of equality"—because the former, unlike the latter, led their fellow citizens to accept the authority of reason *gradually*, first within themselves and only then in the form of the nation-state. This is why he admired the French Academy in Paris: not because he thought there should be a direct equivalent in London (he did not think it possible) but because he saw the value of formally establishing a "recognized authority in matters of intellectual tone and taste."

Arnold was not without his critics. As the nineteenth century drew to a close, his musty Victorianism suffered a sharp riposte in the form of the Aesthetic Movement. In 1873, Walter Pater called for a return to the "original facts" of criticism—namely, the impression of the work of art on the mind of the critic—arguing that the critic need have no motive other than his love of "art for art's sake." There was something notably amoral about the impressionistic critic, who refused to be tied down by *any* interest, practical or intellectual, that forced him to "sacrifice" one iota of his own experience. Amid the many bewildering and entangled interests of the modern world, Pater wrote, the human spirit longed to feel a sense of its own freedom; it was this irrepressible freedom that gave the critic the authority to place his aesthetic experience above all else. "To burn always with this hard, gemlike flame, to maintain this ecstasy, is success in life," Pater wrote in his book on Renaissance art. In the margins of this claim, one could still make out the critic's mission: to keep this flame *alive*, above all within himself. Pater was, in fact, well aware of the moral implications of aestheticism: he later removed the above passage for fear that "it might possibly mislead some of those young men into whose hands it might fall."

And so it did. Oscar Wilde, the great aesthete, went even further than Pater, arguing that the critic had no allegiance even to the works of art he criticized. The critic's only task was to create a *new* work of art equal to—or surpassing—the work under consideration. "That is what the highest criticism really is, the record of one's soul," Wilde wrote in his 1891 essay "The Critic as Artist." His implicit target here was Arnold, whose high seriousness he rejected. (The original title of Wilde's essay had been "The True Function and Value of Criticism.") When Arnold had made a virtue of disinterestedness, he had pictured the critic turning away from himself and toward the social whole, whereas Wilde's critic was *so* disinterested that he answered to no authority but his own personality. Yet even Wilde could not help offering his own notion of citizenship. He made evident his admiration for the ancient Greeks, whom he called a "nation of art-critics"—precisely because each member of the Greek city-state, lacking any "tedious magazines about art," was free to cultivate the critical spirit within himself. This picture was remarkably close to Wilde's highly individualistic understanding of socialism, in which the true personality of man would not admit of "any laws but its own laws; nor any authority but its own authority." (Of course, whether socialism really *could* do without authority was, in the wake of the Paris Commune of 1871, a matter of intense debate. One might have replied to Wilde as Engels did to the anarchists: "Have these men ever seen a revolution?")

One way or another, criticism was now hurtling toward what Arnold had gravely called *anarchy*, the critic's mission having broken down into a narrow individualism that was growing increasingly unsustainable. To many at the turn of the twentieth century, the grounding of the critic's authority in his own freedom had produced not a strong sense of civic duty, as Kant had hoped, but a decadent belletrism that, crucially, was especially difficult to *teach*. "The opinion seems to be gaining ground that the study of literature by itself is unprofitable, hard to disassociate from dilettantism, and not likely to lead to much except a lavish outlay of elegant epithets of admiration," wrote the American critic Irving Babbitt in 1897, fretting that the teaching of the classics had been reduced to "ringing the changes on the adjective 'beautiful!'" The only existing alternative, however, was the hoary discipline of philology, a precursor to linguistics that Babbitt viewed as part of "a dead-weight of information" that had accompanied the rapid industrialization of the Gilded Age. The predicament of the literary critic now, especially in America, was how to find a safe route between the Scylla of amateurism and the Charybdis of positivism. This predicament was not entirely new: it strongly recalled Johnson's frustrated attempt to turn opinion into knowledge without losing his authority *to* that knowledge. But the twentieth-century critic had a technology of social organization at his disposal that, used correctly, promised to solve the problem of authority once and for all. It was called *college*.

5.

The university itself was obviously not a twentieth-century invention. But it was with the rise of the modern research university that criticism first faced the prospect of becoming a *public institution*, both in the sense of an established practice within a liberal society and in the sense of the physical place where that practice might be undertaken. We should not underestimate what it meant for criticism to become an actual building: for one to be able to point across the quad and say, in all seriousness, "That is English." Here one found something of Arnold's desire to set up a "recognized authority" for taste. Yet as the literary scholar John Guillory has recently shown, the university critic was immediately beset by the pressures of being a professional. The literary critic had to show that his discipline was just as legitimate as the other humanities, many of which were already fending off the encroachments of the social sciences. But it was also paramount that the critic neatly distinguish himself from the roundly scorned business of book reviewing, whose reputation had not improved. This put the critic in a familiar position—that of narrowing the scope of his own interests—but with a new wrinkle. The Victorian critic who rushed headlong into political judgment may have offended Arnold but pleased his hungry editors. The twentieth-century literary critic who ventured into territory already claimed more convincingly by history or philosophy might find himself, quite literally, out of a job.

Once again, this needle proved difficult to thread. One major contribution to the new profession of criticism was *close reading*, a concept associated with I. A. Richards, a lecturer at Cambridge. Richards's stated goal was to construct a general theory of value to cut through the existing critical tradition, which he summed up as "some brilliant guesses, much oratory and applied poetry, inexhaustible confusion, a sufficiency of dogma, no small stock of prejudices, whimsies and crotchets, a profusion of mysticism, a little genuine speculation, sundry stray inspirations, pregnant hints and random aperçus." His approach was novel. In the 1920s, Richards hit on the idea of providing his students with a poem a week, stripped of its author, and soliciting their detailed impressions in writing. He compiled these responses, alongside his extensive analysis and commentary, into a 1929 study called *Practical Criticism*. Yet in building his new empirical science, Richards found himself heavily reliant on the existing disciplines of philosophy and psychology. A young American critic, R. P. Blackmur, would remark in 1935 that Richards's theoretical apparatus was so "labyrinthine" that the small amount of actual literary criticism felt like a "by-product instead of the central target." This was one of the dangers of professionalization: that the work of legitimating his own profession might lead the critic, as Blackmur put it, to "leave literature so soon behind."

For if literary criticism could not find a stable source of authority within itself, then it risked being annexed by the greater authority of some neighboring discipline. "English might almost as well announce that it does not regard itself as entirely autonomous, but as a branch of the department of history, with the option of declaring itself occasionally a branch of the department of ethics," wrote John Crowe Ransom in 1937. Ransom was not decrying the professionalization of criticism; he wanted *more* of it, arguing that the pooled effort, resources, and training necessary to establish a "more scientific" criticism were best found in the university. He admitted that criticism could never be a "very exact science, or even a nearly exact one"—but surely this was also true of psychology and economics. When Johnson spoke of science in the 1750s, he had meant a sound set of principles; when Ransom spoke of it, he meant a professional method that would combine the eighteenth-century idea of rational knowledge with the nineteenth-century idea of civic equality. This method, which Ransom sometimes called "pure speculation," was an austere formalist approach to poetry that no other discipline would have dreamed of—enough so that its practitioners would become known as the New Critics.

The authority won through professionalization came with a corresponding duty. Ransom, a conservative agrarian who in his younger days had waxed nostalgic about the "fullness of life as it was lived in the ante-bellum South," seemed to picture the critic as a guardian who stood between the idyllic sanctity of the poem and the advances of the modern world. "A poem is, so to speak, a democratic state," he wrote in a 1941 essay, "whereas a prose discourse—mathematical, scientific, ethical, or practical and vernacular—is a totalitarian state." By this he meant that the ostensible *content* of a poem could easily be paraphrased into assertive prose, which was totalitarian because it had no goal but to maximize efficiency. (One imagines Hamlet beginning his famous soliloquy by announcing, "I am considering suicide.") By contrast, the concrete texture of a poem—Hamlet's repetition of "to be," the image of death as an "undiscovered country"—was by nature free and impossible to paraphrase. The critic's attempt to reduce a poem to prose, Ransom wrote, was not unlike the efforts of a tyrannical government to "despoil its members, the citizens, of the free exercise of their own private and independent characters." The New Critic was thus a sort of attorney for poetry: he was meant to defend the civil liberties of literature from the forces threatening to "despoil" it, whether these emanated from the other side of campus or from what Ransom understood as the general "deracination" of traditional American culture following the defeat of the Old South.

Ransom was not the only critic with this fear. His counterpart in the United Kingdom was F. R. Leavis, another unrepentant elitist who looked out grimly on the "modern" world—a euphemism that could hold everything from the deterioration of the British Empire to the mechanization of society. Of course, they had their differences: whereas Ransom took refuge in science, Leavis sought to revive a "living tradition" of literary culture that, in his opinion, had nearly collapsed. ("With no standards above, inherent in a living tradition that gives them authority, education can be only a matter of so much more machinery," Leavis wrote in 1932.) But like his foil across the Atlantic, Leavis saw the enshrining of critical authority within educational institutions as a matter of desperate moral urgency. It cannot be overstated just how strongly the literary critic of this period, whether New Critic or Leavisite, felt that the general public *could not read anymore*; even Richards spoke darkly of the "sinister potentialities of the cinema." In this sense, critics across the political spectrum tended to present themselves as spokespeople for civilization in the face of an approaching barbarism. They embraced the authority of academic specialization in order to cultivate, as Leavis put it, "free, unspecialized, general intelligence" in the population at large.

As it unified under this basically managerial mandate, criticism began to understand itself as a *liberal institution*, particularly in the United States. We are using *liberalism* here not in the narrow American sense of "left-of-center" but as a general name for the belief that freedom of ideas has an important administrative function within any constitutional republic. Twentieth-century criticism was now becoming a kind of informal state agency, and the critic a kind of bureaucrat, one whose job was the general expansion of thought by technocratic, rather than political, means. We find this institutional model openly articulated by Lionel Trilling, who stood with one foot in Columbia University and the other among the so-called New York intellectuals of the postwar period. Trilling felt strongly that criticism should resist "the dogged tendency of our time to ideologize all things into grayness." (For instance, he argued that Hemingway, having been saddled with "a burden of messianic responsibility" by the critics, went on to write self-consciously political works of lower quality.) For Trilling, the liberal critic must not demand political art. His role was simply to *weather* a diversity of ideas, including those he found politically noxious, in order to restore the original spirit of "variousness" to liberal politics. When Trilling spoke of the "liberal imagination," he did not just mean the mental life of the American liberal; he was also getting at what he conceived as a certain primordial liberalism *within* the imagination himself, as if liberal democracy was the form of government that the imagination would choose for itself if it were a people in search of laws.

At least until the 1970s, criticism in the United States was therefore an amoral institution with an openly political mission: it posited the critic's openness toward *all* ideas as the taproot of a liberal temperament. After all, the future republic looked for by the eighteenth-century critic had in some sense arrived, at least at the level of official ideology. Postwar America, with Jim Crow at home and the Vietnam War abroad, was hardly the innocent embodiment of Enlightenment ideals. Yet it could not be denied that the Americans had been successful in going without a king. Arendt, writing in 1963, would credit this success to the "blind and undiscriminating" worship of the Constitution, whose rational authority was always open to interpretation but could never, like the beautiful in Kant, be finally interpreted. It is against this background that we should read Susan Sontag's *Against Interpretation*, published in 1966, which is usually taken as a polemical assertion of the total autonomy of the aesthetic realm, and in particular modernist art, from "limited social interests and class values." It was this; but it was also a fervent defense of the idea that the "sublime neutrality" of art helped the critic cultivate what Trilling would have recognized as core liberal values— "disinterestedness, contemplativeness, attentiveness, the awakening of the feelings"—which could then be applied freely and without fealty to some ideology. (One remembers that this era of critics was shadowed by Stalinism, in which the neutrality of the state was dissolved in favor of total warfare against the people itself.)

Once more, criticism was charged with defending art against all political interests except the one it happened to serve—as if putting its finger in the dike not to avert a flood but to gain a monopoly over the water supply. An older Sontag would later admit to having been "a pugnacious aesthete" and a "barely closeted moralist" in the sixties. This was no contradiction: aestheticism *was* moralism, and a particularly powerful kind, since it hid this moralism behind the exercise of institutional authority. "Do not imagine yourself a caretaker of any tradition, an enforcer of any party standards, a warrior in any ideological battle, a corrections officer of any kind," John Updike advised his fellow critics in 1975; he was effectively describing the career of a civil servant who kept his head down through successive political administrations. This was what Sontag had meant when she defined the critic's morality as "generic": that criticism was a moral posture without any fixed moral content. In fact, it would not be wrong to say that criticism as the New York intellectuals practiced it was of a piece with the liberal theory of justice put forth by John Rawls in 1971—in particular, the idea that justice consists in equal access to "the most extensive scheme of basic liberties compatible with a similar scheme of liberties for others." There may have been no greater triumph for rational authority within criticism than the claim that the critic's judgments in public and the administration of the state were both based on an identical principle of *fairness*.

But this essentially bureaucratic idea of the critic's authority would undergo a shift in the late twentieth century. As the scholar Joseph North has recently detailed, the last vestiges of the New Critics finally collapsed in the 1970s, giving way to a dense, highly politicized form of literary criticism that integrated left-wing social movement with Marxist critique and recondite French philosophy. This is what Harold Bloom was to call the "School of Resentment," on account of its desire to "overthrow" the authority of the literary canon in the name of social change. North himself calls it a "historicist/contextualist approach to literature," a phrase that bears the mark of what it describes. A better name—all the better for its vagueness—is *theory*. For even as the rear guard accused theory of doing "politics by other means," as David Bromwich wrote in 1992, the partisans of high literary theory were in fact fulfilling an old New Critical dream: the establishment of a hermetic theoretical science with few referents outside of itself. This was not immediately obvious, seeing as theory appeared to fold into itself every kind of practical interest that criticism had long endeavored to exclude. But theory rarely *pursued* these interests; instead it knit them into the text, which it continued to read just as closely as the New Critics ever had. If anything, one could argue, the Reagan-era retreat of leftist politics into literary criticism was a small victory for the right. "A visitor from another world would surely be perplexed were he to overhear a so-called old critic calling the new critics dangerous," remarked Edward Said in 1983. "What, this visitor would ask, are they dangers to? The state? The mind? Authority?"

This would be the final paradox of professionalization: the more institutional authority criticism accumulated, the less political *power* it would ultimately enjoy. Today, theory is almost certainly on its way out—less because it has a compelling successor and more because of the imperiled status of literature departments and the humanities at large. The critic Ryan Ruby suggests that this "hemorrhage" of talent and cultural capital into the broader field of journalistic criticism has allowed the public to reap the benefits of "specialist knowledge" without the "stultifying stylistic protocols" of academic writing. At the same time, criticism as it is practiced in our fine literary magazines, whether out of ideological disgust with the nominal leftism of theory or a humble "love of literature," has begun the pendulum swing back toward a kind of belletrism, contrasting its humane approach with the pressures of social media, the collapse of print journalism, and the general distractibility of the American public. Hence a critic like Zadie Smith, in the preface to a 2018 collection of essays, will go as far as disclaiming any "authority" over her subject matter, neatly summing up her critical method in the phrase "I feel this—do you?"

Here we catch a glimpse of what may be our emerging form of criticism in the twenty-first century: criticism as *experience*. "The critic's assertions are always, read truly, only propositions, impressions, requests for assent," wrote Adam Kirsch in 2014. "This is how it seems to me: does it seem that way to you too?" The critic has become a *witness*, one whose job is to offer up an event within her own experience in such a way that the reader, if she is so inclined, may experience it too. If the concept of authority here is at once totally limp (no two experiences are alike) and exceptionally rigid (no one experience refutes any other), this is because it reflects, in Kirsch's words, "the liberal principle that the individual, the individual's experience of life, is prior to all the languages we use to describe it." The optimism of the experiential critic is, however, belied by a certain desperate politesse that, these days, tends to reflect the great upheaval of the liberal mind brought about by the election of Donald Trump. It is as if the terrifying resurgence of a charismatic authority beyond the reach of all reason has driven the critic to prophy-lactically "democratize" the cult of personality; in the place of a single ruling authority of taste, one finds a nation of tiny dictators. But this emergency measure on the part of the critic has not quieted the thought that most fills her with dread: that the breakdown in critical authority may be a sign that liberal democracy itself is failing for good.

6.

Why do we ask the critic to have authority? It is not out of a romantic desire to improve our understanding of art; nor is it because we wish to be subjected to the tyranny of someone else's opinion. It is because we are inheritors of a history, one in which the critic has consistently been understood as embodying a key political figure: in the eighteenth century, an enlightened king; in the nineteenth, a free citizen; in the twentieth, a state bureaucrat. Implicit in this scheme is a belief that there is something inescapably political about what the critic does—that every act of judgment tests one's ability as a member of society to submit vol-untarily to the authority of the law. We are almost shocked at how often the critics of every age have compared bad criticism to bad citizenship until we remember how often we are told today, by very well-meaning people who surely have our best interests at heart, that criticism prepares us to be "global citizens." In this regard, criticism has long been an ap-prenticeship in thoughtful obedience; its grand historical function has been to make a world without authority entirely inconceivable.

Yet here we are, conceiving of it. Our institutions are crumbling, our sense of civic duty is eroding, our temporal authorities believe they are above the law—so we are told, and with increasing panic, by the keep-ers of the liberal flame. What comes next? "To live in a political realm with neither authority nor the concomitant awareness that the source of authority transcends power and those who are in power," wrote Arendt in 1954, "means to be confronted anew, without the religious trust in a sacred beginning and without the protection of traditional and therefore self-evident standards of behavior, by the elementary problems of human living-together." This was in the first place a sober warning about the rise of totalitarianism—a horrifying vacuum of authority that had been filled with genocidal violence. One can also hear her admiration for the secular religiosity of the American founding fathers, who had managed in her view to reproduce the ancient authority of the Roman Senate in the form of the Supreme Court, the highest literary critic in the land, in which we have lost all confidence today.

It seems to me that if criticism has for so long been a testing ground for authority, we might also ask it to be a testing ground for—well, the absence of it. I do not mean we must strike the word *authority* from our lexicon, or that we must repudiate the authoritative style wherever we encounter it. (I have striven here for just such a thing!) But as a governing concept for criticism, we must admit that authority is an incoherent, inconsistent, and altogether *empty* thing. After all, doing without authority would not mean doing without scholarship, tradition, history, wit, or charisma; for, as we have seen, critics have spent a tremendous amount of time and energy asserting that such things are *not* authority at all. This is good news: if authority has always been at risk of disappearing from criticism, then we shall not have much to miss. But we will have to reckon with our *longing* for authority: our nostalgia, which is the opposite of historical sense; and our idealism, which is the opposite of the future. Nothing may be more dangerous, in criticism or in politics, than the revanchist desire to restore a form of authority that, if we are being honest, never existed in the first place. The great enemy is not the king of France, whose bloody head has been rolling through the streets for as long as anyone can remember. The enemy, my friends, is Napoleon.

2024

V

Holier Than Thou

If you have ever worked with one, you'll know that assholes don't respond well to input. "Coaxing something up there, into the light, can take all day," reports the narrator of Ottessa Moshfegh's "Brom," a 2017 short story about a shut-in feudal lord who spends his days easing foreign objects into his rectum. His name for this practice is *illumination*. "A few things I've managed to illuminate," he tells us, "are worth noting: a small bottle of sherry, my sister's confirmation crown which I snatched from its velveteen case and hammered down straight and flat, a rabbit's foot, a brass corkscrew, an ivory penknife." Brom, you see, believes his colon houses the light of God, safely concealed from his serfs, whom he torments, and his servant girl, whom he imprisons and feeds horse manure. But no man who lighteth a candle hideth it under a bushel, and in the end, hoping to work a miracle on his dying mother, Brom will demand his anus be cut open with a sword.

Moshfegh has dedicated her career to writing about assholes: cruel, pathetic people who do cruel, pathetic things. But the acclaimed author has also spent the last decade writing about the anus. Her early literary fiction is dotted with scatological detail: a smear of bird shit, an anal dildo, buckets for defecating in; ass-to-mouth play, sodomy with a broken bottle, a colostomy bag full of digested Mexican food. Moshfegh's 2015 debut novel, the noirish *Eileen*, follows a laxative-abusing secretary at a boys' prison who stumbles into a mystery involving nightly enemas and anal rape. The book won the PEN/Hemingway Award and was short-listed for the Booker Prize; critics praised it for being a Trojan horse, a study in human depravity hiding in the bowels of a commercial thriller.

Mainstream success did nothing to soften Moshfegh's stomach for bodily functions. If anything, it made her cheekier. The beautiful protagonist of her 2018 novel, *My Year of Rest and Relaxation*, embarks on her quest to sleep for a year by shitting directly onto the floor of the fancy art gallery that employs her. It's tempting to chalk up the butt stuff to a fixation that Moshfegh says dates back to her twenties. The "Marquis de Sade says anal sex is best when the ass is full of shit," she once wrote to a man who had asked her out for ice cream. "What do you think?" Like Sade, Moshfegh also has a philosophical interest in human waste. She finds in it not just pleasure and shock but a serious analogy for the literary act, which she has described as a cycle of defecation and coprophagia. "In writing, I think a lot about how to shit," she once advised her fellow fiction writers. "What kind of stink do I want to make in the world? My new shit becomes the shit I eat."

Moshfegh's latest piece of shit is called *Lapvona*, a dark medieval farce about a woebegone hamlet in quasi-historical Eastern Europe. In the village of Lapvona, shit is everywhere: in the air, in the earth, splattered onto clothes, and crusted onto bodies. "Lapvona dirt is good dirt," the villagers tell one another, referring to the fecundity of the local soil, but when drought strikes, they will resort to eating dried-out cakes of animal dung as well as the dirt itself. Meanwhile, at the manor on the hill, servants fertilize the lord's vegetables with fecal matter from the lord's chamber pots and feed the lord's livestock hay grown in his own ordure. The lord himself, a pervert with no interest in governing, makes his servant girl catch shit-stained grapes in her mouth and present her rump for sniffing. "Cabbage, and something a bit worse than that. Shit, I guess," he discerns. His priest offers the less vulgar term *excrement*. "Excrement," the lord ponders. "Is that like sacrament?"

For Moshfegh, the answer is yes. These days, the leading coprophile of American letters is seeking the sacred. This is no contradiction. "The sacred world depends on limited acts of transgression," wrote the French intellectual Georges Bataille, himself a writer of smut. Think, for example, of the Catholic ritual of the Eucharist, in which the faithful take the body of God in their mouths. But Moshfegh's own sacraments involve a different orifice, so you will forgive her if her search has led her up her own ass. Like the Hebrew holy of holies, the anal canal has two veils—an outer sphincter and an inner one—and its interior is known in formal anatomy as a *lumen*, the Latin word for "light." More than ever, Moshfegh wants to illuminate us. The question is if we'll fit.

Disgusting, I know. Eileen, of *Eileen*, so disgusts herself that she fantasizes about being impaled by a falling icicle: "Perhaps it would have soared down my throat, scraping the vacuous center of my body—I liked to picture these things—and followed through to my guts, finally parting my nether regions like a glass dagger." Of course, readers like to picture these things too. This is the pleasure of reading Moshfegh at her best: letting her plunge something sharp down your throat before you have a chance to gag. She likes to file her metaphors down to a point: a discarded pair of pumps become "two dead crows," fingers clutch a notebook "like the legs of a lizard grappling a rock." Her observations can have the shock of ice water: "He always hid his shame and self-loathing under an expression of shame and self-loathing." Moshfegh prefers to write in a claustrophobic first-person voice, jamming readers up against her characters' darkest thoughts. The narrator of *My Year of Rest and Relaxation* sullenly accompanies her hated best friend to her mother's funeral. "I felt as though she were a stranger I had hit with my car," she coolly reports, "and I was waiting for her to die so she wouldn't be able to identify me." Even the mild-mannered widow who tries to solve a delusional murder case in Moshfegh's 2020 novel, *Death in Her Hands*, can't help imagining grisly ends for the "dull heifers" she sees buying junk food at the grocery store.

As a result, critics have occasionally attempted to locate Moshfegh within the imaginary debate over "unlikable" female characters that has dribbled like a chronic nosebleed down the internet's face since 2013, when the novelist Claire Messud upbraided an interviewer for asking if she would want to be "friends" with her rage-filled female narrator. Two years later, during press for *Eileen*, Moshfegh dismissed the "hoopla" over Messud's novel and rightly declared, to the apparent surprise of one interviewer, that she didn't find Eileen "unpleasant" to begin with. It is wrong to say that Moshfegh writes unlikable characters for the simple reason that many people *do* like them quite a bit; her commercial success testifies to a widespread hunger for having one's appetite ruined. This is often the premise of Moshfegh's fiction: disgust does not preclude delight—and, in fact, it often enhances it.

At first glance, *Lapvona* is the most disgusting thing Moshfegh has ever written. The novel begins with the slaughter of two small children by bandits; their devastated grandfather, Grigor, cuts off a captured bandit's ear and throws it to the birds. Unbeknownst to the villagers, the bandits answer to Villiam, the sadistic lord whose well-appointed manor overlooks Lapvona. In the nearby forest, a slow, misshapen shepherd boy named Marek finds relief from his father's abuse by suckling at the withered teat of Ina, a blind witch who will later gouge out the eyes of a horse to restore her own vision. But when Marek impulsively murders the lord's boastful son, Villiam decides to adopt him instead of punishing him, setting off a cascade of misfortunes.

Yet Moshfegh's trusty razor can feel oddly blunted in *Lapvona*. In part, her characteristic incisiveness is dulled by her decision to forgo the first person in favor of more than a dozen centers of consciousness. This diminishment is also a curious effect of Lapvona itself. The author has always favored vaguely drawn settings, but in the past, with a few exceptions, her stories took place against a backdrop of middle-class America. *Eileen* may refer to her frozen New England suburb only as X-Ville, but her graphic bathroom habits draw their shock value from their proximity to her neighbors' "perfect, neat colonials," which she views with both envy and suspicion. But feudalism features neither polite society nor good taste; there is raw power but little plausible authority. Like a certain Camelot, Lapvona is a silly place, managed by a mostly illiterate priest who pretends to speak Latin and a fatuous lord whose greatest joy is forcing his servants to do comic impressions of him. There is no nice side of town; there is no indoor plumbing. You cannot *épater le bourgeois* without an actual bourgeoisie, and when the malnourished serfs of Lapvona start munching on their neighbors and raping nuns, it's easy not to be offended.

Then again, that may not be the point. Moshfegh may be a cynic, but she has never been a proper satirist—that would require an ideology. Lapvona is the clearest indication yet that the desired effect of Moshfegh's fiction is not shock but sympathy. Like Hamlet, she must be cruel in order to be kind. Her protagonists are gross and abrasive because they have already begun to molt; peel back their blistering misanthropy and you will find lonely, sensitive people who are in this world but not of it, desperate to transform, ascend, escape. True, their methods are alarming. The sleeper in *My Year of Rest and Relaxation* binges sedatives; the widow skitters into paranoid fantasy; Eileen skips town with a kidnapped woman in her car. But as Moshfegh's characters sift through the shit that, like all humans, they carry inside them everywhere they go, they catch a glimpse of something stranger, beautiful even: another world, another way to live. The Lapvonans know this entity as God. They wander their bit of earth looking for God in the filthiest places: They see his love in physical abuse, his faithfulness in starvation, his creation in rape. But their belief is more than a delusion or a heartless trick of the clergy; it is, for Moshfegh, an expression of the divine within each of them, slowly churning, building bulk, until the fateful day it demands to be let out.

At least, this is one explanation for Moshfegh's animosity. There is another: animus. A few critics have complained of gratuitous levels of violence and rancor in her fiction, and it's easy to see why. The self-hating narrator of Moshfegh's experimental novella *McGlue*, set in 1851, makes lavish use of the slur *faggot*, despite the fact that its homophobic sense is not attested until the 1910s. Moshfegh has a similarly blithe relationship to physical deformity: Marek, a child of incest, has a crooked spine, a protruding rib cage, and a distorted skull as well as what we moderns might call an intellectual disability. Moshfegh herself might call him *retarded*, a word that several of her characters brandish like a tiny flag of rebellion. She appears to defend the choice in her short-story collection, *Homesick for Another World*, in which a caregiver at an assisted-living facility reassures readers, "You can call them 'retarded'—that word doesn't offend me as long as it's used the proper way, without pity." Of course, it never is. "How does it feel to be a middle-aged divorcée living with your retarded nephew and working in a computer café?" one character texts his crush. "Is it everything you ever dreamed?"

To be fair, Moshfegh has never tried to defend her characters on moral grounds. She intends that they be outsiders, freaks, malcontents. "I let them say what they want," she told one interviewer. "Usually they're saying something too honest." The effect can be powerful. After Eileen casually humiliates a young woman who is visiting her rapist, she reflects, "I suppose I may have been envious. No one had ever tried to rape me." The sentence slices through you like an icicle—the wit of it, the horror, the heartbreak, the audacity of such poor taste—and the pieces melt away before you can decide how it made you feel. In *My Year of Rest and Relaxation*, the orphaned narrator mentally flicks away her mother's suicide note by calling it "totally unoriginal." The quip is devastating not least because there really is something cliché about the grandeur of depression—and there really isn't a right time to bring it up. If this is what Moshfegh means when she speaks of telling people "the truth they don't want to hear," then good: she is well within the remit of all the best fiction, which rightly holds up a sharp pin for our worst angels to dance on.

But then there is the matter of weight. "I had a thing about fat people," confides one narrator. "It was the same thing I had about skinny people: I hated their guts." Moshfegh's characters are almost universally obsessed with body mass, and their loathing for the "obese" is startlingly vicious and remarkably consistent. The author's first short story, written at the age of thirteen, began like this: "I killed a man this morning. He was fat and ugly and deserved to die." In her mature fiction, fat people—almost always women—are compared to "cows," "hogs," a "sack of apples," a "clapping seal," a "water bed." In two different novels, they are imagined as farm animals awaiting slaughter. They have "huge bloated hands," "swollen thighs," and "throats like frogs," and they waddle around on "thick ankles" that seem "about to snap." They eat "cheesecake" and "hollandaise" and "caramel popcorn"; they eat "a donut" (*Eileen*) or "doughnuts" (*Homesick for Another World*) or "trays of donuts" (*My Year of Rest and Relaxation*) or "what must have been a dozen chocolate-covered donuts" (*Death in Her Hands*). They are "pitiful," "repugnant," "miserable," "lazy," "idiotic" "gluttons." They sit there stupidly, "oozing slowly toward death with every breath."

In literary criticism, we call this a pattern. The funny thing is, this level of verbal abuse could probably be justified if Moshfegh's stories demonstrated even a passing interest in the lives of fat people. But Moshfegh, who has spoken candidly of her struggle with bulimia and recently walked the runway for Maryam Nassir Zadeh at New York Fashion Week, does not write about fat people. She writes about coldhearted, disgusting, strangely sympathetic people slouching toward warped ideas of self-improvement who also happen to be emphatically, existentially thin. A few have actual eating disorders; the rest suffer from orthorexia of the spirit, obsessing over the purity of what they put in their souls. Their fantasies of wellness extend to Moshfegh herself, who speaks of fiction as a kind of ethical colon cleanse: "People should be as hostile as they want in their writing. Do it there, don't do it out in the world to other people." Indeed, if one *did* harbor personal animus, putting it into the mouths of a few loathsome fictional characters would be a clever way to have your cake without the calories.

Moshfegh, for her part, does not believe any topic should be off the table. She is flattered by comparisons to Vladimir Nabokov—she would like to have written *Lolita* herself—and one of her favorite writers is Charles Bukowski, whom she praises for saying "the shit everybody thinks and nobody says." She is an admirer of *American Psycho* author Bret Easton Ellis, in whom she detects a "delicate, invisible layer of self-awareness" often absent in readers. Ironically, Ellis has come to resemble a Moshfegh character in recent years: perpetually resentful, laughably unaware of his own irrelevance. In 2018, Moshfegh joined Ellis on his podcast, where he spends the twilight of his career tilting at millennial windmills. He complained to Moshfegh that literary prizes were being handed out to Black writers who hadn't earned them; she, referring to a book project set in early 1900s San Francisco, told a chuckling Ellis, "If things continue in the way that they are culturally right now, nobody can say shit about my next protagonist because she's a Chinese cross-dresser. You just try to tell me *she's* disgusting." (The book in question has mercifully yet to appear.)

This is as political as Moshfegh ever gets in public. She alludes cryptically to easily offended "people on the internet" and has refused to be called a feminist, suggesting to one interviewer that "men have been turned into children and are no longer allowed to be angry or macho or have opinions or be lustful or masculine anymore." In her own fiction, the novelist is most comfortable avoiding politics altogether. Of course it is perfectly fine not to write political novels. But if Moshfegh has no distinct political beliefs of her own, this has not spared her the inconvenience of the fact that other people do. This attitude makes sense in a writer who has passionately argued that art should free the mind, not

improve society. Last summer, Moshfegh made her case in a widely circulated missive:

> A novel is not BuzzFeed or NPR or Instagram or even Holly-
> wood. Let's get clear about that. A novel is a literary work of art
> meant to expand consciousness. We need novels that live in an
> amoral universe, past the political agenda described on social
> media. We have imaginations for a reason. Novels like *American
> Psycho* and *Lolita* did not poison culture. Murderous corpora-
> tions and exploitive industries did. We need characters in novels
> to be free to range into the dark and wrong. How else will we
> understand ourselves?

This is all well and good; it has the pleasing shape of radical sentiment
without the encumbrance of any actual political commitments. In reality, it is very easy to oppose the banning of a book like *Lolita* while
also pointing out that the author of *American Psycho* is a sundowning
reactionary. But Moshfegh seems to believe that unsettling moral per-
spectives are better found in novels than in readers. For her, the threat
to the novel is posed not by murderous corporations, which are merely
window dressing here, but by a sinister "political agenda" found, like all
political agendas, in the swarming tweets of strangers. The substance of
that agenda is easy to guess—social justice, both real and imagined—
but what Moshfegh really means is what most successful artists mean
when they speak vaguely about the value of art: the absolute indignity of
being told what to do.

Beneath all the bluster, the only political enemies Moshfegh openly
acknowledges are commercialism and agitprop—that is, the desecration
of art by money and power. The narrator of *My Year of Rest and Relaxation* speaks with uncharacteristic reverence of the "ineffable quality of
art as a sacred human ritual" and laments the art world's enslavement to
"political trends and the persuasions of capitalism." She scoffs at a series
of huge, ejaculate-covered canvases by an artist with the cachet of being
Asian American: "He titled the abstract paintings as though each had
some deep, dark political meaning. *Blood-Dimmed Tide*, and *Wintertime
in Ho Chi Minh City* and *Sunset over Sniper Alley*. *Decapitated Palestinian*

Child. Bombs Away, Nairobi. It was all nonsense, but people loved it."
The narrator eventually quits her gallery job by relieving herself on the
floor and stuffing her used Kleenex into the artist's latest installation;
later, well-rested, she visits the Met, where she presses her palm into an
oil painting of a fruit bowl just to prove that "beauty and meaning had
nothing to do with each other." This kind of sacrilege is purifying, not
destructive; it constitutes a limited act of transgression that, like a fecal
transplant, only contaminates the space of art in order to restore it, now
teeming with life, to its original state of health.

This is why we all shit: to be renewed. Everything else—money, political ideology, institutions of all kinds—is a distraction from the fundamental unity of shit and spirit. "We are spiritual and we're human
poop machines," Moshfegh says. "We are divine and we are disgusting.
We're having these incredible lives and then we're going to be dead and
rot in the ground." But few can grasp the enormity of the truth. Out of
all the villagers seeking spiritual awakening in Lapvona, only one gets
close. At sixty-four, Grigor is the oldest and most devout man in the village. When the bandits murder his young grandchildren, he grieves and
asks God to protect their souls. But the summer drought, during which
he survives on leeches and clay from the lake, changes Grigor. He questions how the local lord had food and water during the drought, why the
bandits have never tried to pillage the lord's manor, why God would let
them steal from the poor. Angry and confused, he visits Ina, who opens
his mind with cannabis and nurses him at the breast. "I finally heard the
truth," he tells his daughter-in-law. He imagines leading a revolt against
the lord, but deep in his heart he knows that political remedies are a
fantasy. Instead, Grigor is left with the thwarted liberation of knowing
that the world he lives in is a "sham."

Moshfegh claims to have discovered this secret in kindergarten
when, during a lesson on clock-reading, she realized that she, along with
everyone she knew, was going to die. "Since I was five," she writes in a
rare bit of nonfiction, "all of life has been like a farce, an absurd performance of a reality based on meaningless drivel, or a devastating experience of trauma and fatigue, deep with meaning, which has led me into
such self-seriousness that I often wonder if I am completely insane." The
conviction was strong enough to form the basis of a much-noted short

story in *Homesick for Another World* about a little girl who believes that, if she kills the correct person, she will be returned to the secret world she has been separated from since birth. "I don't know what it is," the girl admits. "But it certainly isn't this place, here on Earth, with all you silly people."

For all its technical mastery, there remains something deeply juvenile about Moshfegh's fiction, colored in with an existential discomfort that the author has not updated since childhood. There were, of course, reasons for the young Moshfegh to feel this way. Her mother was born in then-Yugoslavia; her father belongs to a wealthy family of Iranian Jews whose assets were seized during the 1979 revolution. The couple fled Tehran and ended up in Newton, Massachusetts, the affluent suburb of Boston. Moshfegh grew up lower-middle-class, and she remembers feeling ashamed of the "jalopies" her parents drove around town, one of which was so rusted that "I could watch the ground pass through the hole between my feet."

Class is a frequent theme in her fiction—that detail about a rusty car reappeared in a recent short story—but Moshfegh has no interest in class critique, turning her grade-school scissors instead to a paper-thin picture of "normal people." She is against phonies of all tax brackets, not the commodity form; she means to *widen* consciousness, not raise it. "I just want people to wake up," she has said. In the shocking coda to *My Year of Rest and Relaxation*, the rejuvenated narrator watches footage of what appears to be her unbearably normal best friend, a corporate assistant obsessed with fitting in, leaping from a World Trade Center building on September 11. This is not a searing commentary of political violence but a metaphor for the narrator's enlightened quietism: "There she is," she says admiringly, "a human being, diving into the unknown, and she is wide awake."

By the end of *Lapvona*, a different edifice has been torn down. The village church is dismantled stone by stone by a foreign lord, and no one prays anymore. Moshfegh has said that she could never belong to a religious community herself—too many rules—but she does still believe in God, whom she understands as "the intelligence of the universe." So does Grigor: "Didn't they know that the land was God itself, the sun and moon and rain, that it was all God?" he asks himself. "The life in their seeds of wheat, the manure from the cow, that was God." Desperate to know if "something sacred" remains in Lapvona, Grigor returns to Ina. "Forget that church," the healer tells him. Then Ina takes his hand and commands him to open his heart:

> Grigor's whole arm was pulsating now. His heart beat power-fully in his chest. Ina took him by the other hand, too. He could not fight. She overpowered him, and the force of God entered his body like a rash spreading across his skin, and he felt his heart surge, then stop. He waited for it to start again. He looked at Ina in the eye.
>
> "If you don't let God into your heart, you'll die," Ina said. "That's what kills people. Not time or disease. Now, open up."

Like the art-touching scene at the end of *My Year of Rest and Relaxation*, Ina's miracle is a clear allegory for the very novel it concludes—all the way down to the motif of the hand, which might as well be holding a pen. Moshfegh describes her writing process as an ecstatic experience of "channeling a voice," and she has often expressed a desire to "be pure and real and make whatever is coming to me from God." The epigraph to *Lapvona*, "I feel stupid when I pray," is taken from a Demi Lovato song about feeling abandoned by God. But the phrase also recalls Mosh-fegh herself, who imagines that her "destiny" is to reach into readers and transmit the divine. "My mind is so dumb when I write," she told an early interviewer. "I just write down what the voice has to say." In other words, there's a reason God isn't listening: he's busy praying to people like Moshfegh.

That's a nice thought. It must be convenient to believe in a God whose theological features consist in giving you divine permission to write whatever you want. But even with all the authority of heaven behind her, Moshfegh would rather preach righteousness to an empty chapel than break bread with the weak and the blind. This is the problem with writ-ing to wake people up: your ideal reader is inevitably asleep. Even if such readers exist, there is no reason to write books for them—not because novels are for the elite but because the first assumption of every novel must be that the reader will infinitely exceed it. Fear of the reader, not of

God, is the beginning of literature. Deep down, Moshfegh knows this. "If I didn't like what I read, I could throw the book across the room. I could burn it in my fireplace. I could rip out the pages and use them to blow my nose," observes the widow of *Death in Her Hands*. Yet the novelist continues to write as if her readers are fundamentally beneath her; as if they, unlike her, have never stopped to consider that the world may be bullshit; as if they must be steered, tricked, or cajoled into knowledge by those whom the universe has seen fit to appoint as their shepherds.

It's a shame. Moshfegh dirt is good dirt. But the author of *Lapvona* is not an iconoclast; she is a nun. Behind the carefully cultivated persona of arrogant genius, past the disgusting pleasures of her fiction and bland heresies of her politics, wedged just above her not inconsiderable talent, there sits a small, hardened lump of piety. She may truly be a great American novelist one day, if only she learns to be less important. Until then, Moshfegh remains a servant of the highest god there is: herself.

2022

Big Cry Country

In the first place, *Yellowstone* is not a good show. But that's no pebble in its hoof. Since premiering on the little-known Paramount Network in 2018, the neo-western drama has grown into the most-watched scripted series on cable or broadcast television. The show, which co-creator Taylor Sheridan writes, produces, and often directs, stars Kevin Costner as a fifth-generation Montana cattleman fighting to defend his ranch from threats on every side: land developers, Native activists, biker gangs, U.S. Fish and Wildlife, paid assassins, people from California. The fourth season drew an average of 11.3 million viewers, according to Nielsen data, clocking in below *Thursday Night Football* but above *Monday Night Football*—rawhide sandwiched between pigskins—and a staggering seventeen million tuned in for the fifth-season premiere in November. But critics have largely ignored it. "It's every old western and new western and soap opera thrown together in a blender," Sheridan told *The New York Times* in 2021. "I think it infuriates and confounds some people who study storytelling."

So it does. Costner turns in a muted performance as the wealthy cattle baron John Dutton III, who is more gravel than gravitas. He and his fellow Duttons—from venomous daughter Beth to wary Native daughter-in-law Monica—speak by trading dour maxims about human nature. Meanwhile, the vast Yellowstone Ranch may be "the size of Rhode Island," but it is covered in plot holes the size of Providence. In the first episode, the eldest Dutton son, Lee, is killed in an armed skirmish at the nearby Indian reservation; he is almost never mentioned again. Sheridan prefers violent tableaux to traditional diegesis: People are shot, hanged, gored, trampled, burned alive, and, in one memorable case,

fatally bitten by an airborne rattlesnake. The Duttons murder in such
great volume they have a designated canyon in Wyoming for dumping
bodies. None of this saves *Yellowstone* from having the narrative propul-
sion of a glacier; on the contrary, the constant but rarely consequential
violence heightens the impression that nothing ever happens. After a
Dutton scion strangles a nosy girl reporter from "*The New York Magazine*," her death is improbably staged to look like a kayaking accident.
The magazine never follows up.

In real life, the media tend to wield *Yellowstone* like a sociological
prop, pointing to its heartland appeal and low critical esteem as an indictment of out-of-touch coastal elites. (*The New York Times*, in what
amounts to self-parody, recently assembled a politically diverse group of
fans to find out why people love the show so much.) Really, *Yellowstone*
is popular for the normal reasons: it's a rural crime drama with high
production values and A-list talent, like *Ozark* at higher elevation. Par-
amount+ has already released two prequel series about earlier Dutton
generations, *1883* and *1923*, and there are plans for several more spin-
offs. (Not a moment too soon: following rumors of an ego-driven feud
between Costner and Sheridan, Paramount has announced *Yellowstone*
itself will end when the current season concludes.)

Sheridan reportedly agreed to a nine-figure Paramount+ deal in order to finance his purchase of the historic Four Sixes Ranch, a massive
cattle ranch in Texas featured in the show's fourth season. This is a bit
like if David Simon had created *The Wire* in order to sell drugs. On
Yellowstone, no effort is made to avoid the appearance of self-dealing:
Sheridan cameos as the muscle-bound cowboy Travis, showing off his
reining skills while wearing novelty tees that say things like BEEN DOING
COWBOY SHIT ALL DAY. Travis's pickup truck bears the brand of the real-
life Bosque Ranch, another Sheridan property, where the showrunner reportedly charges Paramount $50,000 a week to shoot as well as $2,000 a
head for the show's growing stable of horses. A particularly bizarre scene
finds the usually rancorous Beth (Kelly Reilly) calling up the Four Sixes
Ranch while perusing steaks you may buy on the ranch's actual website.
"Is this the number to order beef?" she asks politely.

This could all be pulpy fun—the fistfights, the melodrama, even the
brazen self-promotion—if only Sheridan had the good sense to aspire to

less. The creator has the same literary ambitions of any TV auteur, along with a desire to philosophize; his views have ironically been obscured by the "debate" over whether *Yellowstone* represents a triumph of red-state populism. But the show's focus on white-male resentment hardly distinguishes it from other prestige fare—sure, *Yellowstone* is about mad men, but so was *Mad Men*. Sheridan's particular brand of white crisis is not Trumpism, with its bottomless well of victimization. ("Can we just impeach that motherfucker right now?" he said in a 2017 interview.) Nor does *Yellowstone* quite endorse the "great replacement theory" of white nationalism normalized by the likes of Tucker Carlson. Sheridan is principally a moral thinker; if he does have a political ideology, it comes from the *left*. "The show's talking about the displacement of Native Americans," Sheridan told *The Atlantic*, referring to *Yellowstone*'s fictional Broken Rock Indian Reservation, whose members fight ferociously to reclaim their stolen homeland. "That's a red-state show?"

We should believe him. In fact, the whole moral vision of *Yellowstone* is founded on a tendentious equivalence between the genocide of Native peoples and the present-day encroachments on the Duttons' way of life. Sheridan has effectively allotted a place for white resentment *within* a larger critique of settler colonialism. If the show's white characters fear replacement, this is because they are closely identified with the very people they first replaced; the settler has co-opted the language of settlement. On *Yellowstone*, it is the cowboy whose land is now being taken away from him, the cowboy who is now being killed and raped. This forces the cowboy, like the Indian before him, into a posture of existential authenticity; he stands outside the laws of men and sees them for the many guises of empire, land theft, and corporate greed that they are. Cowboys, Sheridan seems to be saying, can be colonized too. In the show's horse-eat-horse world, where no one has a right to anything, the last Indian is the cowboy himself.

Sheridan himself is only part cowboy. The son of a cardiologist father, he grew up weekending at his mother's ranch outside of Waco, Texas; after the divorce, she overleveraged the ranch and lost it. (Sheridan didn't speak to her for years.) At first a frustrated actor—he had a recurring role as a sheriff on FX's *Sons of Anarchy*—Sheridan was in his forties when he sold his first script, *Sicario*, a critically acclaimed thriller set at the Mexican border. He followed that with the Oscar-nominated screenplay for *Hell or High Water*, a film about two Texan brothers who rob banks to save their late mother's ranch from foreclosure. These were vibe-y action films where the slow accumulation of mood was suddenly interrupted by brutal, inglorious violence; they owed much to the bleak existentialism of *No Country for Old Men*, the Coen brothers' 2007 adaptation of the Cormac McCarthy novel. In his film work, Sheridan's worst impulses were curbed by collaborators like *Sicario* director Denis Villeneuve, whose cool minimalism counterbalanced the script's tendency to pontificate. But on *Yellowstone*, Sheridan has demanded what a recent profile called a "maniacal" degree of creative control. In particular, he has eschewed writers' rooms, with the result that every character in the *Yellowstone* universe speaks in the same blunt, peremptory vernacular.

Nonetheless, Sheridan appears to conceive of himself as a kind of cowboy-poet. As a young man, he picked up Gretel Ehrlich's *The Solace of Open Spaces*, a 1986 essay collection by a Wyoming ranch hand. The book left such an impression that Sheridan has John Dutton quote it from memory: "True solace is finding none, which is to say it's everywhere." But Sheridan's own aphorisms come up short. "No, solace must be discovered," John adds nonsensically. *Yellowstone* is full of horse-lipped attempts at cowboy lyricism, ranging from the folksy—"You're either born a willow or you're born an oak"—to the sappy—"Secrets are like a callus on your heart"—to the utterly bovine: "There's no such thing as good men. All men are bad." The idea here is that cowboying produces its own moral knowledge; the Duttons speak in truisms because they live within roping distance of the Truth. But one often feels Sheridan is trying, by poetical brute force, to reverse-engineer wisdom from sheer prosody. "There's two roads in life: One is you're winning or learning, and the other is you're losing all the way to the fuckin' grave," rumbles the ranch manager. This is clearly three roads.

For a better sense of *Yellowstone*'s moral imagination, viewers may turn to Beth, John's only daughter, a ruthless corporate raider on whom *Yellowstone*, in lieu of the frontier, frequently relies for some semblance of life-threatening stakes. "You are the trailer park. I am the tornado," she hisses at a financier in a coffee shop. She is a fan favorite, her would-be withering one-liners adorning official T-shirts and stemless wineglasses.

("I hope you die of ass cancer," she snarls at someone else.) *The Atlantic* recently called Beth "that too-rare figure in the world of prestige TV: an antihero who is also a woman." Critics often remark that Beth can spit, drink, and fight with the best of them, but it should be obvious by this point in the history of TV criticism that only a woman can be written "like a man." (Men are just *written*.) More interesting is the fact that Beth is written as a dude, as in *dude ranch*: a city slicker who shops by "calling the sales manager at Gucci and having her fill a box the size of a fucking refrigerator." Reilly herself is English, and she cannot do an American accent, in particular the short *a* sound found in such words as *ranch* and *Montana*. She compensates for this by delivering every line in an erotic whisper or a hysterical shriek. It is quite simply one of the worst performances on television.

Yellowstone posits Beth as an admirable moral outlaw. "What it must feel like to be that free," her father marvels. As a teenager, Beth received an involuntary hysterectomy; now she rides wild and violent through morality's untamed frontier, liberated by her suffering. (For Sheridan, lady trauma almost always concerns ruined motherhood.) "I subscribe to Nietzsche's thoughts on right and wrong," Beth tells her boyfriend. "I believe in loving with your whole soul and destroying anything that wants to kill what you love." Aside from being terrible dialogue, this is a basic misunderstanding of Nietzsche. For that philosopher, *good* and *evil* were labels created by people who, too weak to form their own values, define themselves by condemning the values of others. "While every noble morality develops from a triumphant affirmation of itself, slave morality from the outset says No to what is 'outside,' what is 'different,' what is 'not itself,'" he wrote in *On the Genealogy of Morals*. By this reckoning, Beth is a perfect Nietzschean slave, a woman whose identity consists entirely of the "submerged, darkly glowering emotions of vengefulness and hatred." She has no values, just grudges. She assaults a woman with a beer bottle for hitting on her boyfriend; she sends another woman to prison for sleeping with her father, whom she still calls "Daddy."

This is not freedom; it is compulsive aggrievement. Beth is the un-leashed unconscious of *Yellowstone*, acting out her family's darkest patterns of grievance; the narcissism that she openly flaunts, they dress up in the language of land and legacy. "As we speak, they're raping the land our family has bled into for more than a century," John growls, even though after five seasons his enemies have barely touched the ranch. The Duttons are a dynasty of losers, in spirit if rarely in practice; their family history is a vast tapestry of hallucinatory persecutions. "Violence has always haunted this family," croons John's ancestor Elsa, a pioneer girl who migrates with her fellow Duttons from Texas to Montana in *1883*. She's not all wrong: the first Duttons face off with bandits, hostile Lakota, and an actual tornado. But if they were innocent in that prequel series—and they weren't, since James Dutton was a Confederate officer, a detail Sheridan drops in but never reckons with—the family's modern descendants hoard their losses as greedily as they do the land. This, not cattle farming, is the land's true purpose: to give the Duttons something to bleed into.

This applies especially to Elsa herself, an ur-Beth whose burial literally establishes the Yellowstone Ranch in *1883*. For that series, Sheridan drew heavily on Larry McMurtry's Pulitzer Prize–winning novel *Lonesome Dove*, about two retired lawmen who drive cattle from Texas to Montana. Both tales end with a protagonist dying of an infected arrow wound following a brutal Indian ambush. In *Lonesome Dove*, the dead man's partner abandons his newly founded Montana ranch to bury his friend in Texas; in *1883*, James Dutton desperately rides *into* Montana with a fading Elsa, having resolved to stake out his allotment wherever she dies. The divergence is telling: the lawman arguably dies for nothing—his loyal partner ends up right where he started with no plans of returning north—whereas Elsa's grave serves to consecrate the land, justifying the act of settlement and providing future Duttons with a monument to their family's abiding martyrdom. This shift may have been inevitable. A troubled McMurtry once observed, regarding his novel's romantic reception, that "instead of a poor-man's *Inferno*, filled with violence, faithlessness, and betrayal, I had actually delivered a kind of *Gone with the Wind* of the West." Sheridan, less worried, shunts the ambivalence of *Lonesome Dove*, at the last moment, into frank colonial sentimentality.

Colonization would come for the Duttons, too. Sheridan has said that *Yellowstone* is about "the gentrification of the West," a reference to the threat posed by corporate vultures and wealthy vacationers to the rancher's bucolic existence—which, aside from the hoofed bits, goes oddly undefined. But the Duttons themselves are landed gentry: They are defined by their crude, feudal relationship to power, and they even command their own militia, lightly disguised as a livestock commission. Their enemies are the grubbing mercantile class, presented as soulless parasites. ("Did seven generations of ranchers infuse six billion dollars into the economy?" asks the cold-blooded representative for a developer of ski resorts.) But John Dutton III refuses to be called rich, and he barely regards his land as a financial asset. Ownership is a legal fiction: He wants to *possess.* This is why the Yellowstone Ranch must be protected with guns, fences, and military-grade explosives; it is why John brandishes a loaded rifle at a busload of Chinese tourists trying to take photos of the view. "This is America," he bellows. "We don't share land here."

Sheridan wants us to hear the irony in that line, which is as much a colonial battle cry as the lowing of a dying breed. As a broke actor, Sheridan ended up driving to the Pine Ridge Indian Reservation in South Dakota, where he says he was invited to participate in ceremony. He based his third film, *Wind River,* on the death of a young Oglala woman, and he provided written testimony to the Senate Committee on Indian Affairs regarding missing and murdered Indigenous women. *Yellowstone* is regularly praised, even by those dern coastal elites, for the depth of its Native American representation. The members of the Confederated Tribes of Broken Rock are as ethically compromised as the white settlers. Tribal chairman Thomas Rainwater (Gil Birmingham, as usual too good for the role) plots to annex the Yellowstone from John by means of a dirty casino deal. "They share a real love for the land, and an intent to keep the land the way it is," Birmingham told the *Times.* John's Native daughter-in-law, Monica (Kelsey Asbille), puts it more directly. "When this land belonged to my people 150 years ago, children were stolen, men were killed, families herded away like cattle," she tells John after a neo-Nazi militia attack on the ranch. "And nothing's changed except you're the Indian now."

This is *Yellowstone*'s gambit: it grounds its defense of the cowboy way of life in an identification with the very Native peoples those cowboys dispossessed. Sheridan did not invent this idea; it is probably as old as the frontier itself, where the cowboy discovered in the Indian not just an enemy but a powerful metaphor for his own impending decline. "We'll be the Indians, if we last another twenty years," sighs the ill-fated lawman of *Lonesome Dove*. "I think we spent our best years fighting on the wrong side." Such sympathy is a defining feature of the revisionist western, supposedly a more morally ambiguous approach to the genre. The obvious example is Costner's Oscar-winning 1990 directorial debut, *Dances with Wolves*, about a white Union lieutenant who assimilates into a Lakota tribe, marrying a white woman raised within it. But the western has always borne the knowledge of its own illegitimacy: In John Ford's 1948 film *Fort Apache*, one of Sheridan's favorites, an arrogant cavalry officer dies in a suicidal charge against the impoverished Apache after refusing to treat them with diplomacy. What has changed, like the slow unfurling of a flag, is simply how explicitly this knowledge is conveyed. "I'd never really known who John Dunbar was," Costner's character reflects in *Dances with Wolves*, sloughing off the settler's guilt. "As I heard my Sioux name being called over and over, I knew for the first time who I really was."

Revised or not, the western has always been a drama of self-discovery, the Indian refracting the cowboy back to himself in the mode of historical tragedy. Sheridan basically writes his own version of *Dances with Wolves* into *1883*, where the free-spirited Elsa falls in love with a passing Comanche warrior who gives her the name Lightning With the Yellow Hair on account of her horsemanship and conspicuous blondeness. When she later is ambushed by Lakota, she shouts her Comanche name at her attackers, who lower their weapons in recognition—although too late to save her life. Call this the romance of Native defeat: Sheridan is eager throughout his work to capitalize on the pathos of white identification with the doomed Indian. If Elsa had only been wearing her beaded Comanche vest and fringed leggings, we surmise, the Lakota would have known her as a fellow Indian. The scene recalls *Hell or High Water*, which Sheridan originally titled *Comancheria* after the Spanish name for the Comanche sphere of influence. "We're like the Comanches, little brother! Lords of the plains!" whoops a bank robber fleeing the law. (He's shot in the head a few days later.)

Actual Native characters do not fare well in a moral universe where white people own the mineral rights to indigenous pain. In particular, Sheridan tends to treat Native women as sponges for historical trauma, before wringing them out on the white man's brow. Monica has endured brain damage, home invasion, attempted rape, police strip search, and a ludicrous car accident *during labor* that kills her newborn son. She is also terrifically dull, a one-dimensional scold whom the show trots out like a museum docent to remind viewers who was here first. (What is worse, the Eastern Band of Cherokee Indians has disputed Asbille's claim to Cherokee ancestry.) A more nuanced—and more graphic—version of Native suffering is found in the prequel series *1923*, where Chairman Rainwater's ancestor Teonna is forced to attend a boarding school run by nuns who beat and rape her. She eventually murders two of them, smashing in the head nun's face with a sack of Bibles. "Know I am the land," the girl whispers in Crow as she smothers her captor. "Know it is the land that is killing you." The atrocity of the Indian boarding schools has been well-documented of late, and somewhere in the torture porn is a welcome dose of anti-colonial violence. (It is enormously gratifying to watch that nun die.) But Sheridan is less interested in the politics of genocide than in the moral idea he can derive from it: When this is your reality—massacre, removal, destruction of culture—you do *whatever* it takes to survive.

In theory, this means *Yellowstone*'s vision of Native resistance is at least on equal footing with that of white grievance. In practice, though, Rainwater's machinations fade into the background as the show wears on, the chief demoted to a sort of spiritual adviser to Monica's white husband. What matters is the *idea* of Native oppression: In a bizarre travesty of the history of forced sterilization of Native women, we learn Beth's hysterectomy was performed at an Indian Health Services clinic. "We're all the descendants of the subjugated—every one of us," Monica declares in a lecture, the notion apparently being that her white students descend from the oppressed peasantry of medieval Europe. Violence levels all social strata; the moral landscape of Montana has not a single mountain. That the white settler was the agent of this violence, historically speaking, does not invalidate his own claim. "No one has a right," John tells a developer. "You have to take the right." Sheridan's language here recalls, in a typical dilution of his influences, the monstrous Indian-hunter of

Cormac McCarthy's *Blood Meridian*, who declares that conflicting parties must "petition directly the chambers of the historical absolute"—in other words, try to murder each other.

That this violence cannot be justified on moral grounds is precisely the point. In asserting their own version of indigenous sovereignty, the Duttons surrender any recourse to the law for protection or remedy. They have just themselves. Their precious freedom turns out to be a predatory loan that can be paid only in blood; the best they can hope for is to pass on this crushing existential debt to their children. For the settler, this is the true tragedy of the West: not Native genocide but the sundered promise of the colonial idea. As Ehrlich writes in *The Solace of Open Spaces*, "Disfigurement is synonymous with the whole idea of the frontier. As soon as we lay our hands on it, the freedom we thought it represented is quickly gone." Sheridan mistakes that irony for poignancy. "In this place where innocence is a mineral in the soil, the filth of our touch is an apocalypse," says Elsa in *1883*, as if she is already mourning the arrival of banks, oil wells, pour-over coffee. That didn't keep the Duttons from putting their grubby paws all over Montana territory—better their hands spoil it than anyone else's. But the cowboy, having instigated settlement, now blames everyone else for it. This makes him something of a masochist of history, forever forgetting how the West was really lost: by being won.

Oddly, *Yellowstone* may be proof of the exhaustion of settler colonialism as a concept. Scholars of Native studies have mixed feelings about the term, which can leave little space for Native power outside of saintly resilience or righteous vengeance, as Ned Blackhawk argues in *The Rediscovery of America*. Historians have recently debated, for instance, whether the Comanche represented an eighteenth-century imperial power in their own right. At least we should dispel the fatuous media narrative that *Yellowstone* is a win for Native American representation purely because it has given Native actors work—especially compared with excellent Native-helmed shows like AMC's *Dark Winds*, a pulpy detective story set in the Navajo Nation, and FX's teen comedy *Reservation Dogs*. The latter's sweet delinquents experience history not as God's paperweight but as a fractured, desultory mess that yields as much humor as grief: a spirit warrior who eats Tater Tots, a blessing that sounds like "Free Fallin'." These kids have no interest in the historical absolute; life has taught them there is no such thing.

As for the Duttons, there is always something unsettled about the settler—this is an internal fact of the colony, not a peripheral threat to it. One asks why the cowboy needed the Indian to make sense of himself in the first place; the simplest answer is that he coveted the exaltation of someone else's suffering. The truly maddening thing about *Yellowstone* is the endless pantomime of inherited necessity, as if generations of attempted land theft have purified the ranchers into historical automata. Of course, the Duttons *can* make choices; they just choose not to. But the kind of freedom that John Dutton III truly admires, the kind that Beth Dutton embodies, is not the freedom to make decisions—that is, ethical freedom—but rather the freedom to act as if one's decisions have all been made in advance. There are no nobler savages than the Duttons, whom their gods have not saddled with the inconvenience of a psychology. They are titanic nothings; they are ideas with guns.

This is the horseshoe-shaped irony of *Yellowstone*: the Duttons, who on paper should be champions of the right, in fact resemble the sentimental, naturally tragic, historically burdened figures who sometimes populate the left's theories of oppressed peoples. There is a real danger to overstating the existential stakes of political violence, not because lives are not at stake—we are speaking, after all, of genocide—but because the very concept of existence is an abstraction of life as the oppressed live it. It is only in the desert of existence that Sheridan can metabolize specific historical wrongs into a general theorem. The white people on *Yellowstone* are under threat not because they are white but just because they are people. It is a bitter irony: the colonizer, having finally extended humanity to the colonized, now uses his own humanity to claim common experience. So if *Yellowstone* has something to teach the left, it is not that some heartland majority is rejecting the woke consensus, or that political polarization is ruining our democracy, or that we must better grasp the roots of white resentment. It is this: Our ideas should be harder to steal. Right now, any cattle thief can do it.

2023

Since the entire Yellowstone *universe appears to exist largely to subsidize Taylor Sheridan's ranching habit, it seemed only appropriate that in my capacity as critic I should not only view every episode—a time of great personal suffering for me—but also sample the man's honest wares. A rib eye, a tenderloin, and a "striploin" (evidently a more exciting name for a New York strip) arrived at my doorstep in a Four Sixes–branded insulated tote bag, along with a cow sticker that said* EAT BEEF. *(The Four Sixes Grit & Glory Ranch Water hard seltzer was unfortunately not available for shipping.) For various reasons, my review-within-a-review did not make the final proof. I am now at liberty to tell you that the steaks tasted fine. I still use the tote.*

Sick Leave

Since Li was young, he and his mother have communicated best in writing. It began with their leaving handwritten notes around the house where he grew up, in Florida; now, even when he visits his parents' home in Taiwan, he still tends to write them emails from his room. Li, in his thirties, has good reasons to view "writing, not speech, as his means to communicate 'at a deeper level.'" For one thing, when he and his parents are with one another, eating fermented vegetables or walking man-made steps up a mountain, they limit themselves to short, simple phrases, speaking a "crude, ungrammatical Mandarin-English mix," thanks to Li's halting Chinese. For another, his parents bicker infectiously, often roping him in as a mediator, or collateral damage, or both.

When Li's parents do attempt kindness, they often require the use of the small family poodle, Dudu, on whom they project emotions too fragile to survive the passage of direct communication. When Li's mother flaps the dog's paw to wave goodbye to her business-tripping husband, Li is moved by "his parents' sly, Dudu-mediated tenderness." In fact, Li's parents often unthinkingly refer to their son as "Du," as if the name were their generic term for a loved one; on his third visit to Taiwan, Li starts doing the same thing to them. In pinyin romanization, *du* may transcribe many different words; pronounced with a rising tone, it could, given the prodigious homophony of Mandarin, mean "reading," "drugs," or "being alone."

As it happens, these are Li's three primary activities in *Leave Society*, the latest autobiographical novel from the author Tao Lin. Lin has spent the past decade novelizing his life in aloof, literal-minded prose; his breakthrough novel, *Taipei*, which fictionalized a drug-fueled relationship, was apparently pared down from a twenty-five-thousand-page draft of recollections. Lin's books of autofiction have made him something of a darling in the Alt Lit scene, where their disaffected sincerity has earned him the title of (although we have so many of these now) the "voice of his generation"—namely, the millennial one, with its infinitely mediated sentimentality.

With "Leave Society," Lin continues his autobiographical project by narrowing its scope even further, until only he and a small handful of others remain. Chronic back pain limits Li's ability to move and work on his novel (the one we're reading); to manage the pain, he relies on LSD and cannabis, both of which he takes freely in his Manhattan apartment but must sneak into Taiwan. A doctor at a rehabilitation center eventually diagnoses Li with ankylosing spondylitis, a rare form of spinal inflammation. But Li, distrustful of Western medicine, refuses a prescription for steroids, preferring the holistic approaches he researches on the internet from his arthritic solitude. He reads about natural health, traditional medicine, volcanic minerals, vegetable capsules. He is constantly identifying new toxins, diagnosing new vectors of inflammation. He fears glyphosate, pesticides, and Crest toothpaste.

If this is hypochondria, it is justified: Western medicine is good at handling acute trauma—for instance, a young Li's frequently collapsing lung—but has a poor track record with chronic pain. But Li is also a hypochondriac of ideas: that is, he often thinks he has them. In bed at night, he thinks about global chronic illness, the CIA's mind-control program, pottery, the nature of dreams, the Dao. He imagines life as a novel, death as finishing it and putting it down. He imagines imagination itself as a forest full of phytoncides and anions, the naturally healing "air vitamins" that he learns about from a sign by a waterfall.

In the course of *Leave Society*, Li settles on a naïve prelapsarianism, straight out of Riane Eisler's dubious eighties classic, *The Chalice and the Blade*. It seemed to Eisler, who, as a girl, witnessed her father being dragged away by the Nazis, that Neolithic "partnership societies," made up of peaceful, Mother Goddess–worshipping egalitarians, had been replaced by "the dominator model of social organization" around 5000 BCE, following the invention of copper smelting. This new model brought to the earth war, patriarchy, and—eventually—the air- and foodborne pollutants that Li spends the novel trying to expel from his body. Li turns Eisler's ideas over in his head, slowly teaching himself to practice partnership qualities like humility and gratitude.

Occasionally, Li's attempts to midwife the universe through mindfulness give rise to brief sunbursts of poetic exuberance, as when he starts noticing (or hallucinating) twinkling particles in the air around Washington Square Park—"translucent, vibrating, meshed hexagons" that he decides to call "microfireflies." But most of the book proceeds with listlike matter-of-factness, as if the author were skimming the ingredients on the back of his mother's Neutrogena hand cream. The first sentence of almost every chapter contains at least one number, often several, like a medical record: "Thirty tabs of LSD arrived on day thirty-five." This kind of prose can be elegant; it can also feel like dieting.

But it's most interesting to consider the book's flat affect as a curious, sidewise effect of Li's linguistic relationship to his parents. Their dialogue is spare and repetitive, their small Beckettian utterances often just missing their marks:

"When you were small, at Fat Uncle's home, you fell off the sink," said Li's mom.
    "Who?" said Li.
    "You," said Li's mom.
    "Where?" said Li.
    "The sink in the bathroom at Fat Uncle's home."
    "Fell from where?" said Li's dad.
    "Sink," said Li's mom.
    "When?" said Li.
    "When you were a baby," said Li's mom.

There is a translated quality to this kind of writing, as if Lin were rendering Mandarin word for word; in fact, given Li's propensity for audio recordings, this is likely exactly what happened. "If Li has a baby, he won't come to Taiwan," Li's father remarks, after Li starts seeing a woman in his apartment building. "Will," Li's mother replies—a single-word answer that scans in Mandarin, a language that often drops pronouns, but sounds off in English. Li and his parents putter around in this gap between languages, leaving readers with a small inventory of calques and loanwords. Lin notes early on that, in Chinese, one usually says "not good" instead of "bad," and the phrase repeats with sweet awkwardness throughout the novel. "I don't feel not good," Li insists, at one point, to his mother, mediating language, emotion, and maternal relation all at once.

Like Tao Lin, whose nonfiction book *Trip: Psychedelics, Alienation, and Change* was well received a few years ago, Li is recovering from years of abusing amphetamines and benzodiazepine. But, more than that, he is trying to "recover from himself." This is a touching notion, as earnest and meek as Li himself, who spends the novel inching tenderly toward his goal of "leaving society"—and, along with it, the existential self-importance of its most voguish genre. "He didn't want to specialize in embodying and languaging confused alienation anymore, as he had for a decade, writing existential autofiction," Lin writes.

Yet autofiction this is. Li reminds his parents that he is recording their conversations; he reflects on how their bickering will play in his novel; and he worries that the book is nudging him to "generate novelty," manufacture drama. Ultimately, Li decides that he likes autobiography's "self-catalyzing properties" too much to abandon it, observing that life is "larger, realer, more complicated" than a novel. Then again, that is the novel's value—not that you can fit a whole life inside of one but that life, in being pared down to the size of a book, necessarily acquires the specificity of form. This act of aspect-giving—of making things look one way and not another—is the primary function of authorship. Think of Oscar Wilde, who once wrote that London wasn't foggy until the Impressionists started painting it that way.

In this sense, all fiction is autofiction; every novel is a record of an author's attempt to transcribe themselves. I don't just mean that all fiction is, intentionally or not, autobiographical. I also mean that all novels refract the veiled subjectivity of their authors. On a walk up a mountain, Li and his parents rehearse a famous story from the *Zhuangzi*, a Daoist classic. It's said that the philosopher Zhuangzi, upon seeing some minnows in a river, remarked to his friend that the fish looked happy. "You're not a fish, so how do you know they're happy?" his friend asked. "You're not me," Zhuangzi replied, "so how do you know

I don't?" What was Zhuangzi doing when he said the fish were happy? Well, writing fiction, of course.

My point is that what makes a piece of writing autofiction is not, in the first place, the self-consciousness suggested by that ponderous moniker but, rather, at least in Tao Lin's case, the brazenness of its self-concealment. In other kinds of fiction, the author hides behind plot, character, or style; in autofiction, the author hides behind his own life. This, too, is form—as Lin has said, his focus in autobiographical fiction is "still on creating an effect, not on documenting reality." But the effect he's created is a kind of fastidious plotlessness, one whose accuracy to life, affected or not ("Li's dad mumbled something that was inaudible in the recording"), has the ambivalent virtue of being, like life itself, mostly boring. If you prefer, we can regard boringness as a perfectly neutral aesthetic category. Even so, it's not a reason that most people read novels.

It is only when Li develops a crush on Kay, a woman who lives in his Manhattan apartment building, that the novel approaches something like a plot. Kay, an almost divorced editor at a stylish small press, shares Lin's contemplative attitude and earnest credulity. They walk around New York, discussing divorce, clinical depression, and Çatalhöyük, a large Neolithic settlement that Li thinks exemplified a partnership society; Kay decides that when a tree trunk splits to form the letter *Y*, this is called the Yoshida Effect, after her last name. The prose is as sedate as ever: "Li went to hug her and they kissed. He asked what she felt about the kiss. 'I liked it,' said Kay." But there is also, for the first time in *Leave Society*, some good old-fashioned dramatic tension. Postcoital in Kay's apartment, they listen to a recording of Bach's Goldberg Variations, and Li begins to think of their dates as numbered variations on a theme, culminating in a planned vacation to Hawaii.

This shift toward narrative is interesting. It's worth saying that, in 2014, Tao Lin was accused of emotional abuse and statutory rape by the poet E. R. Kennedy. During their relationship, Lin was twenty-two; Kennedy, whose poetry Lin published through his small press, was sixteen—the age of consent in Pennsylvania, where the two had sex. The relationship was the subject of Lin's 2010 novel, *Richard Yates*, which included—without permission, according to Kennedy—real email correspondence between the pair. In a Facebook post, Lin denied the allegation of rape and claimed to have approved the book with Kennedy, while conceding that the two "had problems." Suffice it to say that, at minimum, Lin's behavior appears to have been "not good," as we say in Mandarin.

This is all to note that *Leave Society* is not the first time Lin has relied on an autobiographical sex partner to inject narrative energy into his characteristically enervated novels. *Taipei* adapted Lin's marriage to his ex-wife, Megan Boyle, whose poetry collection he also published; Kay is presumably based on Yuka Igarashi, an executive editor at Graywolf Press and a former managing editor at *Granta*, where she once interviewed Lin about *Taipei*. It is surely no accident that Kay is perhaps the only truly differentiated character in *Leave Society* rather than an extension of Li himself. (Compare her with Li's parents, who are not referred to by name.) Yet even as Li's feelings grow, he's aware that he may be instrumentalizing Kay for his book. "I can advance the story with Kay," he writes ambivalently in his notes, realizing that "a relationship might help and deepen and complexify, not necessarily disrupt or distract from, his recovery-novel-life."

The good news is, it does. Li's relationship with Kay gives his novel not just an ending but a happy one: the pair decides to relocate to Hawaii, which counts as "leaving society" for two New Yorkers. The not-good news is that this ending neatly ties together the romantic notions of aboriginality and womanhood that have sustained Li's belief in "partnership" throughout the book. Like the writers he reads, Li imagines aboriginal people as living monuments to a peaceful, prehistoric egalitarianism. When he visits a Bunun village in southeast Taiwan, he fantasizes about staying and doing "nature-based things" with the natives. He buys animal organs, "the most prized food of his aboriginal ancestors," and feels that "wide, aboriginal faces are more beautiful"—including Kay's, which happens to be "less degenerate" than most people's.

This aboriginal fantasy is linked with another: Li's obsession with Goddess worship. He reads excitedly about the "abundance of Goddess symbology" discovered in the excavation of Çatalhöyük: "paintings of childbirth and excarnation; sculptures of the female form; reliefs and cutouts of zoomorphized breasts and pregnant deities." He decides that Chinese culture, in accepting the Dao as "the underlying creative, maternal source of everything," has not "fallen as deep into domination as the West." There is an astonishing naïveté here, on Li's part, if not Lin's; these sections of the book read like *The Da Vinci Code*. Li spends the entire novel learning to revere women as "the ultimate metaphor for nature." No wonder he can't help worrying that his girlfriend is a plot device.

Of course, Kay isn't Li's mother; Li's mother is. His relationship with the latter is hardly harmonious: they bicker and mend and try to love each other in small and hurtful ways. Family, as anyone who has one knows, can be its own kind of chronic pain, no less debilitating than ankylosing spondylitis. This is twice as true of mothering; it's clear that Lin understands this. But that's what makes his dewy-eyed theory of "partnership"—which traces utopia back to ancient, fetishized, matrifocal societies—so laughable. It's easier to leave society than to let your mother be a whole person, and not some infantile ideal. To anyone who would see in that relationship the cosmic echoes of a peaceful egalitarianism, I would simply say: call her.

2021

The Mixed Metaphor

It only takes a few years. An economic catastrophe brings on the partial collapse of American society. As the nation recovers, an ascendant right wing blames the crisis on China. In the years following, the United States is rebuilt as an authoritarian nation under the Preserving American Culture and Traditions Act, colloquially known as PACT, an expansive law that allows the government to ban books, monitor private citizens, and disappear political dissidents, all in the name of preventing the spread of un-American views, a category that grows broader by the month: "Appearing sympathetic to China. Appearing insufficiently anti-China. Having any doubts about anything American; having any ties to China at all—no matter how many generations past."

This is fiction, obviously, even as it clearly brings to mind Japanese incarceration and the rise of McCarthyism as well as the wave of racist attacks on people of Asian ancestry since the pandemic began. The book in question is *Our Missing Hearts*, the third novel from author Celeste Ng, about a twelve-year-old boy named Bird Gardner whose mother, a Chinese American poet, abandoned him and his white father three years before. Ng's little mixed-race hero doesn't speak Cantonese and, as far as we know, doesn't eat Chinese food or know any Asian people. But his appearance alone—"the tilt of his cheekbones, the shape of his eyes"—is enough to subject Bird to the unifying existential threat faced by "anyone who might seem Chinese." This spectacularly anti-Asian version of the United States betrays a new, more openly political ambition on Ng's part: Whereas her previous work focuses on the experience of Asian Americans, she is now trying to write about Asian America itself.

The problem is that such a thing may not exist. It remains a very open question whether the disparate immigrant populations huddled under the umbrella of *Asian American*—a term coined by student activists at Berkeley in 1968—have enough in common to justify a shared politics or even a shared identity. "Nobody—most of all Asian Americans—really believes that Asian America actually exists," contends the journalist Jay Caspian Kang in his 2021 polemic *The Loneliest Americans.* For Kang, Asian American identity is a fantasy created by striving Asian professionals eager to reap the "spoils of full whiteness" while hiding behind a relatively mild, disorganized form of oppression that pales, literally, in the face of the systemic violence visited on Black Americans. "There are still only two races in America: Black and white," he declares. "Everyone else is part of a demographic group headed in one direction or the other."

What interests me here is not Kang's argument per se—he is not the most persuasive writer on the subject, only the loudest—but rather the fact that both he and Ng, arguably two of the most prominent Asian American authors working today, end up placing their ideas on the shoulders of a mixed-race child. In the opening pages of *The Loneliest Americans*, Kang stares ambivalently at his half-Korean newborn's "full head of dark hair and almond-shaped eyes," wondering if she will one day inherit the whiteness that cultural assimilation and accumulated wealth will have bought her. Ng, for her part, is writing about a fictional mixed-race child, though she also has a half-Chinese son in real life, and in any case, as she herself observes in her second novel, *Little Fires Everywhere*, children are always fictional: "To a parent, your child wasn't just a person: your child was a *place*, a kind of Narnia, a vast eternal place where the present you were living and the past you remembered and the future you longed for all existed at once." Indeed, it is quite possible to read *The Loneliest Americans* as the author's attempt to prove that his own mixed-race daughter has a serious shot at whiteness, just as it is hard not to read *Our Missing Hearts* as carefully positing the conditions under which Ng's mixed-race son would be unambiguously Asian.

How is it that the mixed Asian child can be quintessentially Asian American—as Asian American as apple pie, as it were—while also serving as living proof that Asian America does not exist? It is not a question of whether Ng or Kang is right. The looming fact of racial admixture, especially with white people, may be said to form the grit in the pearl of

Asian American consciousness today. This is true in brute demographic terms: roughly three million Americans identify as multiracial people of East or Southeast Asian heritage, but our numbers are rapidly increasing, and almost half of all American-born Asian newlyweds have married outside their race. But this is also true—perhaps even more true—at the level of historical feeling, where the mixed Asian transforms the slow crush of assimilation into a dynamic and emotive physical presence. Even the most racially secure Asian Americans have been known to discover in their mixed counterparts a whiter version of themselves. This creature is beautiful and terrible, striated with desires that feel hard or wrong to name, a literal assimilation of culture, custom, and language, not to mention skin, fat, and bone. "If she can move freely between worlds, why can't you?" the hero of Charles Yu's 2020 novel *Interior Chinatown* asks himself, marveling at the sight of his mixed-race daughter with his immigrant father. "Maybe, if you're lucky, she'll teach you."

That is a lot to ask of a child. It is a strange thing for fully Asian writers to look to mixed Asian people for relief from their racial anxieties when actual mixed-race Asians, who, it turns out, can write their own books, have little reassurance to offer. "I've always blamed my tendency to vacillate on my mixed ethnicity. Halved, I am neither here nor there, and my understanding of the relativity inherent in the world is built into my genes," observes Jane Takagi-Little in Ruth Ozeki's 1999 debut novel, *My Year of Meats*—an early instance of what we might call the mixed Asian novel. In recent years, this little genre has quietly bloomed, given life by a small cohort of novelists who write about characters that, like themselves, are of both white and East or Southeast Asian ancestry. (Accordingly, I'll be using the imperfect shorthand *mixed Asian* to refer to people of that particular ethnic makeup.) These novels are largely about unremarkable middle-class people without political or intellectual ambitions; what links these characters is not only a vague experience of racial non-belonging but also a gnawing uncertainty about how much this experience actually matters, even to themselves. Yet the mixed Asian novel has far more to teach us about Asian America today than Ng's didacticism or Kang's yawp does—precisely because it doesn't have much to say about it at all. Asian America is not an idea for these authors but a sensation, a mild, chronic homesickness; to read the mixed Asian novel will be to ask ourselves if Asian America can be anything *but* a kind of heartache.

In the process, we may also learn to stop reading mixed Asians like novels. There is no better example of the latter tendency than Ng's own debut novel from 2014, *Everything I Never Told You*, in which the favorite daughter of an interracial couple turns up drowned in a nearby lake. Lydia's death is ruled a suicide, and readers are led to believe the girl cracked under competing visions for her life—her Chinese father's eagerness for her to assimilate, her white mother's desire for her to distinguish herself. But the truth is that Lydia never means to kill herself at all. Instead, in a fit of misplaced optimism, she decides to swim the lake despite never having learned to swim. Her mistake is oddly conceptual: Lydia obviously does not need to literally survive a sink-or-swim scenario to figuratively stand up to her parents. It is as if the girl finds herself in a crisis of abstraction, rather than one of family pressures, and it is this essentially *literary* confusion—between narrative trope and material reality—that sends her to the bottom of the lake. Dragged down by the weight not of parental expectation but of her own waterlogged lungs, Lydia dies precisely as she lived: a metaphor.

So how does it feel to be a metaphor? There is, of course, a long history of tragic mixed Black characters saddled with symbolism in American literature: Nella Larsen's 1929 novel *Passing* famously concerns a biracial woman's doomed attempt to blend into white high society. The mixed Asian character, while a comparatively new phenomenon, has its own distinct literary roots. It is often forgotten that Amy Tan's 1989 novel *The Joy Luck Club*—that classic of Asian American fiction—prominently features a mixed-race protagonist. "Most people didn't know I was half Chinese," remarks Lena St. Clair, noting that her resemblance to her mother is limited to dark hair, olive skin, and eyes that look "as if they were carved on a jack-o'-lantern with two swift cuts of a short knife." As a child, Lena is expected to translate for her Chinese-speaking mother and frequently makes up lies; years later, she is languishing in a joyless marriage to her wealthy white boss, who insists they split household expenses. "I'm so tired of it, adding things up, subtracting, making it come out even," she tells him, almost as if she is talking about herself. Her mother, deeply worried, compares her to a ghost.

In one sense, Lena is just a variation on a theme for Tan, who tends to view the character's biraciality as a particularly obvious illustration of the more general plight of the assimilated Chinese American daughter. (If few today remember that Lena is mixed, this is likely because the character was rewritten as fully Chinese for Wayne Wang's 1993 film adaptation.) "Only her skin and her hair are Chinese. Inside—she is all American made," admits a different mother of her fully Chinese daughter. In fact, the members of the older generation of *The Joy Luck Club* often fret that their offspring are Chinese in appearance only, and they hand down sentimental stories of their tribulations in China out of a fear that their presumably mixed-race grandchildren—three out of the novel's four daughters are at various points married or engaged to white men—will end up just as American as their mothers.

Yet at the same time, Lena represents a genuine antecedent to the protagonists of the mixed Asian novel. Like her, these characters are diffident, aimless, frustrated; they are stalled in their careers and ambivalent about their romantic partners, as if the acute experience of racial indeterminacy has diffused into something more banal. This is notably different from the "tragic mulatto" trope dating back to nineteenth-century fiction, in which a light-skinned character, denied the full privileges of whiteness by some remaining quantum of Black blood, descends into self-hatred, depression, or suicide. On the contrary, the mixed Asian hero is not a tragic mixture but an ironic one since, for the most part, she *does* enjoy those privileges—even when she *doesn't* pass. But the fact that this dispensation may be conditional lingers in the mixed Asian psyche as a fuzzy, unsettled feeling that can manifest as anything from shyness to a fear of commitment. In Claire Stanford's *Happy for You*, published this year, a thirtysomething half-Japanese woman named Evelyn impulsively abandons her unfinished philosophy dissertation to help a tech giant develop an app that tracks happiness—even as she is quietly anxious at the prospect of her boyfriend proposing. "I knew I was supposed to be happy about this," Evelyn admits. "And yet when I thought about marriage, I felt only a hollow pit deep in my solar plexus, a vacancy that seemed to be mine alone."

This emptiness—or really the displacement of racial or cultural emptiness into another, more general field of experience—is the first feature of the mixed Asian novel. Something is missing, but it isn't clear what. Several characters end up trying to fill this hole with a child, as if re-rolling the genetic dice will provide a glimpse into the origins of their own discontent. This is easier said than done. Knocked up by her boyfriend, Evelyn will require an emergency C-section after the placenta suddenly separates from her quarter-Japanese fetus, endangering its life. "Somehow, my body had known I was not sure about the baby. My body had acted, unilaterally," she thinks. If mixed Asian protagonists struggle to rear children in these novels, that is because in many ways the mixed Asian still resembles a child, trapped in a state of perpetual immaturity by her failure during the critical window of childhood to inherit a clear narrative about her own racial identity. Willa, the directionless college grad of Kyle Lucia Wu's *Win Me Something*, who works as a nanny for a wealthy white family, is pressured into joining the nine-year-old daughter's private Mandarin lessons, where her precocious charge chastises her for asking questions in English. The scene is a perfect inversion of Willa's kindergarten days, when she would proudly inform classmates that she didn't speak Chinese. Now, to the Mandarin teacher, an ashamed Willa explains, "I didn't grow up with my dad."

Parental abandonment is a consistent theme across these books. Ozeki's fourth novel, *The Book of Form and Emptiness*, opens with the pointless death by delivery van of the central character's half-Japanese, half-Korean father. Willa's Chinese father isn't dead in *Win Me Something*, only absent, having left her white mother to marry a different white woman, resulting in a set of half-Chinese half sisters. Of special note is Rowan Hisayo Buchanan's *Harmless Like You*, about an irritable mixed-race art dealer and the Japanese mother who left him when he was a toddler. In high school, Jay begins to suffer from fainting attacks, and even as an adult he depends on a service animal, a sickly hairless cat that requires a daily suppository. Now, he struggles to relate to his quarter-Chinese, quarter-Japanese newborn daughter, whom he fantasizes about leaving with an expensive-looking white co-ed in the park. "You know the legend about how the goddess who gave birth to Japan had another child first," he pontificates to his wife. "This baby of theirs, he had no bones. Hiruko. The name literally means leech child." Jay is talking about his "leech-like" infant, but he is also talking about himself. It is as if racial amalgamation has resulted in a being whose lack of internal structure leaves it with only one purpose: to feed.

This brings us to a second aspect of the mixed Asian novel: The more the mixed Asian allows the experience of racial dispossession to manifest directly, without displacement, the more this feeling takes on the form of something like a fundamental hunger. Many characters in these novels have strong feelings about Asian food—Willa treasures the memory of eating beef tongue with her father, while Jay nurses a self-parodying love of crab rangoon. By far the most interesting and sustained example of this trend is in Claire Kohda's debut novel *Woman, Eating*, published this year, about a young mixed-race art-gallery intern in London who also happens to be a vampire. Lydia longs to sample the food of her late father's culture—onigiri, soba, Japanese corn dogs—but human food is noxious to her. Nor has she ever drunk human blood, having been raised on a strict diet of pig's blood procured by her half-Malay, half-white vampire mother, who believes vampirism is a monstrous extension of colonial greed. Now, living on her own for the first time, Lydia slowly begins to starve; unable to procure fresh pig's blood from her local butcher, she resorts to buying a powdered version online, then to draining a dead duck she finds along the river. At the novel's end, when she finally drinks the blood of a white art curator, a rapturous Lydia discovers his blood tastes like everything he has ever eaten, including not only Japanese food but Malaysian delicacies like pandan, "something unfamiliar but at the same time deeply familiar, something I didn't know I craved."

There are two ironies here. The first is that Lydia can taste Asian food only through acts of terrific violence that bear an uncomfortable resemblance to the original colonial act. Lydia is also of European stock, after all, and it can be difficult to parse the reclamation of heritage from the crime of cultural theft—hence the narrative contrivance of her inability to source pig's blood, which renders her actions understandable (she's *very* hungry) if not exactly justifiable. For the second irony is that coagulated pig's blood, without the addition of fillers as in blood sausage, is eaten as a food unto itself in several Asian countries, including Malaysia; perhaps some of Lydia's existential problems could have been solved simply by access to a well-stocked Asian grocer. But this is precisely why food matters so much to the mixed Asian: it places the desire for culture *inside* the body, out of the reach of any potential accusation that she is, as it were, appropriating herself. Compare Michelle Zauner's 2021 memoir *Crying in H Mart*, named for the beloved Korean American grocery chain, in which the half-Korean musician reflects on the death of her mother with reference to the fermentation process involved in making kimchi: "The culture we shared was active, effervescent in my gut and in my genes, and I had to seize it, foster it so it did not die in me."

This is poetic but not exactly plausible. There is really only one craving that the mixed Asian invariably carries in their body, and it is not the hunger for cultural memory. "There is no way to look at the face of a mixed-race person and not be immediately reminded of sex," Ozeki observes in her short nonfiction book *The Face: A Time Code*—though this reaction may be more unconscious today than it was when Ozeki was growing up in the sixties. Almost all children, of course, are proof of sexual congress; what the mixed person suggests is not just that people of different races can be attracted to each other but also, more discomfitingly, that people can be attracted to the idea of race itself.

One striking peculiarity of the mixed-race person is that almost any sexual attraction he experiences will by definition be interracial, given that he inhabits no clearly defined racial category to begin with. Racial difference is therefore an inescapable factor in the mixed Asian's romantic choices. The wisecracking author in Peter Ho Davies's *The Fortunes* considers himself "immune to the Western fetish of otherness, even if—perhaps *because*—his father wasn't," though what this means in practice is that "he's never been attracted to Chinese girls" and he calls his white wife his "occident waiting to happen." This dilemma—call it compulsory exogamy—is taken to almost satiric levels in Buchanan's *Harmless Like You*, where Jay putatively wriggles out of the problem by marrying a half-Chinese woman who so strongly resembles him that a friend is reminded of "the Siamese cats in *Lady and the Tramp*." But this is not so much a refuge from the dilemma as a confirmation that even the most precisely calibrated same-race desire is still, for that very reason, a desire for race.

If there is a final feature of the mixed Asian novel, it is that no amount of resemblance can guarantee relation—to a parent, to a culture, to a race, or a racial politic. It is not every mixed-race Asian who can, for instance, walk through Chinatown like Bird in *Our Missing Hearts* and feel "oddly at home" surrounded by faces like his mother's. Compare this with Willa in *Win Me Something*, who anxiously researches restaurants online when her younger half sister Charlotte proposes they meet for soup dumplings. "Sometimes being in Chinatown made me feel a melancholy indigo, skittish with a feather-brushed sadness," Willa admits, recalling the time a man hawking newspapers in Chinese fell silent as she walked past. At the restaurant with Charlotte, who grew up with their Chinese father, Willa puzzles over their differences. "I didn't feel envy. It was just that I wanted her to know what it was like for me," she thinks. "If I could have her understand anything, it was this: *Do you know the feeling of home that you have? I don't have that.*"

But the difference between Willa and her sister, who is just as mixed-race as she is, is the whole point. At the lowest limits of every bond of kinship, one finds not some cultural or hereditary bedrock but a small infinite abyss that must be leapt across, again and again, through acts of will. This is not to say that the only thing standing between the mixed Asian and racial homecoming is her own reluctance to come home—quite the opposite, as the mixed Asian novel amply demonstrates. But what these novels also force us to admit is that there is no racial belonging *without* the desire to belong, that the desire to reach, not without risk, across differences of physical appearance, personal history, and material circumstance is a necessary, even critical, component of race—not just for mixed-race people but perhaps for everyone.

Early in *The Loneliest Americans*, Kang clarifies that the title refers to "the loneliness that comes from attempts to assimilate, whether by melting into the white middle class or by creating an elaborate, yet ultimately derivative, racial 'identity.'" Indeed, Kang so ardently believes in a universal desire to be white among so-called Asian Americans that he reflexively dismisses every indication to the contrary—a taste for tapioca pearls, support for ethnic-studies programs—as little more than yellowface. Eating at an Asian food court in Berkeley, Kang cannot conceive of why a nearby group of Asian undergrads would choose to sit together. "Their insularity feels banal and unwarranted," he complains. "If you're just going to speak English, dress like everyone else, and complain about schoolwork like every other Berkeley student, what, exactly, is the culture you've created?"

We are very good these days at providing elaborate explanations for why people of color may want to be white—an assumption we often make not out of rigor or intellectual bravery but for our own analytic convenience. The world is simply much harder to understand when one stops treating white supremacy like a gas leak—invisible, omnipresent, and expanding to fill every void—and more like an oil spill: sprawling and massively destructive, but also crude, combatable, and, most important, easily surpassed in scale and complexity by the ocean itself. It is a sad irony of *The Loneliest Americans*, for instance, that it never occurs to Kang to ask whether his own half-white daughter might one day want to be Asian. The fact is that a certain minority of people, thanks to an accident of birth, will always find themselves in the curious position of being made to move, just a bit, along the weird, curved plane that is race in America. This movement defies the Euclidean assumption that racial *identity* always exists in direct proportion to racial *assignment*—"the color of one's skin," as American politicians like to say. It suggests, in other words, that a certain small measure of freedom may inhere in the concept of race itself.

To be clear: Such freedom, if it exists, would be largely subjective. It would not be sufficient on its own to alter the objective realities of racism, nor would it have any direct bearing on liberatory struggles; above all, it would not justify race fraud. This freedom would remind us that white supremacy is neither the only nor the best conceptual yardstick for the lived experience of people who are not white—not least because, as the mixed Asian novel shows us, we cannot know in advance who those people are. It is undoubtedly true that race in America is created and maintained through racist violence. It is, however, no contradiction to say that race, once people start living with it, can no longer be reduced to that violence for the staggeringly simple reason that people *do* live with it, every day, gradually patching together new, often temporary worlds of experience in which race may be felt as something *other* than a target on one's back (or, for that matter, a gun in one's hand.) Ng and Kang actually agree that racial identity can be bought only through racism; they are merely, to quote the old joke, haggling over the price. But what this assumption yields is a thin, abstract concept of Asian America, one that is so inhospitable to actual human beings that it recognizes them only when they are in pain. This is why the question "does Asian America exist?" is the wrong one; it is a bloodless logic game masquerading as a political problem.

Here is the better question: Do we want to be Asian Americans? I don't mean this in a voluntaristic, do-you-believe-in-fairies sort of way, but as a real, honest question: Do people of Asian ancestry in this country want to be Asian Americans? The question is not why a mixed-race person should "get" to qualify as Asian despite, for instance, never having been bullied at school or attacked by a stranger; the question is why we cannot imagine any other way to be Asian. And if there is one conclusion to be reached from the mixed Asian experience, it is this: People want race. They want race to win them something, to tell them everything they were never told; they want friendship from it, or sex, or even love; and sometimes, they just want to be something or to have something to be. I do not mean that Asian America will suddenly appear on the horizon tomorrow if enough of us choose it tonight. What I mean is that many people across the country, including many of us who are mixed, are already choosing it, and it is enough for now to ask why. There is, after all, a reason that people sit together: they don't want to be alone.

2022

Likely People

Zadie Smith's first book, *White Teeth*, was the English comic novel on bath salts. Published to universal acclaim in 2000, it loosely centered on the Iqbals and the Joneses, two zany families living in Willesden Green, the diverse North London neighborhood where Smith grew up. Her madcap creations lost their teeth, fucked twins, gave birth during earthquakes, predicted the end of the world; there were Irish pubs owned by Iraqis, genetically modified mice, and an Islamic fundamentalist group named KEVIN. ("'We are aware,' said Hifan solemnly, pointing to the spot underneath the cupped flame where the initials were minutely embroidered, 'that we have an acronym problem.'") All the while, one never lost sight of Smith herself, bursting with exuberance and sincerity. Critics celebrated her for breaking "the iron rule that first fictions should be thin slices of autobiography, served dripping with self-pity," even as the author's biographical details—her age (twenty-four), her race (Jamaican mother, white father), her looks (good)—would make her an object of fascination. "Is Britishness cream tea and the queen?" asked *The New York Times*. "Or curry and Zadie Smith?"

But Smith also had her critics. In an infamous review, James Wood dubbed *White Teeth* a work of "hysterical realism," arguing that Smith's characters, though they did possess a certain "shiny externality" reminiscent of Dickens, were "not really alive." For Wood, a passionate defender of the realist novel, this meant that *White Teeth* lacked "moral seriousness." In response, Smith conceded that *hysterical realism* was "a painfully accurate term for the sort of overblown, manic prose to be found in novels like my own." As early as 2002, she began to speak of "the morality of the novel," relocating herself within a tradition that included

George Eliot, Henry James, and E. M. Forster. For Smith, this tradition was united in the belief that by enlarging the sphere of plausible
others—what Forster once called "likely people"—the novel could act
to widen the reader's moral sympathies. "When we read with fine attention, we find ourselves caring about people who are various, muddled,
uncertain, and not quite like us (and this is good)," Smith wrote in a
2003 lecture on Forster, whose *Howards End* would inspire her genteel
third novel, *On Beauty*. That same year, she tried to read *White Teeth* for
the first time since publication: "I got about ten sentences in before I was
overwhelmed with nausea."

It's a shame. A novelist has a sacred right to hate her first novel, but
White Teeth remains by far the best thing Smith has ever written; what
bad luck to have done it by twenty-four! Smith has apparently concluded
that *White Teeth*'s greatest strength, its audacious unreality, was in fact
its fatal flaw. Today, she is firmly within the realist camp despite her
recurring feints at departure. Her much-debated 2008 essay "Two Paths
for the Novel," which pitted the "lyrical realism" of Balzac and Flaubert
against the twentieth-century avant-garde, reads now like two paths for
Zadie Smith. Every time she has set out down the second path, it has
looped consolingly back into the first. *On Beauty* was a novel of ideas;
NW, Smith's fourth novel, dabbled in Joycean modernism. But each new
form has represented a fresh attempt to write the morally serious novel
that *White Teeth* had failed to be. This is Smith: radical for the sake of
tradition. In another 2008 essay, this one on *Middlemarch*, Smith argued that a heightened moral sensitivity drove Eliot to "push the novel's
form to its limits." But for this very reason, the "George Eliot of today"
would need to invent her own forms; she certainly wouldn't be writing a
"nineteenth-century English novel."

Now Smith has done just that. *The Fraud*, her first historical novel,
depicts the celebrated Tichborne trial of the 1870s through the eyes of
Eliza Touchet, real-life cousin by marriage to the minor novelist William Harrison Ainsworth, an erstwhile rival of Dickens. Eliza, a sensitive soul who longs to discover "what could be known of other people,"
soon becomes obsessed with key witness Andrew Bogle, an enigmatic,
formerly enslaved Jamaican; her fascination will ultimately inspire a
novel of her own. *The Fraud* is thus that irresistible creature: a novel

about novels. Like *Middlemarch*, it is divided into eight volumes, and Eliza even spies Eliot (who privately went by Mary Ann Evans Lewes) among the trial's attendees. "Was this what the admirable Mrs Lewes felt as she worked?" wonders our budding lady novelist as she prepares to write. More than ever, Smith is asking herself the same question. Her two paths for the novel have become a perfect circle: What could be more avant-garde in an age of data harvesting and identity politics than a heartfelt nineteenth-century novel? The socially minded Eliot believed that through sympathetic portraits of ordinary people, the novel could provide readers with "the raw material of moral sentiment." With *The Fraud*, Smith delivers her most passionate defense of this idea to date. Whether it persuades is another matter.

Years of living with a novelist have made Mrs. Touchet suspicious of the whole breed. Smith imagines Eliza as a thwarted intellectual—every Zadie Smith book must have at least one—but the subtle, liberal-minded housekeeper still loves her cousin enough to withhold her dismal view of his turgid historical novels. Eliza has an even poorer opinion of his friend Charles, in whose dark charms she glimpses the "vampiric" attitude of all novelists toward real life. Smith apparently relished writing Dickens's death into *The Fraud*; the novel is almost too easily read as a final attempt to wash off the ancient stain of hysterical realism. Wood wrote that Smith had substituted "information" for character, and so here we find a drunk William Thackeray telling Eliza that her cousin "too frequently mistakes information for interest." Wood accused Smith of Dickensian caricature; Eliza bitterly charges Dickens with turning the people he meets into "cartoons barely worthy of Cruikshank's inkpot." One wonders if the sting of these criticisms really has lingered for twenty years; at least we can assume that Eliza too would have hated *White Teeth*. "God preserve me from novel-writing," she thinks. "God preserve me from that tragic indulgence, that useless vanity, that blindness!"

But one never seriously supposes Smith has lost her faith in the novel. Eliza must have a change of heart. It comes in the form of the Tichborne case, in which the courts weighed an Australian butcher's dubious claim to be Sir Roger Tichborne, the long-lost heir to a baronetcy. From the beginning, Eliza regards this "Sir Roger" as an obvious fraud, "a man with no centre, who might be nudged in any direction." But Bogle, formerly a valet to Sir Roger's uncle, is something different. Eliza sees "nothing hidden or masked" in his face, but this makes him totally "impenetrable," a cipher without evident motives. Inexplicably, Bogle testifies that the Claimant is the genuine Sir Roger, even as his testimony costs him his pension from the Tichbornes. This sets off a moral crisis in Eliza, whose wonted perspicacity has finally met its match: a man who must be speaking falsely and is nevertheless radiant with truth. As she walks the streets of London taking in the foreign faces—Chinese sailors, an African doctor, a delegation of men in fezzes—Eliza ponders the question raised by Bogle's very existence: "What can we know of other people?"

Desperately curious, Eliza poses as a journalist and convinces Bogle to tell her "everything." But his history—his life as an enslaved man in Jamaica, then a manservant in England—provides few clues to his motives in supporting Sir Roger; it reveals only a cautious, clever man who has won his freedom through "obscure and underhand" means. Upon learning this, Eliza senses that the door to ultimate reality has suddenly come loose: "Finally, she could open it! But to her astonishment, it opened inwards. She had been standing inside the very thing she'd been looking for." The secret is that there is no secret: Andrew Bogle is simply a person, and as Eliza inwardly exclaims, "A person is a bottomless thing!" One need not believe Bogle to find him *believable*, the way a character in a good novel is believable. He is one of Forster's likely people: fully, unfathomably alive. For Eliza, this had always been the failure of her cousin's drab historical novels; never had there been room for "stories like her own—or for that matter like Mr. Bogle's. Stories of human beings, struggling, suffering, deluding others and themselves."

In fact, there is one novel Eliza likes very much. "Just a lot of people going about their lives in a village," her cousin scoffs when he spots her reading the second volume of *Middlemarch*. "Is this all that these modern ladies' novels are to be about? People?" The heart leaps up: *Precisely!* In that second volume, we find what Smith once called "the most famous lines" in all of *Middlemarch*: "If we had a keen vision and feeling of all ordinary human life, it would be like hearing the grass grow and the squirrel's heart beat, and we should die of that roar which lies on the other side of silence." As Eliza opens herself to Bogle, this roar will begin to split her ears. Just who does she think she is? Certainly Eliza Touchet, whose late husband's family made their fortune in the transatlantic slave trade, is not the "right" vessel for an enslaved man's careful ascent to freedom. Bogle's firebrand son distrusts Eliza's reformist attitudes, and the life story of Andrew Bogle, presented here in two stand-alone volumes, often resembles the Caribbean slave narratives dictated to well-meaning English abolitionists in the early nineteenth century. It is quite possible that Eliza's novel, like the silly ladies' novels Eliot abhorred, will be "less the result of labor than of busy idleness."

So perhaps *The Fraud* expresses an anxiety about the novel equal to its defense of it. "We mistake each other," Eliza admits, reflecting on how "everything conspires" against the enduring cognizance of other people. But for Smith, the inevitable fraudulence of the novel is precisely what gives it its moral urgency. In a provocative 2019 essay about cultural appropriation, Smith opposed the "popular" idea that "we can and should write only about people who are fundamentally 'like' us: racially, sexually, genetically, nationally, politically, personally." The novelist does presume to know the lives of others, she wrote, but only in order to light up our hidden commonalities as human beings; without this presumption, "we could have no social lives at all." Eliza's blind spots, far from disqualifying her, testify to the slow, uncertain work of becoming morally serious. Like Dorothea in *Middlemarch*, she is reaching imperfectly toward "the fullest truth, the least partial good." Who does Eliza think she is? Well, a person.

Now Smith would be the first to claim that her defense of the novel, that "indefensible art," is inherently contradictory. "Ideological inconsistency is, for me, practically an article of faith," she wrote in the introduction to her first essay collection, *Changing My Mind*. Smith has often made a virtue of negative capability, Keats's phrase for how Shakespeare wrote so empathetically that he appeared to hold, in Smith's words, "no firm opinions or set beliefs." In a talk given after the 2008 election, Smith ascribed negative capability to Barack Obama, whose biracial heritage had blessed him, as it had her, with the ability to "see a thing from both sides." There was tremendous credulity here; as the critic Namara Smith has noted, the argument lacked any awareness that the two sides in question "might not be competing on level terrain." Doubtless, many would no longer stand by what they said in the afterglow of 2008. But the optimism here, far from an Obama-era relic, is just an early instance of a very *consistent* feature of Smith's career as a public intellectual: her almost involuntary tendency to reframe all political questions as "human" ones.

This humanist impulse has made for some perennial wrongheadedness. Smith rather famously compared the opponents of a white artist's controversial painting of Emmett Till to "Nazis," arguing that all art deserved to be "thought through" on its own terms. The truth is that Smith herself struggles to think in groups of two or more; her habit of sympathizing with the least sympathetic party in any given situation frequently drives her to the political center. In fairness, the Trump years have made her more receptive to Black radicalism, but Smith will still always favor a psychological interpretation over an ideological one. Thus we are asked, in the wake of Brexit, to spare a thought for the white working-class voter who lacked "the perceived moral elevation of acknowledged trauma"; thus we are asked not to call the Charleston church shooting a hate crime since, "when it comes to murder, what other kind of crime is there?" At the same time, Smith regularly confesses that she has "no qualifications to write as I do," downplaying her own essays as "the useless thoughts of a novelist." This is disingenuous: they are the thoughts of Zadie Smith. But Smith appears to have decided at some point that being faintly ridiculous all of the time is preferable to being wrong some of the time.

No surprise that Smith's most ardent wish these days is for fiction to be a space of freedom from the long teeth of identity. She traces her own desire "to know what it was like to be everybody" back to that "big, colorful, working-class sea" that was Willesden Green. But, for her, negative capability gently dissolves the specific contents of whatever consciousness birthed it. One need not be biracial to write a great novel because all great novelists *might as well be* biracial, so vast are their powers of empathy. Smith is just as happy to attribute the "empathic imaginative leap" of fiction to David Foster Wallace, a white guy from Illinois who once speculated that "straight white males" may be more alienated than anybody. Smith has similarly warned us off the absolutist belief, vaguely burbling up among her writing students, that a novel's characters should be judged for how "correctly" they represent the distinctive behaviors of an identity group—that a gay character, for instance, should do things only a "real" gay person would do. "How can such things possibly be claimed absolutely," Smith asks, "unless we already have some form of fixed caricature in our minds?"

This is a good point. But one should never trust an argument that depends on the anonymous defenestration of undergraduates. Smith's 2018 short story "Now More Than Ever," in which professors point enormous arrows at one another to decide who should be canceled next, is proof enough that nothing breeds reaction in the liberal mind like appointment to an American university. "Speaking for myself, *I'm* the one severely triggered by statements like 'Chaucer is misogynistic' or 'Virginia Woolf was a racist,'" Smith wrote in a self-effacing review of the film *Tár*. "Not because I can't see that both statements are partially true, but because I am of that generation whose only real shibboleth was: 'Is it interesting?'" This is a willful misunderstanding. Of course Woolf's racism *is* interesting to those whom Smith calls, with not enough irony, "the youngs." The problem is that it isn't interesting to *her*. But when young people rate a novel poorly because they disagree with its politics, it is more convenient to assert that they have simply abandoned the old-fashioned field of aesthetic inquiry altogether than to reckon with the possibility that criticism *itself* is being remade. And so Smith congratulates the new generation on preferring politics to aesthetics; the best way to get someone off your lawn is to direct them to a lawn of their own.

This is literary NIMBYism: *Yes, politics, but over there.* Smith grants that language has become a "convenient battleground" for political aggression given the meager success of intractable (but so admirable!) material struggles around, say, wealth inequality or prison abolition. Still, she insists that fiction cannot afford the "ideology of separatism" that naturally springs up among historically oppressed groups; its business is "with the people, all the people, all the time." But this too is a political position. As Forster once said of himself, Smith would rather be "a humanist with all his faults, than a fanatic with all his virtues." She admires the veil of ignorance, a thought experiment devised by the liberal philosopher John Rawls in which a group of rational individuals must organize a society without knowing their place within it. For Smith, the novel is just such an experiment in thinking beyond our closely held identities. It's true that many bad novels have substituted ideology for interest. It's equally true that Smith envisions the novel as a little liberal machine for making more little liberals. "We hope all of humanity will reject the project of dehumanization," she wrote in an essay on Toni Morrison last year. "We hope for a literature—and a society!—that recognizes the somebody in everybody." Fine words! But they are all gums.

Suppose Zadie Smith is right. How does fiction arouse our sympathies? One good way is to present people who are "finely aware and richly responsible," as Henry James wrote, explaining that readers care "comparatively little for what happens to the stupid, the coarse and the blind." This makes sense: We are moved by Hamlet's *feeling* for poor Yorick, not by Yorick himself. But the Jamesian sensitive soul is by now a cliché; it is why so many debut novels maroon us in the minds of characters who sound suspiciously like novelists. Perhaps we will have better luck with one of the blind. Consider Mr. Casaubon, the irritable pedant of *Middlemarch*. Urging us to make "room" for Casaubon, Eliot tells us that his soul has always been too weighed down by self-doubt to experience true passion: "It went on fluttering in the swampy ground where it was hatched, thinking of its wings and never flying." Over a century of readers have been moved by this image. But we know that this leaden theologian could never devise a metaphor so fine and delicate—this is Eliot speaking, making him into a likely person. In this respect, Eliot is no different from Hamlet: the more sympathetically she paints her characters, the more we are stirred by her own powers of sympathy.

So how is the author to get out of the way? A traditional solution is free indirect style, a technique as old as Austen, in which the narrator speaks in the voice of a character. Here is Elizabeth Bennett, reading that fateful letter from Mr. Darcy:

> How differently did everything now appear in which he was concerned!

Now here is the same sentence, rewritten as quoted speech:

> "How differently everything now appears in which he is concerned!" Elizabeth thought.

Not as compelling! Rather than look down from above, Austen briefly sacrifices her authorial omniscience in order to get in character, narrating Lizzy's shock as if from within. This technique is now exceedingly common; one finds it all over contemporary fiction, and Smith is quite good at it. "Did he think her a vampire?" she writes in *The Fraud*, adopting Eliza's anxiety about Bogle as her own. "She only wanted to know what could be known of other people!"

But Eliza is right to be anxious: one can never quite tell if free indirect style is a gallant deferral *to* a character or a jostling encroachment *on* him. Here is Bogle in his part of *The Fraud*, passing contemplatively by an English forest:

> Bogle admired a gold and russet forest as it went by, swaying in the gathering wind. One lifetime was not enough to understand a people and the words they used and the way they thought and lived.

The second sentence is classic free indirect, a clear back-shifting of the contents of Bogle's consciousness. But that "gold and russet forest"— whose thought is this? Perhaps it really is Bogle's, as sensitively dictated to Eliza: *I was admiring the forest—gold and russet, as I recall.* Or perhaps we are reading from Eliza's novel about Bogle, also called *The Fraud*, in which case that gold and russet forest may be her detail, a sympathetic embellishment not unlike Mr. Casaubon's fluttering soul. Then again, perhaps it is the work of Zadie Smith, lightly indulging in a novelist's word for brown.

Now if I am Smith's ideal reader, finely aware and richly responsible, then I will find here not a single vibrating consciousness but as many as *three*, crammed into a handful of words. Which one should I pity? Especially given that they are not on equal footing: Bogle is in Eliza's hands, and both of them are inexorably in Smith's. The irony of Smith's career is that she has never actually excelled at constructing the kind of sympathetic, all-too-human characters she advocates for. (The closest she came was the affecting portrait of a crumbling marriage in *On Beauty*.) In truth, Bogle is far less interesting than advertised, the latest in a line of increasingly dull characters dating back to the technically proficient but lackluster *NW*. Their studied ordinariness makes us long for Smith's true strength, which lies not in character but in *voice*. We read her because she possesses that rare and precious gift of sounding always like herself. As an early admirer said of Eliot, "We are in the presence of a soul." True, anyone who has read the irritating experiment in first-person narration that was *Swing Time* will agree that the last thing we want Smith to write about is herself. "I have been both adult and child, male and female, black, brown, and white, gay and straight, funny and tragic, liberal and conservative, religious and godless, not to mention alive and dead," she wrote in 2019. But what moves us is the reverse: These people have all been *her*.

So if I really do encounter an ethical other in *The Fraud*, it is Smith herself: her rippling intellect, her unmistakable sound. Eliza, Bogle, and the rest are *other others*, strangers who, precisely because Smith has so finely enmeshed her consciousness with theirs, necessarily overflow my ethical capacities. I will simply never get them alone. Smith admits that fiction runs "the continual risk of wrongness"—racial caricature, for instance—and she allows that Eliza may be treating Bogle like a lifeless "scarecrow," one she is determined to stuff with a soul. For Smith, this is the great ethical drama: *How will we mistake each other this time?* Perhaps she is even right that the infinite rehearsal of this drama can teach readers a fine feeling for humanity. But the humanist's mistake is to suppose that politics is just lots and lots of ethics. Ethics asks us to recognize that the other has a soul; politics asks us to reject the soul as a precondition for moral interest. In this sense, fiction has always been an exercise in political consciousness. It asks me to care about people I do not know and will never meet, people who *might as well not exist* as far as my own life is concerned but whose destinies are nonetheless obscurely intertwined with mine. Not for nothing do we call it the third person.

The author of *White Teeth* knew this. The Iqbal twins, long separated by gulfs of geography, ideology, and personal feeling, try to bury the hatchet by meeting in a "neutral place." But soon, they "make a mockery of that idea," reenacting memories, quoting mentors, relitigating the hoary tale of their mutineer ancestor. A novel is never a neutral place: every attempted encounter with the other is interrupted by the hysterical crowd, their noses pressed up against the glass. It was true that Smith's creations in *White Teeth* were "luminous disks of a pre-arranged size," as Forster once said of flat characters, their inner and outer lives forming a single glossy Möbius strip. And it was true that Smith sometimes wrote too blithely of people unlike herself. (There was an Arab family that named all their sons Abdul.) But Smith's characters did not lack humanity so much as she lacked a use for it. Her eye was trained on a collectivity: the vibrant Willesden Green of her youth. In her own way, Smith had written a condition-of-England novel not unlike *Middlemarch*; with Icarian optimism, she had launched herself directly at the social whole, and in falling, she seemed to fly. Accordingly, Smith never asked too much of her unlikely people. They hit their marks, said their lines, and disappeared, check in hand, back into the crowd. You could tell they had better things to do than be furniture in someone's novel.

So sympathize away! No one can stop you. But neither the novel nor its people are so weak that they would collapse if our hearts did not bleed for them. Indeed, it is precisely *because* we feel that characters in novels are real that we can politically object to the way a writer treats them. This may be what the youngs were saying—not that they feared for their own sensitive souls but that they wished to know how to do real justice to imaginary people. How might Smith have answered them? She dislikes the adage "Write what you know" on the grounds that it is now used to keep novelists within the bright chalk circle of personal identity. So for her sake, let us look somewhere more morally serious. The midcentury literary critic F. R. Leavis once wrote, in his very serious book *The Great Tradition*, that Austen's genius was to take "certain problems that life compelled on her as personal ones" and impersonalize them, tracing carefully out of herself and back into the world. What Leavis admired was not that Austen had stayed in her lane; it was that she'd had the good sense to ask where it led. This is a splendid notion. It suggests that, for any novelist, there exists a small number of historical problems that, for reasons of luck and temperament, she *naturally* grasps as the stuff of life. The genius lies in knowing which ones they are.

2023

You Must Decide

In Octavia E. Butler's novelette "Bloodchild," a quantum of humanity fleeing Earth finds sanctuary on a distant planet—but at a price. The native Tlic, a species of intelligent, centipede-like aliens, establish the Preserve, where humans can work, marry, and raise children without interference; in return, some humans are implanted with eggs by Tlic females, whose larvae must feed on living flesh. First published in *Asimov's Science Fiction* in 1984, "Bloodchild" won Butler the Nebula, Hugo, and Locus Award for Best Novelette—a sci-fi Triple Crown. Narrated by a young human host who begins to question the whole arrangement after witnessing a gruesome larval delivery, the story represents Butler at the height of her powers, patiently unfolding the consequences of an upsetting moral premise with horrific serenity. The author herself viewed "Bloodchild" as an unusual kind of love story as well as "a story about paying the rent"—one that took seriously what it might cost humanity to survive on an alien planet. "It wouldn't be the British Empire in space, and it wouldn't be *Star Trek*," Butler wrote in a 1996 afterword to the story. "Sooner or later, the humans would have to make some kind of accommodation with their um . . . their hosts."

But many readers found a different kind of parable. "It amazes me that some people have seen 'Bloodchild' as a story of slavery," Butler wrote. "It isn't." She later recalled telling this to a college student who had written a paper on the topic. "Well, the author doesn't always know!" the young woman replied. In a sense, both of them were right: The question of what exactly to make of the disturbing relationship between Gan, the human narrator, and T'Gatoi, the Tlic politician to whom he has been promised since birth, is not only the thematic core of "Bloodchild" but also a topic of heated debate among the story's own characters. "We were necessities, status symbols, and an independent people," Gan says of humanity's standing among the Tlic, even as he defends the practice of implantation after his bitter older brother accuses him of being a willing host animal. But Gan will still end up staring down T'Gatoi, pointing an illegal rifle at his own throat, demanding to be seen as more than her property. "What are we to you?" he whispers, terrified. "You know me as no other does," the alien gently answers. "You must decide."

Butler made her own decision, coolly telling an interviewer in 1996, "The only places I am writing about slavery is where I actually say so." Yet she had often seemed to say so. In fact, slavery had been present in Butler's work from the very beginning: her debut novel from 1976, *Patternmaster*, was the first in a hugely ambitious saga about the millennia-long breeding of a telepathic master race known as the Patternists who eventually enslave some of Earth's population and drive the rest off-world. Three novels later, in 1979, Butler found mainstream success with *Kindred*, in which a present-day Black woman is mysteriously transported to the antebellum South to repeatedly save the life of her slave-owning white ancestor. That novel was followed by *Wild Seed* in 1980, the fourth in the Patternist series, about two sparring African immortals set against the backdrop of the Atlantic slave trade.

In this light, longtime fans could be forgiven for taking "Bloodchild" as one more of Butler's slave stories. But there was another explanation for readers' response. "So many critics have read this as a story about slavery, probably just because I am Black," Butler observed. For decades, Butler was nearly the only Black woman writing science fiction in America, a position she occupied with dignity and frustration, and this kind of reading—the slavery reading—would dog her throughout her career. But there was more to this than the racist notion that Black people have nothing better to do than pick at historical wounds. What Butler also faced was the enduring idea, not exclusive to white people, that African American literature represents one long, elaborate riff on the slave spirituals that first awakened a young Frederick Douglass to "the soul-crushing and death-dealing character of slavery," as he wrote in 1855. In other words, if the slavery reading prevailed among Butler's readers, this was perhaps because they were working, even in all good faith, from the simple, seductive assumption that the underlying impulse of all Black art is to get free.

Yet to make this assumption, at least in Butler's case, is to miss one of her finest qualities as a writer of science fiction: her often ruthless commitment to writing about highly rational people who choose to *give up* their freedom, or their chance at going free, in exchange for something they need or want more. To be sure, they typically make these choices under threat of violence, enslavement, or death, and they almost universally resent being made to choose. But they do not strike their bargains simply in order to survive—a trade-off easily understood from the standpoint of Hobbesian liberalism—but rather because they ultimately judge that, in their specific situations, freedom has less value than, for instance, hope or pleasure. Even *Kindred*, in its depiction of the protagonist's ambivalent relationship with her slave-owning ancestor—she briefly considers becoming his lover before killing him—toys with the idea that such bargains could exist *within* the actual historical institution of American chattel slavery. Arguably, the true object of Butler's interest was not slavery per se but rather the real possibilities opened up when freedom is no longer humanity's north star.

It's not hard to see why Butler might have been skeptical of slavery as a theme. Issues of colonization, enslavement, and empire had after all been the bread and butter of science fiction since Asimov; the colonized Fremen people of Frank Herbert's 1965 classic *Dune*, one of Butler's favorite novels, were originally envisioned as transported penal laborers called "freedmen." At the same time, the genre had all but sealed itself off to nonwhite characters during Butler's time. Early in her career, she participated in a panel alongside an editor who cheekily suggested that Black characters were superfluous in science fiction since "you could always make any racial statement you needed to make by way of extraterrestrials." (The experience would inspire her 1980 essay "Lost Races of Science Fiction.") Even now, science fiction remains the preferred genre of white slavery narratives; a Black science-fiction writer wishing to write about slavery may achieve little more than redundancy in a genre whose appeal has long consisted in ethical carte blanche to restage historical wrongs like the Atlantic slave trade, the British Empire, the Holocaust, or the dropping of the atom bomb so long as half of the people involved are blue.

But what Butler may not have anticipated was a later generation of admiring readers who would actively *want* her stories to be about slavery. It is increasingly difficult to separate Butler the author from the hagiography that has sprung up around her since her untimely death in 2006; this is especially the case in academic and activist circles, where she is hailed as a prophetic voice, a public intellectual, and an Afrofuturist visionary. Her work is sometimes called utopian, even as Butler herself was a political pessimist with a lifelong aversion to utopian thinking, and scholars have praised her novels for being "queer," overlooking her relentless focus on sexual dimorphism and biological reproduction. (The unusual male pregnancy of "Bloodchild" also happened to spare Butler, who had weathered homophobic insults growing up, the prospect of a phallic female impregnating another female.) In 2015, the editors of the fiction anthology *Octavia's Brood: Science Fiction Stories from Social Justice Movements* went so far as to draw a straight line from Butler's legacy as a Black science-fiction writer all the way back to "our ancestors in chains dreaming about a day when their children's children's children would be free." Indeed, it is no great mystery why the neo–slave narrative *Kindred*—a good novel, but not a great one, and one that Butler never considered a work of science fiction—remains her most widely read and taught book today.

Butler, who in 2000 would tell Charlie Rose that she had no interest in saying anything about race other than "Hey, we're here," made it a point to avoid critical theory of all kinds. "It's just an impression of mine, but in some cases critics and authors seem to be massaging each other," she remarked. "It's not very good for storytelling." She regarded herself first and foremost as a writer; her biographer Gerry Canavan would call writing "a holy thing for Butler, a constant and daily devotion." Yet her novels are rarely afforded the full privileges of literary criticism, perhaps because this would puncture the apotheosis to which she is sometimes subjected. Her prose, sometimes called spare, is just as often lackluster. Her heroines—most of them idealized versions of Butler herself (tall, androgynous, highly driven)—tend to occupy the vantage point of lucid species-consciousness at the expense of their interior lives. "They rarely notice anything that doesn't pertain to their emergency, as though the world were a fluorescent-lit escape room," observed Julian Lucas in *The New Yorker* last year. None of this is to say that Butler is undeserving of remembrance or critical evaluation; on the contrary, it is to say that, like many writers, she was often good, sometimes bad, occasionally brilliant, and almost never satisfied.

Butler would go so far as to disavow her 1978 novel, *Survivor*, which she blocked from being reprinted in perpetuity. (A used copy can run you hundreds of dollars online.) In fact, as a decent execution of a derivative premise, *Survivor* is no worse than Butler's first novel, *Patternmaster*, to which it serves as an oblique prequel, describing the fate of a group of human colonists called "Missionaries"—quasi-Christian religious refugees who have fled the Patternist telepaths on Earth and hope to reestablish humanity among the stars. On a faraway planet they name Canaan, the Missionaries enjoy a cautious peace with the Garkohn, a tribe of bioluminescent aliens whose social roles are determined by their fur coloration. When the Missionary heroine, Alanna, is captured by the rival Tehkohn clan, she learns that the Garkohn have been quietly enslaving her fellow humans with a highly addictive drug, and she persuades the Tehkohn chieftain, with whom she has begun (unwillingly, at first) a sexual relationship, to help liberate them.

Butler would disparage *Survivor* as her "*Star Trek* novel"—her childhood crush on Captain Kirk notwithstanding—on account of what she saw as the book's scientific absurdities and simplistic picture of interstellar exploration. She was deeply embarrassed by the fact that the novel's aliens just so happen to have reproductive organs compatible with human ones, such that Alanna ends up giving birth to a Tehkohn daughter. Butler's later Xenogenesis trilogy, in which a postnuclear humanity is forced to reproduce with a race of extraterrestrial gene traders, may be read as one long, fastidious atonement for *Survivor*'s interspecies sex scenes. But worse than this for Butler, who rarely wrote hard science fiction anyway, was the fact that she had naïvely repeated the old colonial encounter that had characterized so much of the stories she had read in her youth, one in which the colonists must conquer the natives or risk being subjugated themselves. When the Garkohn leader learns of humanity's designs to escape, he confidently offers them a familiar bargain: Be fruitful and multiply in the south in exchange for submitting to Garkohn customs and rule. "You Missionaries find it very easy to say you would rather die than do this or that," he says, trying to call their bluff. "You will realize that there is no shame in your submission." But the colonists successfully escape anyway, resettling in harsh but conveniently uninhabited territory in (of all places) the north.

This was Butler's biggest issue with *Survivor*: Humanity goes free. It was a mistake she endeavored never to repeat. Originally, she had planned for *Survivor* to be the first of several Missionary stories, each set on a different planet, and in her journals she privately acknowledged that "Bloodchild," with its vague allusions to the flight of Gan's ancestors, could have easily been another. Yet in its published form, "Bloodchild" presents a very different scene of negotiation from that in *Survivor*. What Gan demands, loaded rifle under his chin, is that T'Gatoi allow him to give up his freedom on his own terms. "No one ever asks us," he tells the alien, but when she offers to take his sister instead, he stops her. "Do it to me," he says, letting T'Gatoi lead him to bed and slide her ovipositor into him: "The puncture was painless, easy. So easy going in. She undulated slowly against me, her muscles forcing the egg from her body into mine." T'Gatoi hesitantly asks Gan if he has offered himself in order to spare his sister. "And to keep you for myself," he answers, nuzzling into her. The question is not whether this qualifies as lovemaking but what kind of love is being made. Pressing his naked flesh against T'Gatoi's velvety body, Gan accepts the risks of being unfree; in return, he wins fidelity, purpose, and a deeply compromised version of love—overclose, carnivorous—that may nonetheless form the basis of a good life.

To return to "Bloodchild" today is to be confronted with the prospect of a Black writer for whom freedom was rarely, if ever, the highest good. That this may appear paradoxical says less about Butler than it does about a contemporary tendency to compensate for poor representation of minority artists by inflating their art until it reflects, tautologically, the experience of not being represented. This is to respond to pigeonholing by overstating the value of being a pigeon. Undoubtedly, Butler's fiction was informed by her personal experiences of racism and misogyny; but we must never assert the obvious fact that Butler managed to be both a fiction writer and a Black woman as if this were a specifically *literary* accomplishment instead of a social one. What recommends Butler's work today is not her status as one of the few Black science-fiction writers of her time but rather the fact that, despite this overwhelming professional isolation, she never gave in to what the critic Ismail Muhammad recently called "the pressures of easy legibility that Black writers have always faced in America." For Butler, nothing was harder, or more important, than the act of writing. If we do owe her a debt, as devotees sometimes claim, we may pay it by having a harder time reading her.

For what do we think that literature actually *does*? In the eighties, Butler's speaking gigs would inevitably result in a Black person asking her about the value of science fiction for Black people—a question to which she never found a satisfying answer. "I resented the question," she wrote in a 1989 article for *Essence*. "Still I'm asked, what good is science fiction to Black people?" Her answers there were brief and predictable— imagination, creativity, thinking outside the status quo—and Butler seems to have known they were unsatisfying. "What good is all this to Black people?" she asked again in the essay's final line. It's as if Butler was the alien now, legs akimbo, staring down at the reader from yellow, unblinking eyes: "You must decide."

2022

Epilogue

This has all been a rather long walk to say that the critic is always a social critic, something that any student of literary history as well as anyone who skims the newspapers probably could have told you. I am saying it again here at the end in case you are skimming the book (I envy you the experience) and also because it may be so obvious, especially to those of us who do criticism for a living, that we forget what it actually means. It does not mean that the job of the critic is to "improve society," an empty phrase that functions as a kind of foxhole for the most reactionary views. In fact, the critic must *not* improve society, if by this we mean feeding the public endless bromides about the hygienic effects of "critical thinking." When the liberal critic tries to persuade us that the willingness to have political principles is the only political principle worth having, he is telling us, in effect, to think more and do less.

So if all the critic does is provide food for thought, I say: Let thought starve. The only criticism worth doing, for my money, is not the kind that claims to improve society in general; it is, as the late John Berger once wrote, the kind that helps to destroy *this particular one*. To be clear, I do not wish to overvalue the business. I have no illusions about the political power of a staff writer at a print magazine owned by a corporation: I do not think it is much, though I am not foolish enough to suppose it is nothing. But I do believe that criticism, at its best, can be a small act of freedom. Not, I should say, "freedom of thought" as the liberal understands it—that is, the freedom to entertain every idea and commit to none. This is not true freedom; it is merely license, and always depends on the approval of some authority. Coleridge's image of criticism as a windmill, grinding every person's grist into the same indifferent flour, was a better metaphor than he knew: for someone owned the mill. When the good critic urges us to form our political beliefs the way we might contemplate a work of art—that is, from a safe distance—he is casting himself as our Sancho Panza, that faithful squire. In truth, he is worried that, in charging the windmill, we will discover that it really was a giant all along.

This is why we cling to authority: it guarantees our freedom while relieving us of the burden of exercising it, turning it into something fine and handsome and altogether useless, like an old suit of armor. What, after all, was Don Quixote's great delusion? Cervantes tells us: *To put into practice everything he had read.* We know the man of La Mancha was a terrible critic—he used to stay up all night torturing meaning out of trashy romances. But in one respect, he was absolutely right: he re-fused to believe that the things he read about existed in a *different world* from the one he already lived in. That this strikes us as the behavior of a madman tells you just how impoverished our concept of intellectual freedom remains today. We want reading to free the mind; we do not want it to free the reader. For my part, I am with the old hidalgo. When he rode full tilt at that giant in disguise, he was acting on the correct as-sumption that reading was not enough. This, it seems to me, is the only way to do without authority: to go out and *do* it.

Acknowledgments

This book would not exist without two phenomenal women. Dayna Tortorici, the editor of this book and my old editor at *n+1*, took a chance on a disgruntled graduate student with nothing to her name but a paper on Hegel. She, and not any half-cocked professor, taught me that the life of the mind was within reach. Gazelle Emami, my editor at *New York* magazine, shepherded nearly half of this book into existence with infinite care and cool delight. I should like to write for her forever.

I thank all of the editors who touched these pieces and made them better, including Arielle Angel, Ari Brostoff, Madeline Leung Coleman, Mark Krotov, Michael Miller, Kaitlin Phillips, Nikil Saval, Sharan Shetty, and David Velasco. I thank David Haskell, editor-in-chief at *New York*, for letting me get away with things that few in his position would; and I thank everyone in the New York Magazine Union for continuing to fight for fair pay and better working conditions for all of us in a time of great upheaval in our industry. I also thank my fact-checkers at *New York*, including Britina Cheng, Jack Denton, and Sophie Hurwitz: they have been calcium for the bones. My fact-checker for the new material in this book was the formidable Juliet Kleber, whom I first met in the basement of the Ace Hotel after she had fact-checked "On Liking Women." Any remaining errors are my own.

My publishers at Farrar, Straus and Giroux have been very patient in waiting for this book. I thank Eric Chinski for believing in the first idea and believing in the next one; and Tara Sharma and Eliza Rudalevige, for answering every email. For his industriousness, I thank my agent, Chris Parris-Lamb, a fellow North Carolinian who runs on New York time. For invitations to speak, I thank Kyle Dacuyan, Merve Emre,

Sophus Helle, Sophie Herron, Ricardo Alberto Maldonado, and the eminent Bernard Schwartz. For conversation, encouragement, references, and the odd translation over the years, I thank Arielle Angel, Rachael Bedard, Ari Brostoff, TJ Calhoun, Madeline Leung Coleman, Daniel Drake, Andrea Gadberry, Allison Hughes, Brandy Jensen, Alex Jung, Sarah McCarry, Michael Macher, Michael McCanne, Lakshmi Padmanabhan, Ethan Philbrick, Torrey Peters, Ned Riseley, Corey Robin, Jasmine Sanders, Charlotte Shane, Lila Shapiro, Christopher Shay, Thora Siemsen, Tony Tulathimutte, and Harron Walker. A very special thanks to anyone who let me explain Kant to them for twenty minutes.

Deep gratitude to Paisley Currah, who took me in and held on tight; Sally Weathers, who had the grace to let me go; Sarah Chihaya, my wife of the mind; Sarah Ax and Rebecca Crawford, my confidantes and cheerleaders; Janet Kwon, apple of my eye; my parents, who got there in the end; and Aros, Braak, Enid, Nim, Nora, Nowhere, and Wymar, who followed me into hell and trusted me to lead them out again.

Finally, I am nothing without Jenny Xu, my treasure, my rock, my Arrakis, my Dune. Thank God I already had this book under contract when you reached out to see if I wanted to write one.

Index

A NOTE ABOUT THE AUTHOR

Andrea Long Chu is a Pulitzer Prize–winning essayist and critic at *New York* magazine. Her book *Females* was published in 2019 and was a finalist for the Lambda Literary Award in Transgender Nonfiction. Her writing has also appeared in *n+1*, *The New York Times*, *The New Yorker*, *Artforum*, *Bookforum*, *Boston Review*, *The Chronicle of Higher Education*, *4Columns*, and *Jewish Currents*.